ETHICS

SOCIAL

AND LAW

FOR

WORKERS

SAGE was founded in 1965 by Sara Miller McCune to support the dissemination of usable knowledge by publishing innovative and high-quality research and teaching content. Today, we publish more than 850 journals, including those of more than 300 learned societies, more than 800 new books per year, and a growing range of library products including archives, data, case studies, reports, and video. SAGE remains majority-owned by our founder, and after Sara's lifetime will become owned by a charitable trust that secures our continued independence.

Los Angeles | London | New Delhi | Singapore | Washington DC

ETHICS

SOCIAL

AND LAW

FOR

WORKERS

ROBERT JOHNS

Los Angeles | London | New Delhi
Singapore | Washington DC

Los Angeles | London | New Delhi
Singapore | Washington DC

SAGE Publications Ltd
1 Oliver's Yard
55 City Road
London EC1Y 1SP

SAGE Publications Inc.
2455 Teller Road
Thousand Oaks, California 91320

SAGE Publications India Pvt Ltd
B 1/I 1 Mohan Cooperative Industrial Area
Mathura Road
New Delhi 110 044

SAGE Publications Asia-Pacific Pte Ltd
3 Church Street
#10-04 Samsung Hub
Singapore 049483

Editor: Kate Wharton
Production editor: Katie Forsythe
Copyeditor: Rosemary Morlin
Proofreader: Clare Weaver
Indexer: Gary Kirby
Marketing manager: Camille Richmond
Cover design: Shaun Mercier
Typeset by: C&M Digitals (P) Ltd, Chennai, India
Printed and bound by CPI Group (UK) Ltd,
Croydon, CR0 4YY

Library of Congress Control Number: 2015936967

British Library Cataloguing in Publication data

A catalogue record for this book is available from
the British Library

MIX
Paper from
responsible sources
FSC
www.fsc.org   FSC® C013604

ISBN 978-0-85702-909-6
ISBN 978-0-85702-910-2 (pbk)

At SAGE we take sustainability seriously. Most of our products are printed in the UK using FSC papers and boards.
When we print overseas we ensure sustainable papers are used as measured by the Egmont grading system.
We undertake an annual audit to monitor our sustainability.

This book is dedicated to generations of social work students who demanded of law prescriptions it could not offer, and of ethics absolutes it could not deliver. Here's the reason why.

Contents

About the Author

Before moving into social work education, Robert Johns worked for a number of years in a range of social work roles, predominantly in the public sector. He has experience of all aspects of social work, ranging from mental health to youth justice and work with vulnerable adults, but with specialist experience in courtwork, representing the interests of children involved in care proceedings. Academically, his major abiding interest has been social work law but he has also taught social policy and social work values and ethics, hence this book. Currently, he teaches at the University of East London, where he has been Head of Social Work and programme leader for the qualifying MA offered in conjunction with the Tavistock and Portman NHS Foundation Trust. He is the author of *Using the Law in Social Work*, now in its sixth edition, *Social Work, Social Policy and Older People* and, most recently, *Capacity and Autonomy*.

Introduction: But I Want to Be a Social Worker, Not a Philosopher!

The Challenge of Ethics and Law

This book addresses a challenge. It is a challenge all social work practitioners must tackle, and it is a particular challenge for students on social work qualifying and post-qualifying programmes, for whom the book is particularly intended. In a nutshell the challenge is this: how do social workers, practising within the UK legal context, act ethically and legally?

Behind this lies a more fundamental question: what do we understand by ethics and how does social work law relate to it? Social work practice in all countries incorporates a clear, unstinting commitment to social justice, but what is social justice? A preliminary understanding of ethics and ethical theory together with clarification of what is meant by social justice, is absolutely essential for anyone intending to practise social work.

From the social work practice perspective, a number of issues then arise. Given that the majority of social workers are employees or agents of state-sponsored agencies that must operate within clearly defined legal boundaries, what dilemmas arise for social work? What challenges do practitioners face when they try to reconcile their commitment to social justice with their legally circumscribed duties to service users? What tensions might arise between their loyalty and obligations to their chosen profession and the legal context within which they operate? How does the law itself address such issues? What decisions have the courts made when balancing conflicting ethical demands, for example the duty to protect people and the commitment to empowering people to make decisions for themselves? How has the legal system adjudicated on ethical issues related to social work? For some social workers there may also be issues of reconciling their own personal beliefs and values with those of a profession that requires compliance with a code of conduct that is, ultimately, enforced through legal requirements. Is this possible for social workers in everyday practice without resorting to legal-technical or bureaucratic responses? How can social workers move beyond asking what the law says, in the hope that this tells them what to do, towards the professional maturity that can use the law as a means of empowerment and can also challenge laws that are oppressive or fail to meet service users' needs? Ultimately, to put it succinctly, how can social workers respond to laws that both constrain and empower?

While this book cannot answer all of those questions, it aims to address many of them. There is certainly a gap between the texts on ethics and law which this book bridges. Specifically, there is a substantial and growing literature on ethics in social work (for example: Banks, 2012; Beckett and Maynard, 2013; Gray and Webb, 2010; Parrott, 2015). Also there are a number of authoritative texts on social work law (for example: Brammer, 2015; Braye and Preston-Shoot, 2010; Brayne, Carr and Goosey, 2015; Johns, 2014b). All are valuable, yet some of us who, as social work practitioners and educators, teach social work law, have identified a tendency for social work students to treat ethics and law as two distinct animals. This, of course, is compounded in many social work programmes by having ethics and law as two distinct modules, which in many cases is an unavoidable necessity. Yet it can yield undesirable consequences. Students feel challenged, and sometimes deeply perturbed, by the ethical debates in which they are compelled to engage, and in some cases by the disjunction between their personal beliefs and professional values. In the case of social work law, students then demand more than it can give: they expect the law to tell them what to do in every circumstance. In some cases they hope the law can help them reconcile ethics and practice, and are often disappointed when told that the law simply sets the boundaries within which they as practitioners must decide the best course of action. After all, the Highway Code and the rules of the road lay down the principles of good driving and penalise poor driving, but they do not direct drivers as to what to do in every circumstance which they may encounter when actually driving along a road.

This book is practical. It cannot, of course, tell anyone what to do in any particular circumstance and would never seek to do so. However what it can do is explore some of dilemmas that social workers encounter in everyday practice where they need to reconcile social work ethics and law. It does this not by a deep theoretical exposition – although there will be summaries of ethical theory and theories of justice – but by inviting readers to reflect on how to address the everyday complexities of social work practice. Every chapter will draw on case study material which, as a general principle, will be as current and real as possible. Such cases will, naturally, be anonymised unless they are in the public domain. Every chapter will also include reference to statute law and case material that is relevant to that chapter's considerations. However readers should note that, not only can laws change and therefore may have changed since the publication of this book, but also that some legislation is country specific. Some of the regulations that apply to England, for example, do not apply to Wales although there may be equivalents. Some legislation itself does not apply to Scotland or to Northern Ireland. This book should not be taken as an authoritative statement of law as it applies to all countries in UK, therefore, although it was as accurate as it was possible to be at the time of publication.

WHO IS THIS BOOK FOR?

This book is primarily intended for students undertaking modules on courses that lead to a professional qualification in social work. It would also be highly suitable for qualified practitioners in their first year of practice or later in their careers when they are undertaking further studies on post-qualifying modules, most especially in mental health, mental capacity (for example, as Best Interest Assessors) or advanced child care practice.

In qualifying programmes, both at undergraduate and postgraduate level, it is almost certain that there will be at least one law module, and at least one that incorporates values and ethics – although, interestingly, rarely one that incorporates both. Law teaching was specifically itemised as a compulsory area of teaching for qualifying programmes by the Department of Health in their programme requirements for the (then) new degree in social work (Department of Health, 2002). Social work practice is imbued with both ethics and law in the shape of rights and social justice. This is made transparently clear in the Professional Capabilities Framework that applies to social workers in England, the National Occupational Standards for Social Work that apply to social workers in Wales, Scotland and Northern Ireland and in the various relevant codes of practice (see below).

It is recognised that readers will come from variety of backgrounds, with different levels of experience. Some of the case studies in this book raise complex issues and presuppose some limited familiarity with professional practice. Nevertheless even readers with minimal practice experience will be able to engage with the kinds of issues which arise from the case study examples, and indeed sometimes it is beneficial to adopt a fresh approach that does not make any assumptions about how practice is currently carried out. Readers will find it enormously helpful to undertake wider reading in order to enhance understanding and learn about different ways in which different people approach complex ethical issues. At various points in the text there are indications as to where further reading may be helpful. The book has deliberately been designed for readers to engage in its interactive approach, and to this end some critical thinking exercises are incorporated into the text. These are intended to spur thinking in a more analytical way, but crucially also to help students and practitioners apply the benefits of this analysis to the kinds of practical situations which they are likely to encounter in social work practice.

Requirements of Social Work Education

Social work is a moral activity that requires practitioners to recognise the dignity of the individual, but also to make and implement difficult decisions (including restriction of liberty) in human situations that involve the potential for benefit or harm. Honours degree programmes in social work therefore involve the study, application of, and critical reflection upon, ethical principles and dilemmas. As reflected by the four care councils' codes of practice, this involves showing respect for persons, honouring the diverse and distinctive organisations and communities that make up contemporary society, promoting social justice and combating processes that lead to discrimination, marginalisation and social exclusion. (QAA, 2008: 4.6)

Social work education is governed by regulations and requirements set out separately by the governments of the four countries that comprise the UK. While there are some minor differences between these, in general terms they consist of expectations in relation to practice (the Professional Capabilities Framework for Social Workers in England, National Occupational Standards for Social Work for Wales, Scotland and Northern Ireland), academic requirements as set out by the Quality Assurance Agency for Higher Education, and codes of practice emanating from the Care Councils. The next three sections highlight the relevance of this book to these sets of requirements.

The Professional Capabilities Framework and National Occupational Standards

Two sections of the Professional Capabilities Framework, applicable to social workers in England, are directly relevant to this book. In the values and ethics section social workers are expected to 'conduct themselves ethically' and to this end need to demonstrate 'confident application of ethical reasoning' and be able to 'recognise and manage con-flicting values and ethical dilemmas'. Social workers are expected to be 'knowledgeable about the value base of their profession, its ethical standards and relevant law'. In a similar vein under Rights, Justice and Economic Wellbeing, the Framework states that social workers should 'recognise the fundamental principles of human rights and equality' in law and policy and as part of their role should 'routinely integrate the principles of, and entitlements to, social justice' (The College of Social Work, 2012).

Elsewhere in the UK, the National Occupational Standards for Social Work reflect similar expectations. In the original version (General Social Care Council, 2002) Key Role 3 expected social workers to 'advocate with and on behalf of individuals, families, carers, groups and communities' while Key Role 6 required social workers to be able to 'manage complex ethical issues, dilemmas and conflicts'. National Occupational Standards for Social Work for Wales, Scotland and Northern Ireland are all currently being revised but doubtless will include very similar requirements in the future.

The Quality Assurance Agency Subject Benchmarks for Social Work

Subject Benchmarks apply across the UK to all universities. The Quality Assurance Agency Subject Benchmark Statements for Social Work (QAA, 2008) set out expecta-tions about standards of knowledge, skills, understanding, and competence that students would be expected to attain by the end of an honours degree in social work (not Masters programmes yet). They indicate both areas of knowledge and skills for social work practice.

Listed below are the benchmarks that are generally covered in this book, with considerable emphasis on benchmarks falling under 5.1.3.

Subject Knowledge and Understanding

5.1 During their degree studies in social work, honours graduates should acquire, critically evaluate, apply and integrate knowledge and understanding in the following five core areas of study.

5.1.1 *Social work services, service users and carers, which include:*

- the social processes (associated with, for example, poverty, migration, unemployment, poor health, disablement, lack of education and other sources of disadvantage) that lead to marginalisation, isolation and exclusion, and their impact on the demand for social work services
- explanations of the links between definitional processes contributing to social differences (for example, social class, gender, ethnic differences, age, sexuality and religious belief) to the problems of inequality and differential need faced by service users
- the nature of social work services in a diverse society (with particular reference to concepts such as prejudice, interpersonal, institutional and structural discrimination, empowerment and anti-discriminatory practices)
- the nature and validity of different definitions of, and explanations for, the characteristics and circumstances of service users and the services required by them, drawing on knowledge from research, practice experience, and from service users and carers
- the focus on outcomes, such as promoting the well-being of young people and their families, and promoting dignity, choice and independence for adults receiving services
- the relationship between agency policies, legal requirements and professional boundaries in shaping the nature of services provided in interdisciplinary contexts and the issues associated with working across professional boundaries and within different disciplinary groups.

5.1.2 *The service delivery context, which includes:*

- the location of contemporary social work within historical, comparative and global perspectives, including European and international contexts
- the changing demography and cultures of communities in which social workers will be practising
- the complex relationships between public, social and political philosophies, policies and priorities and the organisation and practice of social work, including the contested nature of these
- the issues and trends in modern public and social policy and their relationship to contemporary practice and service delivery in social work
- the significance of legislative and legal frameworks and service delivery standards (including the nature of legal authority, the application of legislation in practice, statutory accountability and tensions between statute, policy and practice)
- the current range and appropriateness of statutory, voluntary and private agencies providing community-based, day-care, residential and other services and the organisational systems inherent within these
- the significance of interrelationships with other related services, including housing, health, income maintenance and criminal justice (where not an integral social service)

- the contribution of different approaches to management, leadership and quality in public and independent human services
- the development of personalised services, individual budgets and direct payments
- the implications of modern information and communications technology (ICT) for both the provision and receipt of services.

5.1.3 Values and ethics, which include:

- the nature, historical evolution and application of social work values
- the moral concepts of rights, responsibility, freedom, authority and power inherent in the practice of social workers as moral and statutory agents
- the complex relationships between justice, care and control in social welfare and the practical and ethical implications of these, including roles as statutory agents and in upholding the law in respect of discrimination
- aspects of philosophical ethics relevant to the understanding and resolution of value dilemmas and conflicts in both interpersonal and professional contexts
- the conceptual links between codes defining ethical practice, the regulation of professional conduct and the management of potential conflicts generated by the codes held by different professional groups.

5.1.4 Social work theory, which includes:

- research-based concepts and critical explanations from social work theory and other disciplines that contribute to the knowledge base of social work, including their distinctive epistemological status and application to practice
- the relevance of sociological perspectives to understanding societal and structural influences on human behaviour at individual, group and community levels
- the relevance of psychological, physical and physiological perspectives to understanding personal and social development and functioning
- social science theories explaining group and organisational behaviour, adaptation and change
- models and methods of assessment, including factors underpinning the selection and testing of relevant information, the nature of professional judgment and the processes of risk assessment and decision-making
- approaches and methods of intervention in a range of settings, including factors guiding the choice and evaluation of these
- user-led perspectives
- knowledge and critical appraisal of relevant social research and evaluation methodologies, and the evidence base for social work.

5.1.5 The nature of social work practice, which includes:

- the characteristics of practice in a range of community-based and organisational settings within statutory, voluntary and private sectors, and the factors influencing changes and developments in practice within these contexts

- the nature and characteristics of skills associated with effective practice, both direct and indirect, with a range of service users and in a variety of settings
- the processes that facilitate and support service user choice and independence
- the factors and processes that facilitate effective interdisciplinary, inter-professional and inter-agency collaboration and partnership
- the place of theoretical perspectives and evidence from international research in assessment and decision-making processes in social work practice
- the integration of theoretical perspectives and evidence from international research into the design and implementation of effective social work intervention, with a wide range of service users, carers and others
- the processes of reflection and evaluation, including familiarity with the range of approaches for evaluating service and welfare outcomes, and their significance for the development of practice and the practitioner.

Academic Skills Development

As far as skills are concerned, this book will mirror the importance attributed in Social Work Benchmark 4.7 to accountability, reflection, critical thinking and evaluation. The skills to be acquired by the time students graduate are specifically addressed and developed in certain chapters of this book and at the start of each chapter those that are most relevant to that chapter will be listed. Readers will be encouraged to learn to think logically, systematically, critically and reflectively (Benchmark 5.5.1) and to acquire higher-order skills as follows:

Skill 1 demonstrating understanding and application of theoretical ideas

Skill 2 comparing and contrasting different viewpoints and experiences

Skill 3 relating different views to underlying philosophies or ideologies

Skill 4 evaluating different perspectives and ideas

Skill 5 evaluating evidence

Skill 6 synthesising arguments

Skill 7 reflection

Skill 8 reviewing, re-evaluating and reformulating your own views

Codes of Practice

The current codes of practice applicable to social workers across the UK are:

England: Health and Care Professions Council Standards of Practice for Social Workers in England (Health and Care Professions Council, 2012)

Wales: Code of Practice for Social Care Workers (Care Council for Wales, 2011)

Scotland: Code of Practice for Social Service Workers and Employers (Scottish Social Services Council, 2009)

Northern Ireland: Codes of Practice for Social Care Workers and Employers of Social Care Workers (Northern Ireland Social Care Council, 2002)

For the sake of brevity what follows highlights the key expectations common to all codes of practice that are most relevant to this book.

Perhaps not surprisingly, codes of practice generally are quite specific in their insistence that social workers act ethically. In the Professional Capabilities Framework, for example, social workers are explicitly required 'to be able to practise within the legal and ethical boundaries of their profession' (Health and Care Professions Council, 2012, section 2). In all of them there is an expectation that social workers will:

- treat each person as an individual;
- respect the views and wishes of service users and carers;
- promote dignity;
- respect confidentiality;
- declare conflicts of interests;
- respect diversity in all its forms;
- promote independence and people's rights;
- challenge abusive or discriminatory behaviour;
- practise in a safe way;
- be honest and trustworthy;
- be reliable and dependable;
- be accountable for their actions and quality of their own practice.

Furthermore social workers will not:

- abuse neglect or harm people;
- abuse people's trust;
- engage in inappropriate relationships;
- behave in a way that calls into question their suitability for professional practice.

From this selective list the ethical dimension is apparent, but it may also be worth noting at least two requirements that require social workers to be certain kinds of people, rather than act in certain kinds way. For example, social workers are required to be honest and trustworthy, reliable and dependable. We will see later in this book that there is a debate about whether ethics is a matter of principles that require people to act in certain ways, or whether ethics is a matter of how people are, about the characteristics and qualities that make someone the kind of person who would know how to act ethically or even 'be ethical'. We will also see later in the book that there is a debate about the law and what constitutes justice, an issue which is of great importance in social work with its strong commitment to the pursuit of social justice.

THE FOCUS OF THIS BOOK

The book is interactive and practice focused. Each chapter in this book brings the two strands, law and ethics, together. They do this by focusing on an area of practice, highlighted by one or more selected case studies. The majority of case studies comprise decisions handed down by the courts, rather than examples directly from social work practice. Necessarily they are highly selective; they have been chosen to represent specific points at which law and ethics intersect, focusing on those that present the most acute issues for social work practitioners. It is not practicable in a book of this size to cover every aspect of social work practice or to present definitive answers which imply that there are right or wrong answers. In social work there is rarely just one right answer, and it would be quite deceptive for any textbook to pretend that this is the case.

Each chapter starts with an introductory paragraph explaining the coverage of the chapter. In each chapter there will be one or more case studies. Readers will be challenged to think about how to identify the ethical components and to recognise the relevant legislation. Reference will be made to the law of England in force at the time of the book's publication and where possible reference will be made to law in other countries of the UK. Use will also be made of the various national codes of conduct or ethical guidelines laid down by regulatory or professional bodies. The discussion in each chapter is geared towards the needs of student social workers, assisting them to analyse and evaluate those aspects of the case that relate to law or to ethical considerations. There will be some tentative guidance as to how to approach various issues but this is not an instruction manual!

The book assumes basic knowledge of social work law, although it will remind readers of the relevant legislation. The discussion in each chapter is intended as a worked through analysis of legal and ethical issues, and to this end will incorporate some reflective exercises to enable readers to distinguish the various components of the practice dilemmas that they face. The book will not pretend that there are easy, quick fix solutions to profound ethical dilemmas. It will however encourage readers to identify what these dilemmas are, and to devise avenues whereby they might set about seeking to address or even resolve them. Towards the end of the chapter there will be encouragement to draw up a balance sheet reflecting on legal requirements, ethical dimensions, and strategies for addressing them. Finally each chapter will include a summary that points to a wider context and may refer to opportunities for further reading, consideration of relevant case law, or for reflection on practice.

WHAT IS IN THIS BOOK?

The book opens with a consideration of social workers as ethical actors. How do we judge whether something is 'ethical'? What theories help us to understand this? Here will be found an overview of the different key approaches to ethics: principle-based ethics (deontological, utilitarian) and person-based ethics (virtue ethics, ethics of care). The discussion then turns to the importance of ethical practice and its connections to the law that underpins this.

Leading on from this, Chapter 2 has a strong focus on social justice, which is a core principle underpinning much of social work practice. It is social justice which most readily connects ethics and law in social work. Identifying the key components of social justice, the chapter provides an overview of different philosophies that promote human rights and principles of empowerment, again key social work values. Necessarily this includes a discussion of what rights are being promoted and what is meant by social justice. This chapter offers an important analytical approach that is taken forward in subsequent chapters when specific aspects of social work practice are analysed. Towards the end of the chapter, analysis of the case study is used to exemplify the different approaches to social justice. This serves to highlight some of the potential dilemmas that may confront social workers when addressing the needs of service users on whom social policy changes have had a particular impact.

Chapter 3 focuses on the issue of accountability. The underlying principle behind codes of ethics that undergird social workers' professional practice is respect for service users and promotion of their interests. There is potential for conflict here with expectations from employers and the public. The chapter therefore begins with some examples of where social workers may encounter that conflict. This may be between their own personal values and the formalised codes of ethics to which they are officially committed, or it may be between what they see as ethical practice and the law. There may be ways in which social workers as professionals may be required to do more than just observe the regulations and requirements of their employers, and likewise how employers and professional bodies are entitled to expect social workers to observe ethical principles in all that they do. The different avenues of accountability are highlighted and explained. This chapter concludes with an example of gross abuse of trust which was only revealed after a sustained personal campaign by a residential social worker determined to stop the abuse of youngsters in the care system and to pursue justice on their behalf. This raises the question of safeguards for professionals who bring malpractice to public attention and asks readers to reflect on the fundamental question: what are social workers' duties and obligations and to whom are they responsible?

In the second part of the book, duties and obligations within an ethical social work framework as a theme is then applied to specific areas of practice. The selected areas are not meant to be comprehensive, but offer valuable examples for an exploration of how law and ethics relate to each other in social work. So from this point onwards the focus moves towards consideration of challenges and dilemmas relating to particular service user groups.

We begin in Chapter 4 with one of the most challenging areas: how to balance the protection of children with support to parents. In the vast majority of cases it can be taken as read that providing support to parents has the benefit of promoting the upbringing of children in their own families, which conforms exactly to the principles underpinning the Children Act 1989. However in a very small percentage of cases needs of children must be addressed separately from those of their parents, yet the law requires practitioners to work in partnership with parents even in those cases, and to avoid legal action such as care proceedings unless it is absolutely necessary. How should practitioners interpret these requirements? What does the law say? Some recent case decisions have brought this issue into the limelight, and it is one in which practitioners need to be very clear about their objectives and ethical principles.

What is good enough parenting? Are there any circumstances in which parents can be compelled to give up children for life? If so what should the circumstances be? How do social workers operate within a legal context that allows for compulsory adoption, as the Adoption and Children 2002 does? What are the ethical considerations here? How do practitioners address this issue within the context in which there are different cultural views concerning the value of adoption? These are all issues which are considered in Chapter 5.

In Chapter 6, there is further consideration to notions of justice through an examination of the whole notion of youth justice with its emphasis on putting clear boundaries around the behaviour of young people. What is the social work role in this and how does it connect to the ethical commitment to social justice? It helps here to learn from history so the chapter explores an attempt to place children and young people's needs first in the youth justice system by adopting a purely welfare approach to offences committed by them. Lessons learned are salutary and indicate that there needs to be a balance between the needs of young people and the rights of the wider society, as the remainder of the chapter explains.

The focus then shifts to adult care for Chapter 7. Much practice is dominated by what policymakers call personalisation, which in essence is a comparatively straightforward notion of ensuring that services are configured so as to meet the needs of the individual, rather than the individual having to fit into available services and resources. This is facilitated by laws such as the Health and Social Care Act 2008, the Health Act 2009, and latterly the Care Act 2014, that encourage service user choice, including individual budgets and similar measures that fall under the umbrella of personalisation. In practice, personalisation can raise substantive ethical and practice issues, which often centre on the question of how need is to be defined and what is the best way of ensuring that need is met. The parallel between people choosing services and choosing goods from a supermarket does not quite apply when service users may not be able to evaluate the extent to which services will truly meet their needs, or how best services should be organised to ensure that they do so fairly – taking into account the needs of others. Issues of empowerment and rights to self-determination need to be balanced here with the social work imperative of ensuring that services meet all people's needs.

Chapter 8 concerns the issue of mental capacity. This is a very topical issue in social work, being of critical importance in social work both with children and adults. In work with children, case law has attempted to clarify how practitioners decide if children are competent to make their own decisions. In adult care, following implementation of the Mental Capacity Act 2005, practitioners now have a comprehensive set of values and ethics enshrined in legislation. The ethical principles that underpin the Act reflect a particular approach to social justice that demands respect for individual autonomy, yet permits decisions to be made on behalf of otherwise autonomous individuals in certain circumstances. The chapter therefore includes an exploration of examples where serious life-changing decisions may need to be made on behalf of others. Inevitably, this means that the majority of the chapter focuses on deprivation of liberty which – excluding very specific provision in mental health – is relevant to two service user groups in particular: older people and people with learning disabilities. In the course of analysis the chapter addresses real crunch ethical issues that the law has tried to address, namely assessing competence to make decisions and the extent to which people lose the right to make decisions for themselves.

Finally, Chapter 9 adopts a slightly different approach in that it offers several examples of practice that was alleged to be unethical and on which the courts have had to adjudicate. Included here are examples from the field of mental health, where professionals are charged with making decisions in the public interest and protection of the public. When it comes to the critical issue of detention or deprivation of liberty, the law has to tread a fine line between the rights of service users (or patients as people are often called in this context) and the rights of the public at large, and has to operate in accordance with European Convention on Human Rights principles which ultimately reflect a particular approach to individual liberty and social justice. Furthermore, family members themselves may have legal rights which, when exercised, could impede professional decision-making. Likewise, child care social workers can be tempted to skirt around the edges of the law and ethical practice when they are convinced that a certain course of action is in a child's best interests.

Astute practitioners will no doubt note that this means that some key areas of practice have been overlooked. In one book it just is not possible to cover all areas of practice, even if some of these do raise substantive legal and ethical issues. Principally here there is not space to devote to more specialist areas of practice such as work with refugees and asylum seekers, work with the homeless, hospice or end-of-life care. All are, of course, important in their own right, and their omission here is certainly not intended to indicate otherwise. Rather, the overall ambition is to help social workers, especially those comparatively new to the profession, to learn more about how to engage generally with social work law and ethics, and thereby to be equipped to practise better in whichever field they choose.

The book concludes by reflecting on the interconnections between earlier discussions of ethical theories, social work law and social justice. The challenge to be addressed is how social workers can balance a natural desire to follow what the law requires with a commitment to person-centred ethical social work practice. Ultimately there is a need for a commitment to social justice that brings together law and ethics into a viable framework for practice. Understanding law is important, understanding ethics is vital, understanding both is imperative.

1

Judging Actions or People?

INTRODUCTION AND CHAPTER OVERVIEW

This chapter begins to connect law and ethics by focusing on an example of an incident involving a newly qualified practitioner. The key issue to be addressed here is not their social work practice as such, but how to judge whether an action is 'ethical', decide which standpoints to adopt in order to evaluate their behaviour, and how all of these relate to the law. Inevitably this raises questions concerning what is moral or acceptable behaviour, and hints at issues of responsibility and accountability that recur in this book.

Exercises integrated into this chapter are designed to promote the attainment and development of the Critical Thinking Skills 1 and 2: demonstrating understanding and application of theoretical ideas, and relating different views to underlying philosophies or ideologies.

This chapter starts with a case study in which a social worker appears, at first sight, to have acted unethically and may have broken the law. This leads into a discussion of:

- how we judge whether particular actions are ethical: whether we judge just the actions themselves, or whether we judge the people who engage in a particular action;
- how these judgments relate to ethics and moral philosophy;
- why ethical practice matters and to whom it matters;
- how ethical practice connects to the law;
- returning to the case study, what conclusions can be drawn about this particular action and how should we judge it in terms of ethics and legality?

In the two subsequent chapters of Part 1 of the book we go on to focus on areas where law and ethics meet in social work. In Chapter 2 we focus on an important principle that underpins much of social work practice, namely the concept of social justice. In Chapter 3 the attention moves to the wider issue of accountability, which includes the process that judges the ethics of practice, as well as the constraints on practice that are enshrined in the general legal framework that contextualise social work practice in UK.

Part 2 of the book attempts to integrate law and ethics by looking at some key issues in social work practice. Necessarily, these are selective. There is no way in which it would be possible for one book to explore all the issues that would ever arise, but there are always challenges and controversies in social work, and the intention is to look at a sample of these in relation to as wide a diversity of social work practice as possible within the limitations of a single volume.

CASE STUDY

Unethical, illegal or just disorganised?

A senior social work practitioner invited a newly qualified social worker who had just joined the team to go on a visit to a specialist residential unit which she believed the new worker would find of interest. The unit was 40 miles from the office where they were both based, and so they travelled together in the senior practitioner's car. At the end of the month, both of them submitted claims to the agency for reimbursement for the costs of the 80 mile round-trip. The manager checking the claims noticed this, and the newly qualified worker immediately admitted when questioned that he had not used his car for the journey and so had made a false claim. However he said this was a mistake; he had used his diary to work out what he should claim from the employer for the previous month and had forgotten that on that particular day someone else (the senior social work practitioner) had driven them to the residential unit. The newly qualified social worker was suspended immediately and informed that disciplinary proceedings would be instigated with a view to a possible prosecution for attempted fraud, and that the matter might also be referred to the professional body's conduct committee.

Critical thinking exercise 1.1

While you might have all sorts of initial responses to the employer's reactions, try to set these aside and reflect on how you would set about analysing the ethics of what the social worker did.

1. Where would your focus be on deciding whether this conduct was ethical?

   On the legality of the action?
   On the social worker's explanation?
   On the quality of the social worker's other work and their general approach to it?

2. Having decided this, how serious do you think this matter is?

This scenario, which is loosely based on a real event, raises a number of questions about ethics and the law. In reflecting on what the social worker did, you may have asked yourself a number of questions. Why was it wrong for the new worker to make the claim? Would they have a defence against the allegation that they acted dishonestly? Was the employer's action too hasty? Would a conviction for a criminal offence be appropriate in this case? Should this action result in them losing their licence to practise? Does it make any difference that the person who made the false claim was a registered social worker?

These are the kinds of questions that are likely to engender a lot of discussion, some of it heated, as indeed it did at the time. However, the purpose of this chapter is not to present a series of personal views about what the newly qualified worker did, but to relate their action to ethics and the law, which was why the exercise asked such specific questions about how you would set about your evaluation. In order to achieve that objective we need to start by setting out different views of ethics, relating these to the law and also to the role of social workers as people of whom certain standards of behaviour are expected.

JUDGING ACTIONS OR PEOPLE?

Ethics is a branch of philosophy, specifically moral philosophy. Ethics therefore, in effect, means love of wisdom about morality, so an ethical debate about what someone has done focuses on morality. But is it morality of the action or the actor? Is something wrong because the action itself is simply wrong, or does the degree to which it is right or wrong depend on who carried out the action, in what circumstances, with what intent, and for what purpose?

Essentially this is a distinction between two sets of ethical theories which have been particularly influential in the West for many years, and they are the kind of theories that form the focus of any basic text on ethics. Students of social work will probably be already familiar with the work of Banks (2012), Beckett and Maynard (2013), Parrott (2015) and Gray and Webb (2010), and any one of these can be commended as a general introduction to ethics and social work.

For the purpose of determining the relationship between ethics and law in social work we need to start with theories of ethics and then connect these into the legal and regulatory system within which social work operates. For our purposes it may help to follow distinctions set out by Gray and Webb (2010: 9–13) who suggest that there are two sets of ethical theories which can be divided into two groups: principle-based and person-based, non-naturalistic and naturalistic. If this idea is adapted and converted to a table, this is the result:

Table 1.1   Two sets of ethical theories

Principle-based or non-naturalistic	Teleological, naturalistic
Deontology, absolute principles, duty, universal, categorical, transcendental, objective	Purpose and ends, human needs and nature
Plato, Kant, for example	Aristotle, Bentham, for example
For social work this means acting out of a sense of duty or obligation	Everything is designed towards a final result; goal is human flourishing
Codes of ethics, rules, principles which social workers are duty bound to follow	Social workers to be judged by the consequences of actions or whether they themselves are morally good
Rightness or wrongness of an act is determined by the character of the act itself	Rightness or wrongness of an act is determined by the outcomes of the act or the character of the agent

Readers who are familiar with ethical theories may prefer to jump to the next section on why ethical practice matters, but if you are not, or want a reminder of the different approaches, read on.

Critical thinking exercise 1.2

As you read through the following summaries of theory, underline and note the keywords that will help you remember the theories, and then use them to distinguish between them.

Right at the end of the chapter, there will be a comparison between the theories that use some of the keywords that have hopefully been identified.

Deontological (Principle-based or Non-naturalistic) Theories

Let us start with the theories that are principle-based, or are based on absolutes.

If you have a strong religious faith you might well say that your principles are derived from it, and naturally there is nothing wrong with this but here we are looking for principles or absolutes that apply to all people at all times. Furthermore we are not here talking about people's values, in which faith may play an important part, but ethical principles that should govern everyone's behaviour. In this context it would be counter-productive to come up with principles derived from one particular religious faith and try to apply it universally. Such an attempt would meet a huge amount of hostility, not least from those who did not share that faith. In addition it assumes consistency, an agreement about exactly what principles derive from a particular faith and this might well be contested even by those who subscribe to it, witness the recent controversies within the Christian Church about the role of women, gay marriage, and in former times the death penalty and even the acceptability of slavery. If you are interested in the topic of faith and social work in this context, there is a chapter devoted to values and religion in Beckett and Maynard (2013: Chapter 3).

In the search for absolutes, all philosophy texts will identify Kant as the chief proponent of such an approach, and in terms of modern philosophy (that is, from the eighteenth century onwards) this is quite understandable, although inevitably few now accept his original views and formulations in totality. His significance, however, is beyond dispute since his contribution is to seek some kind of universality that does not derive from adherence to religious beliefs or principles. Instead it focuses on absolutes that relate to the notion of duty, hence deontological (*deon* being the Greek word for duty).

Kant maintained an a priori basis for his use of ethics; there is a moral law, first principles, that we have an absolute duty to obey – the categorical imperative. Yet this morality is not based on religion or feelings about what is the right thing to do, but on reason. Reason should guide all behaviour. All moral concepts have their origin a priori, that is they are independent of experience, and precede everything else. Since they are objective and inherent in the universe, they are binding. Human beings know how to behave without reference to consequences.

To be more precise about how to work out what is right and what is wrong, someone should ask themselves these questions before taking a particular course of action:

> What rule would I be following if I were to do this action (the so-called maxim)?
>
> Would I be willing for this rule to be followed by everyone all the time and in all places, in other words if it became a universal law? (sometimes referred to as universalisability)
>
> If the maxim can be universalised then do it, if it can't, don't! (Jenkins, 1999: 43)

Another way of formulating a categorical imperative is always to act in such a way that humanity is never treated as a means to an end but always as 'ends in themselves'. Thus it can never be right 'to use human beings as a means to the end of our own happiness or to treat any group of people as a minority that does not matter. This principle enshrined the idea of the equality of each and every human being irrespective of class, colour, race, sex, age or circumstance' (Vardy and Grosch, 1999: 58). In this sense there is a clear link to notions of social justice.

So returning to our example of the false mileage claim, the action was simply wrong because it could be categorised as theft or fraud: trying to take or claim something to which someone was not entitled. What would happen if everyone made false claims, that is everyone trying to take something to which they were not entitled? Clearly it would not be desirable for everyone to do this; therefore, as it could not become an acceptable universal practice, it is obviously wrong. Since the social worker knew that such actions were wrong, a priori, they should have thought twice before claiming, double-checking its validity, in order to avoid breaking this categorical imperative. As they clearly not did not, their actions were bad, or unethical and they could be punished as 'bad' since they failed to observe their moral duty to act totally honestly.

Utilitarian (Consequentialist or Naturalistic) Theories

Utilitarian ideas were devised at the same time roughly as Kant, originally by Bentham and later adapted by a number of other thinkers, principally Mill. Utilitarian ethical principles are in many ways a complete opposite to deontological notions since they direct attention towards the intentions or consequences of individual actions. The end product is what matters; this is what is meant by teleological (*telos* being the Greek word for end). In utilitarianism the general aim is to look for good consequences, and as many as possible, which are interpreted by Bentham as pleasure or happiness. This enables him to summarise his theory in the well-known phrase 'the greatest happiness of the greatest number'. This assumes that there is some kind of calculation, an approach Kant profoundly opposed. A utilitarian looks at the results of an action, to decide whether it is right or wrong. Consequently the end justifies the means, and thus a thinker from this school of thought would judge the rightness of an action by the result it produces, 'the greatest good for the greatest number', what Bentham called the 'principle of utility'. A choice that results in a good end is morally better than a choice that results in a bad end.

Applying this to our example is not quite so easy as it was with deontological approaches. Nevertheless it is clear that a utilitarian would focus on the results of the actions. In this case the arguments that the social worker was disorganised, claimed to have made a completely accidental mistake, and that the attempt to make false claims was unsuccessful, would all be relevant. In addition one could argue that pursuing action against the errant social worker risks damaging the greater good of having a skilled practitioner able to help a large number of potential service users, even if they are disorganised in doing so!

It needs to be acknowledged that there have been developments in utilitarian theory, and of particular interest here would be the development known as rule utilitarianism (propounded by Mill among others). A concise way of summarising this approach is to say that it looks to the long-term general interests of society as a whole. Rule utilitarianism does not conduct a simple calculation of what might be the best in these particular circumstances for these individuals, but does prioritise the need to have consistency of rules and laws which it is argued creates the greatest good for all in the longer term. So, in our example, despite the fact that there might be convincing reasons for not pursuing action against the social worker at this stage, and this might relate to the potential value of the social worker to service users, a rule utilitarian could argue that action to enforce a rule about mileage claim honesty serves the long-term interest of all potential service users since it convinces them that the profession of social work upholds very high standard of ethics and probity. Therefore in this case our disorganised social worker ends up in front of the professional standards committee because this proves to the outside world that this is the case.

The Third Way: Virtue Ethics

There has recently been a revival of interest in some ideas originally put forward by Aristotle, which, when modified, break into the diametrically opposed ideas of deontologists and utilitarians (McBeath and Webb, 2002: 1020–102). Aristotle was concerned not so much with rules as rules, or the consequences, but the virtues of the person engaged in the action. A virtuous person is someone who may be, for example, courageous, honest, kind, loyal, or conscientious, although not to an excessive extent – after all, someone who is excessively brave could become foolhardy (this moderation is referred to as the 'golden mean'). So an action is right if it is what a virtuous person would do; their goal being *eudaimonia* (Greek for human flourishing). Key concepts and ideas in Aristotelian virtue ethics are the pursuit of good which fulfils the end purpose (telos) of humanity which is to be rational, the development of character and asking the right questions. The emphasis is on practical wisdom (phrenesis) which is the tension between emotions and reason.

Modern philosophers, such as Elizabeth Anscombe, have reasserted the value of this approach. Anscombe was scathing about ideas such as the right action is the one that produces the best possible consequences, which she labelled 'consequentialism'. Likewise legalism was not ethics, but what mattered was practical reasoning and virtue. In this approach such concepts as 'intention' really matter. Virtue ethics 'makes foundational the qualities of one's character, which are manifest in one's actions' (Gray and Webb, 2010: 110). Note above all that virtue ethics is agent-centred rather than act-centred: a virtuous person will know how to act ethically in any given situation. One attractive feature of this approach is that it is holistic, which may explain the resurgence of its popularity.

In social work terms, what matters therefore is the qualities, character and disposition of the social worker themselves. The social worker's virtues and character really count. So in judging whether behaviour is ethical, what really matters is the virtuousness of the agent, not the action in terms of its observance of rules (deontology), or the action in terms of its consequences (utilitarianism). From this it is easier to judge what makes a good social worker: someone who displays all the positive qualities previously listed but, in addition, shows compassion towards service users, respect for people as human beings, and integrity in their dealings with them. Other commentators (summarised in Pullen-Sansfacon, 2010: 403) have suggested virtues for social workers such as temperance, magnanimity, gentleness, truthfulness, wittiness, friendliness, modesty, justice, professional wisdom, care, respectfulness and courage. Such workers in their training would be encouraged to develop qualities of reflection, empathetic understanding and sensitivity. This would invariably endorse a person-centred or relationship-based approach to social work.

Thus a good social worker would by their nature be anti-discriminatory in their practice. They would not become anti-discriminatory because they were observing rules telling them not to be, or because they were aware of the consequences of dis-crimination and consider these to be against people's overall interests. As McBeath and Webb (2002: 1026) put it: 'Doing the right thing in social work is not a matter of applying a moral rule, it is not the work-as-activity that is morally right, but rather the worker-as-agent expressed in the range, and subtlety of use, of the virtues.' Note that a virtuous social worker would not necessarily be an administratively competent one(!), so in our example of the illegitimate mileage claim, what would really matter is the kind of person who made the claim. Never mind their lack of organisation, are they committed, conscientious and caring social workers?

It is tempting to embrace virtue ethics as a refreshing, heartening approach, with a social work-like focus on the person rather than the action. Yet beware of some of its pitfalls.

Critical thinking exercise 1.3

What do you think the pitfalls of a virtue ethics approach might be?

Here are some of the points that might occur to you.

First, there is a real danger, fairly predictably, of inconsistency. A court or tribunal would not concern itself with what someone actually did, but focus more on what kind of person they were, and whether they generally acted ethically.

Then, at a deeper level, there is an almost inevitable circularity in any arguments that one may be tempted to put forward. If a 'good' social worker is one who has certain qualities, then we might end up by saying if they say they acted ethically, they did! Furthermore, presumably a 'good' social worker can only be really judged by other 'good' social workers. Does this then presuppose that people without those qualities cannot adjudicate on the actions of social workers – so the managers in this social work agency would themselves have to be 'good' social workers and, ultimately, only those who display virtuous qualities can be trained to be social workers?

Leading on from this, if judgments about whether social workers act ethically can only be made by other 'virtuous' social workers, must these judgments then confine themselves to determining the motivation and character of the social worker in question? In other words is there a danger of divorcing decisions from rules, laws, or consequences of actions? We will return to this debate later in the book, since decisions as to how to handle particular cases necessarily cannot conform exclusively to a deontological, utilitarian or virtue ethics approach.

Indeed, within these three distinct kind of theories there are variations which have different emphases.

Variations and Developments of Basic Ethical Theories

One obvious, principle-based, deontological alternative to Kant is that which rests on rules laid down by divine command. In such an approach rules are literally God-given. In Judaism and Christianity the most famous set of rules would be the Ten Commandments, but similarly Islam would also be quite prescriptive about what is right and wrong, with authority deriving from the Qur'an. So in effect if you want to know what is right and wrong in a given situation, or what your duty is, you need to ascertain what is the will of God. Clearly this presupposes that you accept divine authority and that you adhere to the specific religion which accepts and promotes that authority (for further discussion on connections between religion, values and ethics see Hugman, 2013: Chapter 7).

Utilitarianism has developed branches to meet some of the objections to the original Benthamite ideas. 'Rule utilitarianism' is an example already mentioned. Instead of judging each particular action by its consequences, the principle of 'utility' can be brought to bear on the code of rules which govern society, and do not have to be applied to individual actions in every particular case. In short, rule utilitarianism means 'an act is right if and only if it is in line with the code or set of rules whose widespread acceptance would result in at least as much utility as any alternative code' (Stewart, 2009: 26). Telling the truth and not stealing would be examples of such rules. More recently has been the development of the theory of preference utilitarianism which suggest that instead of calculating amounts of happiness and pain that result from actions, which in reality would be very difficult, all that is necessary is to find out what most people would prefer to happen and then do that.

One variation or alternative approach to virtue ethics is put forward by some feminists who hold that what underpins 'virtuous' social work, for example, is that social workers care about their clients: 'We keep confidentiality because we care about our clients. There is something intrinsic to our relationships with clients centred on mutuality and trust. We behave in a trustworthy manner because we care' (Gray, 2010: 1797). Drawing on the work of Levinas and others this leads some feminists to assert the importance of relationships as being central to ethics. If you are interested in exploring these ideas you may find articles that apply the thinking of Levinas and Habermas to social work interesting and relevant: see, for example, Rossiter (2011) and Gray and Lovat (2007).

Related to this alternative approach is what has become known as the 'ethics of care' approach. This derives from the work of Gilligan (1982) who took issue with the way in which other schools of ethics had drawn their conclusions. In particular there seemed to be an assumption that male rationality or male virtues were what mattered with little acknowledgement that the form of reasoning adopted by women is different from men. Because of socialisation processes and concern to develop the cohesiveness of the family, women seek compromises, resist blaming people and prefer an approach to competitiveness that seeks a result in which everyone gets something (Fisher and Lovell, 2009: 107). There is wisdom in this perspective that is referred to as 'care'. This should be regarded as highly as justice and is an approach that seeks equitable resolution of conflicts, with an emphasis on maintaining future working relationships and co-operation.

WHY DOES ETHICAL PRACTICE MATTER?

For the remainder of this chapter we need to consider, though, why ethical practice matters and say something about how it connects to the law in a general way. This may help us to draw some conclusions about the case study with which this chapter started. In Chapter 3 we will then return to this to consider how ethical practice relates, not just to the law in the sense of rules and principles, but to the specific legislation that governs ethical practice in social work.

Critical thinking exercise 1.4

Why does ethical practice matter? How would you start to answer this question?
It may help you to approach the question from a different angle by asking: to whom does ethical social work practice matter?

There are a number of ways of answering this question, and indeed a number of different levels at which could be answered. Let us start at the broadest: the international level.

International answer

> Social work grew out of humanitarian and democratic ideals, and its values are based on respect for the equality, worth, and dignity of all people. Since its beginnings over a century ago, social work practice has focused on meeting human needs and developing human potential. Human rights and social justice serve as the motivation and justification for social work action. In solidarity with those who are disadvantaged, the profession strives to alleviate poverty and to liberate vulnerable and oppressed people in order to promote social inclusion. Social work values are embodied in the profession's national and international codes of ethics. (IFSW and IASSW, 2004)

This statement by the International Federation of Social Workers (IFSW) starts by reminding us of the background to social work as a general concept, indicating a very strong ethical base. This is clearly linked to human rights and social justice, a theme to which we will be returning in Chapter 2, but what is significant about the IFSW statement is that it points to the global characteristic of social work, namely that it is essentially an ethical enterprise. So we could answer the question by saying that ethical practice matters because by definition social work has to be ethical. Social work practice in the UK that was exclusively bureaucratic, which relied on no separate ethical principles other than those that apply generally to people employed by public authorities, would therefore by definition not be social work. There is a global aspect of social work that binds everyone who describes themselves as a social worker together across nations, and those ethical principles are shared universally, even allowing for minor cultural and national differences.

At an international level, ethical practice also matters because of certain global trends that affect the context in which social work is practised. In a critical commentary article on social work ethics, Banks identifies a number of these:

> High-profile environmental, medical, scientific and socio-political issues such as climate change, developments in genetic technologies and global terrorism are bringing to the fore new versions of perennial ethical questions about human responsibilities, the nature and value of human and animal life and social justice in the recognition of diversity and distribution of scarce resources. These factors influence the context in which social work is practised and theorized. The 'postmodern' turn in sociological and philosophical thinking has contributed to a questioning of universal values, all-embracing foundational theories (including ethical theories) and the legitimacy and roles of 'expert' professional practitioners in relation to service users. There has also been a heightened concern to monitor and manage risk in social welfare work; a restructuring of welfare systems in many countries; the introduction of mechanisms for surveillance and control of citizens and service users; and increasing regulation of the work of professional practitioners. These factors are contributing to a continuing concern with professional power, legitimacy,

credibility, conduct/misconduct and a questioning of the traditional professional–client relationship – all themes that fall within the scope of social work ethics. (Banks, 2008: 1239)

These are not going to be explored further in this chapter, but they certainly set the scene for discussions later in the book. Social justice is a theme right through the book, and the exposition of this begins in the next chapter. Concern for the value of life, risk-taking, and the challenge of empowering service users while protecting the most vulnerable is a key theme running through Part 2 of the book. It is obviously a critical issue in relation to child protection and deprivation of liberty issues in the fields of mental health and mental capacity.

The Individual Service User

Now let us go from the macro to the micro, from the broadest level to the single individual. Why does ethical practice matter to the individual service user?

At this level the shortest answer to the question is that ethical practice matters because individual service users must have the assurance that people who describe themselves as social workers will act in accordance with certain important principles. Just as one assumes that a doctor has their patient's best interests at heart and will only recommend medicines that are the most appropriate for the condition which the patient is experiencing, so too social work service users have the right to expect that assessments are impartial and independent, and that social workers always place service users' needs first. Neither should they be influenced by commercial considerations, nor should they agree to compromise their advice or opinions simply because of organisational requirements.

For example, it may be expedient to arrange for someone who has mental health problems to be moved into hospital from the community, and may indeed be what a considerable number of people want, but arranging this and imposing it raises huge ethical questions, which the social worker must resolve through independent judgment of what is in the person's long-term interests operating within the broader legal framework. When dealing with very vulnerable, frail older people it is very tempting to conclude that they ought not to be left living at home on their own, and that residential care would provide a safer environment, even if they are reluctant to move. Relatives may well tell the social worker that residential care is the 'obvious' solution, that there is no alternative, and that the social worker is being obstructive in not arranging it immediately. However the safest option is not necessarily the ethical option. Ethics must be taken seriously and it is essential to understand what the law says – in this case, it is dubious to compel people to enter residential care simply on the grounds of frailty and hypothetical potential risk.

In child protection work it is axiomatic that, because of the tight legal structures that rightly apply to compulsory intervention in families, social workers need to be clear about their professional role. Parents and children need to know that social workers are making their decisions based on evidence, and not on the basis of prejudice, assumptions, organisational demands or even public opinion. If children are separated from parents, they need to know that the people who will be looking after them are 'fit and proper' people to do so. This means more than just police checks, but includes knowing how to respect children's rights, how to promote their well-being and how to make appropriate plans that are centred on children's own needs.

Doubtless readers will be able to think for themselves of a whole host of other ways in which individual service users need to have confidence in the ethical practice of social workers. However there are two other groups to whom it matters that social workers act ethically.

The Profession Itself

If you are a registered social worker, how other social workers behave matters to you. Any case attracting publicity invariably incites non-social workers to ask challenging questions. Why did they do that? How could they act in that way? Why did anyone think that that was the right thing to do? Responding to these can be a very uncomfortable and unnerving experience, not only because sometimes the actions of others appear to be indefensible, but also because by association with someone as a fellow professional who has acted unprofessionally, other social workers feel implicated.

This is particularly the case where children or young people have been abused by the care system itself; the most notorious example of this being systematic sexual abuse in North Wales residential homes in the 1990s which resulted in the Waterhouse Inquiry (Department of Health, 2000b). The history of institutional abuse, which makes for rather unpleasant reading, has at least had the beneficial effect of producing a whole welter of legislative measures to screen out people potentially likely to act unethically towards vulnerable groups. The Safeguarding Vulnerable Groups Act 2006 is the most recent example of legislation in this area.

So in this sense the existence of agreed ethical standards, together with a system to oversee the implementation of those standards, is a protection for the profession itself. As this runs alongside 'protection of title', meaning that only people who are registered can call themselves social workers, the consequence is that service users and other social workers know that if they are talking to someone who says they are a social worker, that person is bound by codes of ethics which are backed up by legislation. In the case of social workers, ethical practice is enforced by a professional body established by Parliament and required to implement the protection of title legislation (Care Standards Act 2000 as amended).

The Wider Public

If you are a registered social worker you doubtless know that your name can be accessed through the Internet in order to check that you are genuinely and currently registered. All a member of the public has to do is to go to the website of the relevant Care Council and click on the Register and check your name. What does this mean though, and why is it important?

Apart from the obvious answer – that it confirms whether someone is telling the truth or not – registration means that there is a process whereby someone can complain if a social worker acts unethically or unlawfully. This is in addition to complaining to the organisation that employs the social worker. For the public this is an important safeguard since there is an independent forum for judging whether social workers are acting responsibly and ethically. This means in some cases that social workers will not just do what the management of an organisation tells them to do, for organisations sometimes require people to cut corners and act in a way that does not fully promote people's rights. Occasionally there may be some cases in which the complainant believes that the social worker in question ought not to be in practice as a social worker anywhere. Through the enforcement of ethical standards there is a procedure for professional registration being withdrawn. This is important because this goes over and beyond someone simply being dismissed from employment. If there is evidence of gross violation of ethical principles, it seems only right and proper that the public should have the confidence to know that someone can be debarred from practice altogether.

Another way in which the public at large need to have confidence in the ethics of social workers is where they want to secure the services of a social worker themselves. In Britain this is unusual since the majority of social workers are employed by local authorities, agencies contracted to work for local authorities, or by independent organisations. However in other countries, for example the United States, it is commonplace to purchase social work services directly from the professionals. Nevertheless in Britain there are some circumstances in which the public will encounter independent social workers: those commissioned by courts to write independent reports, for example, or expert social work witnesses who are commissioned by solicitors acting on behalf of members of the public who are seeking redress.

HOW DOES ETHICAL PRACTICE LINK TO THE LAW?

We can address this question by returning to the case study in order to consider how this particular example relates to both ethics and the law, which will enable us to draw some conclusions about how they interconnect. We need to begin by unpacking some of the issues in this specific case.

The starting point as regards ethics is debatable. Absolutist, or principle-based, guides to ethics and acceptable behaviour will refer to concepts such as duty, categorical imperative or principle – some of the words you may have identified from completing Critical thinking exercise 1.2. Thus the social worker's actions could be condemned because they had a moral duty to act totally honestly and their actions were dishonest, whatever their intentions or consequences. If we start with utilitarian principles, then we are concerned with the consequences of the actions, what happens in the end, what is their result – these are the key concepts you ought to have identified in the Critical thinking exercise. The utilitarian argument against penalising the apparently unintentionally dishonest social worker is that it risks damaging the greater good of having a skilled practitioner able to help a large number of potential service users. Virtue ethics would be very much concerned with the nature of the person who is considered to have acted wrongly, whether they are virtuous, their character – again these are words you could have identified from the Critical thinking exercise. Hence the fundamental question raised: is this a committed, conscientious and caring person?

The starting point in law is clear cut: everyone must obey the 'law of the land' which in effect means that law that declares some behaviour unlawful or illegal. If this is true for everyone then there is a heightened expectation that so-called professionals will always obey this law. So law sets the overall framework for expectations at the very broadest level. In this case the law (principally the Theft Acts of 1968 and 1978) declares that any attempt to acquire money by falsely declaring that someone owes you money, when they do not, is an offence. While there is no universal agreed definition of fraud, generally speaking it is an act of dishonesty that intends to reduce one person's assets (in this case the employer) in order to increase those of another (the social worker). Fraud refers to the action of misrepresentation for this purpose. Note that throughout intention is important, so an action would not be fraud if it was accidental, or if someone had good reason to believe that they really were owed money.

In this case, what do you make of the social worker's defence that this was a genuine error? You may, or may not, find the explanation – they had used their diary to work out what they should claim from their employer for the previous month and had forgotten that on that particular day someone else had driven – convincing. But for the sake of argument let us suppose that it is true, and then apply what has been discovered thus far about ethical theory in order to help illuminate what action should be taken. We can then see how that matches the law.

Table 1.2   Matching ethical theory to the law

	Deontological principle-based theories	Utilitarian consequentialist theories	Virtue ethics	Law
Submitted false claim	Clearly wrong in principle	Whether it is wrong depends on the consequences	What was the social worker's intention?	A successful claim would be fraud
Said it was unintentional	Irrelevant, it is still wrong	Of no relevance, what matters is consequences	Of critical importance: is this a normally virtuous person?	Determines whether this was a 'criminal' act or not
Claimed disorganisation led to the claim	Professionals should not be disorganised so this reason compounds the wrongness of the action	Does this affect the potential value or utility of the professional for the greater good of society?	May help demonstrate that this is a person who is usually virtuous	May be used as evidence of lack of intent to commit crime

	Deontological principle-based theories	Utilitarian consequentialist theories	Virtue ethics	Law
Should this person be punished?	Yes, both for the false claim and for being disorganised!	Depends on overall consequences	No! This is a good social worker	Depends wholly on whether they intended to deceive or not
Likely action	Some kind of penalty	Depends	Point out that being disorganised is not a virtue and encourage reform	Lay evidence before court

So, from a law perspective, so much depends on the explanation as to why the false claim was submitted. If the court accepts the contention that this was the result of disorganisation, then clearly intention is not proven and no offence has been committed. But if the court does not, it would be bound to conclude that the fraud was deliberate and that the social worker tried to cover it up by making up a plausible excuse. This compounds the offence. So a great deal would hang on whether the social worker's explanation was believed or not. Did the social worker intend to gain money to which they were not entitled? It is this decision that ultimately defines whether an offence has been committed or not.

Critical thinking exercise 1.5

To what extent does this correspond to ethical theories?

Deontological principle-based theories: agree that the action is wrong in principle but diverts from this in that the law considers the agent's reasons for acting in the way that they did.

Utilitarian consequentialist theories: the law does not seem relevant to this, but in practice, courts would take the potential or actual consequences to others very much into account when determining the sentence.

Virtue ethics: very relevant in consideration of whether guilty of breach of criminal law, and virtuousness or 'good character' would certainly be taken into account when deciding the severity of the punishment or sentence.

From this it is clear that ethical theory does relate to the law but no one ethical theory appears to determine exactly how the law will operate. Inevitably, law represents an amalgam of different aspects of ethical theory and, furthermore, as we shall see later, which ethical theories are influential depends on what kinds of laws and in what contexts those laws operate. We explore this further in later case-study chapters but next we need to consider how the ethical theory relates to the other aspect of law – those principles of justice meant to underpin the whole political and legal system.

CONCLUSION

This chapter used a not entirely fictitious example of a newly qualified practitioner making a false expenses claim. Was the practitioner acting unethically? The question was posed in order to explore different theories about how judgments are made about ethics, in other words it introduced the realm of moral philosophy. Here three broad distinctions were made. First, there were theories that were deontological, principle based, and 'non-naturalistic'. Then there were utilitarian, consequence based or naturalistic theories. The third approach was labelled virtue ethics. Other theories, derived and developed from each of these were acknowledged, and it would be well worthwhile following these up if this chapter has whetted your appetite.

The discussion then broadened to address the fundamental question as to why ethical practice matters. Answers ranged from the international, to the individual, then to the professional and to the wider public. There are others, of course, but those four appear to be the key areas; their order is not meant to indicate a hierarchy of importance – far from it.

Finally the three different ethical approaches were connected to the law, returning to our hapless newly qualified social worker to explore how their actions might be judged. It is interesting to note how much the different ethical standpoints matter since they imply quite different judgments about the social worker's actions, and none correlates exactly with how the law would interpret these in reality.

The exercises in the chapter have hopefully helped develop skills in demonstrating an understanding of theoretical ideas. You should now be able to see how these apply to an analysis of actions and have also learned how to relate different views to underlying philosophies, in this case moral philosophy. This experience also helped one newly qualified social worker learn of the potential disaster of unwittingly making a false expenses claim. For in the actual case their otherwise exemplary behaviour and commitment to service users enabled virtue ethics to win the day, and no further action was taken – apart from the inevitable and necessary reprimand for their lack of organisation and accurate record keeping.

2

Social Workers, Social Justice and the Law

INTRODUCTION AND CHAPTER OVERVIEW

This chapter explores a fundamental principle that connects ethics and law in social work, namely social justice. What do we mean by social justice? In order to answer this, we need to explore different philosophical viewpoints of justice: what it is and how it is to be attained. Here reference will be made to the thinking of Aristotle, Hobbes, Adam Smith and J.S. Mill among others as a prelude to an explanation of the debate that dominates contemporary thinking between those who argue for a form of social justice to be attained through the welfare state and those who say that such ambitions are unjust, thwarting individual freedom and development. Among these more recent exponents of social justice theory this chapter will refer to the work of Miller, Nozick, Rawls and Sen. Later chapters will build on this discussion by applying different perspectives of social justice to ethics and practice in social work.

This chapter is particularly relevant to the justice aspect of the Professional Capabilities Framework which requires social workers at various stages in their career to advance human rights and promote social justice and economic well-being (The College of Social Work, 2012). It also relates to at least two other aspects of the Professional Capabilities Framework: under the heading 'knowledge' social workers are expected to apply knowledge of social sciences, law and social work practice theory. In addition social workers should be able to engage in 'critical reflection and analysis' in order to inform and provide a rationale for professional decision-making.

Exercises integrated into this chapter are designed to promote the attainment and development of Critical Thinking Skills 1, 2 and 3: demonstrating understanding and application of theoretical ideas, and relating different views to underlying philosophies or ideologies.

In addition its content is particularly relevant to 5.1.2 and 5.1.3 of the Social Work Subject Benchmarks (for list see Introduction).

This chapter begins with a case study that raises issues of fairness and justice for a parent who, despite their disabilities, is found to be 'fit for work'. This raises important issues concerning:

- the plight of people living on the borderline between barely coping and falling into acute poverty and debt;
- the distribution of resources more generally;
- notions of justice in a social context, referring principally to issues of equality and fairness;
- what is meant by justice – justice for whom?;
- how social workers should respond to social justice issues.

This moves us away from the discussion in Chapter 1 which focused purely on ethics and ethical actions. Here we are considering the importance of the concept of social justice in social work, which raises fundamental questions about the relationship between the individual and the state, mediated through the law, and also about the ethical role of social workers in combating injustice. However before we can discuss the role of social workers, we need to be clear about what is meant by social justice and the theories that underpin this notion. In passing we need to highlight that sometimes the law promotes social justice, but in other cases may itself appear to be unjust, as may become apparent from the following case study.

CASE STUDY 1

Fairness and justice: the plight of a disabled parent

Martha, who has multiple sclerosis and is a lone parent caring for three school-age children, confides in family centre staff that she is feeling suicidal following a recent threat to withdraw her benefit. She has been found 'fit for work' after a recent assessment. Although she has worked part-time in the past, she found it increasingly difficult to go to work due to the fluctuations in her condition. However she has been told she is fit enough to work from home and therefore is not incapable of work. Martha describes the news that her benefit may be withdrawn as the 'straw that breaks the camel's back' since she was only just about coping with her finances when she did have the allowance. She says that after paying her rent and heating bills, there was just sufficient left for food for her and her children. She cannot see any way she can cope and believes that her children would be better off without her by being adopted by someone who could look after them.

Critical thinking exercise 2.1

While you might have all sorts of reactions to this scenario, try to separate your own feelings from the situation described and try to think about what it is telling us about concepts of justice. It is all very well to respond that this situation is, for example, fundamentally unfair, but why might it be unjust? Ethically, what would be your response? So the questions you need to answer are:

1. What do you understand by the term 'justice'?
2. What do you understand by the more precise term 'social justice'? In answering this it may help to consider whether you think social justice is inextricably linked to notions of well-being and fairness, or to notions of equality.
3. How would you respond to the issues raised by the case study?

These are fundamental and challenging questions and the remainder of this chapter is given over to answering them. The plan is to address them stage by stage, beginning with an analysis of that most basic concept of all in law, justice, and then moving on to explain the meaning of social justice and concluding with a consideration of how this all links to law and ethical practice.

WHAT IS JUSTICE?

Perhaps not surprisingly the answer to this question depends on the starting point concerning how one judges people and actions, and that of course is precisely where we started in Chapter 1. Different interpretations of justice relate to the different perspectives adopted by theorists. So for an absolutist, deontological, view of what constitutes justice we look to Kant. For some kind of balancing act between the needs of people in order to determine what would be in the interest of the majority, we can look to the utilitarians who adopt a consequentialist approach. For a view of justice that draws on the notion of virtue and the concept of a good life, we look to Aristotle.

This is worth exploring further by looking at some case examples (we will return to consider our first case study towards the end of the chapter). This section concerning more general notions of justice starts with a dilemma which philosophy teachers love to put to their students: is torture ever justified? Should the law allow it? Is it just? Is it ethical?

CASE STUDY 2

An unpalatable dilemma

A man has been arrested on suspicion of terrorism. The police know that a bomb has been planted but do not know where, but do know that it will go off in three hours' time. They also know that their suspect knows where the bomb is, but he adamantly refuses to tell the police, despite the fact that the explosion will inevitably lead to substantial loss of life. Desperate for time and faced with an absolute refusal to give them the information they require which would save lives, would the police be justified in using torture to extract the information?

Critical thinking exercise 2.2

There are obvious debates for and against, but do try to decide whether on balance your answer to the question is yes or no.

So how would you set about resolving this ethical predicament? Would you use torture. If so, why? If not, why not?

Your answer to the questions does not matter quite so much as how you got there, although inevitably this challenging dilemma does give rise to some interesting and sometimes heated debates. It may help to think back to the theoretical positions explored in Chapter 1 which will enable you to anticipate how the different views – deontological, consequentialist, and virtue ethics – respond to this.

Kant's position, predictably, is that torture in these circumstances is unacceptable, whatever the consequences for other people. More specifically he would say that justice means respecting human dignity in the sense that we cannot use people as a means to an end. So in this example we cannot use torture to find out essential information even if the purpose in doing this is utterly honourable, namely to save the lives of others. There is a categorical imperative to treat each other with respect and we cannot resort to resolving debates about how to act by some kind of calculation. Instead we can only act out of duty; we must do the right thing for the right reason. Now of course one could argue that the terrorist has acted with considerable lack of respect for other people and is quite prepared to treat them for their own ends, yet the absolutist view would have to be that this does not justify jettisoning categorical imperatives (or fundamental principles if you prefer) in retaliation. For Kant the principles are inviolable, and for this reason Kant is generally regarded as being the father of human rights, since his position is that certain rights are unchallengeable, inalienable, non-negotiable with no exceptions permitted, whatever the consequences.

For the utilitarians, such as Bentham, the decision as to whether or not to use torture depends on the consequences. In this particular case there is a potentially good outcome to be achieved by adopting a strategy that would inevitably cause irreparable harm to one person's life but would also save dozens of other lives. Hence this would clearly result in the best result for the greatest number of people. Issues of principles of ethical behaviour become subsumed in the overriding question of what is in the interests of the majority of people. Put in its simplest term, in this example one person has to suffer in order to ensure that more than one person does not. Do note in passing, though, that it is assumed that we know what the consequences of the actions will be.

Virtue ethicists ask a different question. Their question concerns the character and intentions of the person who makes a decision about whether or not to use torture. There are no absolute rules about right and wrong in this situation, but there are considerations as to whether people making decisions are the right kind of person to be trusted with important decisions. So in this particular example there is no recourse to principles as such, but simply questions posed as to how honourable are the intentions of the police officer who makes a decision about what strategy to employ in order to secure essential information from the suspected terrorist. If that police officer believes that the only way of getting information is by using torture then that is acceptable if they are the kind of person to whom that sort of decision-making can be entrusted.

So the question as to whether torture is ever justified, whether it is ethical and whether the law should allow it, has different answers according to these different perspectives.

The next example looks at how these different perspectives may be put into practice in a legal context. Does the law implement absolute principles and make judgments on the quality of the action, rather than its consequences? Or are the consequences really what matters, so a sentence has to be proportionate to the harm caused? Or should the outcome of a legal case simply reflect what the court believes to be the character of the person involved: if they are not the kind of person who is likely to intend harm, should their sentence or punishment be different from a person who does not seem to care about other people?

CASE STUDY 3

The perils of speeding

Harry is driving along a country road and is approaching the top of the hill, where there is a bend in the road. The broken white lines in the middle of the road give way to double white lines and there are two warning signs: one says that there is a speed limit of 40 mph, and the other says that there is a road junction coming up, with a road off to the right. As soon as he drives round the bend at the top of the hill, Harry realises that there is a car stopped at the junction down the other side of the hill ahead of him signalling to turn right, and turned slightly to the right. There is also a lorry coming the opposite direction, some distance away. The car is now travelling at 45 miles an hour so he brakes, but unfortunately he cannot stop in time and hits the back of the car waiting to turn right. This pushes that car into the path of the lorry travelling in the opposite direction causing the lorry to brake and skid, unfortunately mounting the pavement and killing a pedestrian.

Critical thinking exercise 2.3

In the ensuing court case, what do you think happens?

Harry is convicted by a jury of causing death by careless driving, but acquitted of the more serious charge of causing death by dangerous driving. He is given a six-month prison sentence, suspended for 12 months, and disqualified from driving for 18 months.

Your initial response to this case, which is based on a real one, may be to ask why the other drivers were not also prosecuted, given that one had incorrectly positioned their car in order to execute a right turn, and the lorry driver was unable to stop in time without skidding. However the court takes the view that the chief fault was with the driver who is travelling down the hill too fast who had not taken sufficient account of the various hazards, including the junction, for which there was a warning sign. For our purposes, though, note that:

- the court judges the consequences of the actions in determining the nature of the offence – causing death by careless driving is far more serious than simply careless driving – and so there is an element of consequentialism in courts' considerations;
- had there been no accident, had Harry managed to stop in time, the offence would have been speeding for which there would have been a fixed fine on the grounds that there is a principle that cannot be violated – drivers must not drive at more than the legal speed limit – so sometimes penalties are applied on the basis of absolutist principles regardless of circumstances;
- the severity of the sentence would be partly determined by an assessment of the character and response of the accused motorist – a virtuous, remorseful motorist would be treated more leniently than one who was cavalier and tried to defend what they had done, and someone with a previously unblemished record would be treated differently from someone with previous convictions for speeding.

So in reality courts take a mix of approaches, sometimes within the same case: an absolutist approach with regard to the speeding, a consequentialist approach in terms of determining the severity of the offence, and an element of virtue ethics in determining what would be the appropriate sentence for this particular offender.

We will return to all of this in Chapter 7 when we examine youth justice since deciding how to assess young people's responsibility for their actions, and determining appropriate sentences, is a major issue reflecting all these sorts of arguments. In addition there is the ethical consideration of the extent to which young people can be held responsible for their actions when they are brought up in adverse circumstances, which naturally brings us into the broader area of social justice.

The case study at the start of this chapter also raised wider issues of social justice. The case of the disabled parent does not concern court cases or the application of criminal law, but rather focuses on the law as it sets out the framework for the welfare benefits system, and the way in which the law regarding entitlement to benefits is implemented. This brings us firmly into the realm of welfare state provision, so we now need to consider how general approaches to ethics and justice connect to the whole notion of social justice. This will enable us to provide a fuller answer to the question posed in Critical thinking exercise 2.1 and ultimately help to formulate deeper thinking about what constitutes an ethical social work response to case study 1 and the issues it raised.

WHAT IS SOCIAL JUSTICE?

In essence social justice refers to the application of principles of justice in a social context, concerning how society is organised and how people relate to each other, and the extent to which they have responsibilities towards each other. This moves beyond basic human rights that are, globally, enshrined in a number of different conventions, protocols, declarations, covenants and treaties. Many of these will already be familiar to readers: for example, the United Nations Universal Declaration of Human Rights, the Convention on the Rights of the Child, the Convention on the Rights of Persons with Disabilities (for a fuller exposition see Taket, 2012: Chapter 2). Fundamentally social justice concerns the distribution of wealth: social policy determines the extent to which a country is going to redistribute wealth among its citizens, and the law sets up the mechanisms for implementing that policy. Welfare benefits legislation is an obvious example of this, but so too might be included equal opportunities legislation, provision for enforcement of human rights, education, protection of children, adult care services, and a whole welter of other legislation aimed at promoting people's well-being.

This next section of the chapter introduces some markedly different views about what constitutes social justice, which of course incorporates notions of fairness and sometimes makes assumptions about equality.

Aristotle (384–322 BCE)

Aristotle is generally associated with virtue ethics, and the preoccupation with virtue continues into this Greek philosopher's approach to social justice. Aristotle was concerned to cultivate virtue, and therefore the good life. Natural justice was not necessarily the same as what the law said, since natural justice is independent and applies to everyone. In determining what were right and just actions, it was important to emulate the behaviour of virtuous people, and generally distribution of goods and wealth in society should be according to virtue, which would determine who should be honoured. Presumably this meant that those with the greatest virtue get most.

Hobbes (1588–1679)

One of the classical theorists is Thomas Hobbes who in the seventeenth century was writing in an England during the turmoil of the English Civil War. His work explores the relationship between the individual and the state. He declared that justice is simply a covenant or agreement between the individual and the state whereby in return for being ruled by a sovereign ruler, individuals gave up their freedoms and thus gained the right to live in a well-organised, disciplined society.

> In the natural condition of mankind, everyone had the natural right to do anything that was conducive to their preservation. There is both an obligation under the law of nature and natural rights to preserve oneself. The natural condition of

mankind was one of war of each against everyone else, and therefore one of great insecurity. Reason required men to authorise a sovereign to act on their behalf. All men were obliged to obey the sovereign, provided that he did not threaten their preservation (quoted in Freeman, 2011: 22)

Justice therefore rests on some kind of agreement; it is not intrinsically something natural or given. The assumption is that a sovereign will act justly but essentially Hobbes' theory supports the notion of absolute authority of the sovereign who 'has a right to do whatever he thinks fit, so that his commands are never a breach of justice' (Raphael, 2001: 68). So social justice becomes whatever the sovereign determines, which might mean a very uneven distribution of wealth.

Smith (1723–1790)

In the eighteenth century the Scot Adam Smith, who is probably best known for his economic theories as expounded in the *Wealth of Nations*, also wrote about justice and moral philosophy in the *Theory of Moral Sentiments*, published in 1759. Smith distinguishes three kinds of justice. Commutative justice means abstaining from harming other people – either the body of the person themselves, their estate or property, or their reputation. Violations of this kind of justice are to be punished. A second sense is the notion of valuing something or someone:

> valuing or pursuing an object with that degree of esteem or ardour that the impartial spectator would think it deserves, as when we speak of doing or failing to do justice to a work of art, or indeed to ourselves in a matter of self-interest. (quoted in Raphael: 115)

The third kind of justice comes closest to what we might identify as social justice. This is a form of distributive justice (although that may be too strong a term for it) that Smith calls 'proper beneficence', meaning doing positive good to those connected with us, or using what we have for charity. Charitable enterprise therefore becomes a form of social justice.

Mill (1806–1873)

The Victorian John Stuart Mill starts from a utilitarian approach, therefore sharing a common starting point with Bentham, whose work was briefly discussed in Chapter 1. Bentham justified workhouses because the majority of people disliked seeing people begging on the streets, and it was in everyone's interests that the poor should be set to work. Mill moves beyond this to consider the whole notion of justice in 'Utilitarianism' published in 1861. Mill starts from the basic premise that the requirements of justice contribute to general utility and analyses this in relation to six kinds of things which would come under the concept of justice.

- First there are legal rights. It is just to respect them and unjust to violate them.
- Second there are moral rights whereby certain laws may be considered unjust on the ground that they infringe somebody's right.
- Third, there is 'requital of desert', returning good for good and evil for evil.
- Next comes keeping faith, which basically means keeping promises.
- Allied with this is impartiality, for example: people in public office remaining neutral and unbiased is essential.
- Finally there is equality which connects with the basic utilitarian notion of producing the greatest possible happiness of the greatest possible number. This, Mill says, includes two principles: one aggregative, that is referring to the total amount of happiness produced, the other distributive referring to the way in which happiness is shared among people which implies some notion of social justice.

Those who follow Mill also argue that an action is right if it conforms to a valid rule within the system of rules, since following these rules leads to the greatest 'utility', the best result for the majority. Judging individual actions as to whether they lead to the greatest utility would, in practice, prove incredibly time-consuming and cumbersome, so it is best for human beings to agree to observe some general rules which would create the maximum benefit to most. This is often referred to as rule utilitarianism. Textbooks on ethics often quote an example of such a rule utilitarian approach as the generally accepted principle 'do not lie'. For our purposes, a general rule might be that people should be treated equally by the law, that law should be respected, and that it is the role of government to pursue the overall interests of the majority. In the economic context this might translate into the general requirement for governments to pursue what is in the economic interests of the country as a whole. The debate about how that is to be achieved then, of course, begins!

Miller (1946–)

Moving on to contemporary British theories of social justice, David Miller wrote specifically on this topic in his book entitled simply *Social Justice* written in 1976. Miller starts with a key distinction between conservative and ideal justice. Conservative justice is about rights which are publicly acknowledged rules and practices, while ideal justice links to the principle of desert, which is connected to need. There are then three principles or interpretation of justice: distribution in accordance with rights, distribution in accordance with desert, and distribution in accordance with need. The essential challenge is that these three are liable to conflict with each other, particularly desert and need which, he says, cannot be reconciled, since 'a distribution according to desert is incompatible with a distribution according to need' (Raphael, 2001: 185). The notion of need is, of course, fundamental to social justice. Miller distinguishes three types of need: instrumental (such as authorisation to do something); functional, relating to task performance (such as needing a computer in order to write an assignment); and intrinsic (we all need food; some people need interpreters). Miller says intrinsic needs are not wants, meaning simply objects of desire, but rather needs. Needs incorporates the notion that someone will suffer if something is not provided.

In a market society, Miller notes, desert was straightforward since each person was an independent agent producing goods or providing services so the gain obtained from the operation of the market constituted the just reward. In a capitalist economy goods and services are provided by groups of people working collaboratively so the desert of an individual cannot be assessed from the value of the product or service that can be assigned to that individual alone. Instead the organisation calculates the value of a position in that organisation and grades it accordingly. It then appoints to the position according to merit: those best suited for the post with the most appropriate qualifications and skills are appointed and then paid according to the value of the post. Hopefully readers will be familiar with this process! So in a sense while an employee merits their post because of their qualifications, experience and skills, the reward they receive is based on the value of the post to the business or organisation.

Desert and need are therefore in conflict with each other, for the process whereby someone is appointed to a post presupposes an acceptance of inequality with the most able being appointed. The reward they receive rests on recognition of inequalities of skills and ability. By contrast need relates to the notion of justice but presupposes a sense of human equality. The only kind of society that challenges this would be a planned egalitarian community, based on strong principles of solidarity and comradeship, where equality is all, and workers are not paid according to their market position.

Miller is careful not to draw any conclusions from his analysis but simply to set it out as a means of understanding the underlying tension between 'desert' and 'need'. The key question, of course, is to what extent measures should be taken to balance desert and need, in other words, to take from those who benefit from the way in which rewards are allotted, and give to those who lose out to the extent that what they 'earn' does not match what they 'need'. This clarity of analysis may be useful when questions of social justice are being considered, although it will not offer definitive answers to dilemmas posed by it.

Nozick (1938-2002)

What measures should be taken to balance desert and need? One straightforward answer is none at all, and this would be the response offered by the American Robert Nozick. His answer is simply that there is no obligation to redress this balance; there are no measures that ought to be taken. He comes to this view by putting forward a particular view of morality, which could be summarised as simply obeying the rules of the game.

In *Anarchy, State and Utopia* published in 1974, Nozick declares that someone is entitled to have what they have so long as they acquired it legally, or in a way which their society defines as legal. Thus people who work are entitled to the products of their labour, however unfairly those products may be distributed, and someone who is awarded a post is entitled to the salary that goes with it no matter how unfair that salary may appear to other people. Nozick maintains that in a fair and just society there are three key principles. These relate to: the just acquisition of what an individual has, the just transfer of what they have – which means selling or trading – and the just rectification of that if something has been acquired illegally. There is no greater or higher obligation of redistribution. There is no moral requirement to do anything about the way in which people gain their 'desert' so long as they do so lawfully. For Nozick contends that we are moral if we live according to the rules of society. Each individual's fundamental responsibility is to themselves; there is no higher social justice obligation, which is the starting point in the debate that took place in the 1970s between Nozick and our next philosopher, Rawls.

Rawls (1921-2002)

John Rawls, writing in the United States, comes to very different conclusions from Nozick, primarily because he puts forward the notion of some kind of social contract, transferring this social contract notion to the concept of justice.

In *A Theory of Justice* (Rawls, 1972), Rawls sets out five key assumptions about people and how they engage in a social contract with each other in order to agree how to live. The assumptions are:

1. self-preservation is natural and normal and therefore people are naturally self-interested;
2. people have the same right, are equally able, to participate in society and share in deciding how it is run since no one can justifiably claim more power than anyone else;
3. people are rational, that is they can think through the consequences of a social contract;
4. people have access to information;
5. people are ignorant about their own particular futures, for example, future health needs.

In order to explain how he gets to these assumptions, Rawls asks us to imagine people being able to rid themselves of all biased previous thinking and getting together to agree the basic principles for running society. It is rather like starting with a blank sheet, which Rawls prefers to call the 'veil of ignorance'. Being both self-interested and rational, people can then devise a set of principles by which benefits in society are distributed, and by which deserts and needs are reconciled. Therefore his conception of social justice centres on the idea of a social contract 'whereby people freely enter into an agreement to follow certain rules for the betterment of everyone, without considering the implications of these rules for their own selfish gain' (Robinson, 2010: 79).

The starting position is that people are equally able to participate and therefore any deviation from this could only be justified if it benefited everyone, especially those who are 'least advantaged' (Raphael, 2001: 198). Therefore all social primary goods – by which he means liberty and opportunity, income and wealth, and the bases of self-respect – are to be distributed equally unless an unequal distribution is to the advantage of the least favoured. Thus social justice is essentially about distribution, it is about 'assuring the protection of equal access to liberties, rights, and opportunities, as well as taking care of the least advantaged' and whether something is social justice 'depends on whether it promotes or hinders equality of access to civil liberties, human rights, opportunities for healthy and fulfilling lives, as well as whether it allocates a fair share of benefits to the least advantaged members of society' (Robinson, 2010: 79).

The question then is how: on what basis is distribution to take place? One basis, advocated by utilitarians, certainly would be to regard the principle of utility, or that which is likely to lead to the greatest happiness, to determine what should be done. However utilitarianism

> really consists of two principles, one prescribing the maximum increase in the total sum of happiness, the other prescribing the distribution of happiness to as many persons as possible. These two principles can conflict. In a particular situation, an individual, or, more realistically, a set of legislators, may be faced with two alternative policies. The first seems likely to increase the total national wealth more than the second, but the second seems likely to spread it more widely. Which policy is to be preferred? Utilitarianism gives us no answer. (Raphael, 2001: 201)

Rawls instead suggests that we should get away from looking for one single overriding principle yet there is one priority which is important, namely to ensure that all citizens' basic needs are met since only then can they exercise their rights and liberties (Rawls, 1993: 7). His views tend towards a concept of justice that favours egalitarianism and distribution according to need. For, in starting with a blank sheet of paper and drawing up some rules by which to engage in society, people would invariably conclude that there ought to be some kind of social contract based on two principles. The first principle would be that people should be as free as possible to pursue the kind of life that they wanted to have. The second principle would be the principle of difference, meaning people have different aims or goals. Yet since according to his fifth assumption people are ignorant of their own futures, it would be sensible to use a pattern of distribution that most favours the least well off. Rawls calls this the 'maximin' rule of game theory.

Elsewhere I have likened this theory to a board game.

> Imagine a board game in which a player has to throw a six to start. The player who throws a six at their first go is like someone who starts life with a large inheritance and wealthy parents. They then progress smoothly and rapidly and often win the game. The player who takes a long time to score the compulsory six before they are allowed to start is like the person who is born into a socially deprived area with parents who face multiple problems including inadequate housing and few social amenities. They progress much later, if at all, and rarely win. This is manifestly unfair and so the 'maximin' strategy ought to be to give

everyone the opportunity to play on a relatively equal playing field. In other words no one should have to throw six to start so that everyone should then have the potential to progress at a relatively equal pace, although, of course, some will win or do better than others. Therefore, Rawls argues, we are under a moral obligation to assist those who are worse off than ourselves. (Johns, 2011a: 64)

Since there can be no guarantee that we are born with manifest advantages it would be prudent to opt for social arrangements that supported this maximin principle. Therefore society ought to embody two principles of justice. The first is that everyone has an equal right to the greatest range of liberties compatible with liberty for all. The second principle is that social and economic inequalities where they exist should be to the greatest benefit of the least advantaged, and that all positions (such as employment or official posts) should be open to all – through what we might call a robust equal opportunities policy (Rawls, 1972). Of these two principles the first, liberty, is the more important; liberty is not to be limited either on the grounds of utility (hence Rawls opposes utilitarianism) or for the sake of equality. As regards the second principle, equality of opportunity must take precedence and here some equalisation of difference would be acceptable – what Rawls calls the difference principle – if they are to benefit the least advantaged. To explain this, Fitzpatrick (2011: 33–34) invites consideration of the following distribution:

Table 2.1 Possible distribution of opportunities

	Amanda	Bill	Carol
Blue	12	6	1
Purple	10	5	3
Red	4	3	2

Logically, those opposed to egalitarianism would opt for Blue, while true committed egalitarians would presumably opt for Red. Yet Rawls would opt for Purple on the basis that this benefits most the least well-off person, Carol. Redistribution in favour of the least well-off is justified up to the point when it starts harming their interests, for example, when the process begins to affect the economy. Thus Rawls' theory 'incorporates a strong element of social justice that seems to require redistribution and the equalisation of income, wealth and power but not equality for equality's sake' (Fitzpatrick, 2011: 34). His theory also promotes self-respect, an important concept in Rawls' writing on justice, since it establishes a fundamental basis of equality and this promotes 'public affirmation of all individuals' value as moral persons' (Zink, 2011: 333). So Rawls offers a sophisticated but quite specific interpretation of social justice, to which we will shortly return in our consideration of the connections between social justice, law and social work practice.

Sen (1933-)

The work of Amartya Sen, an Indian philosopher and economist, is worth considering briefly as Sen offers a different perspective, one which is global and practical, as well as being a direct challenge to Rawls.

Sen is impatient with justice simply as a theoretical idea, contending that there is too much abstract talk about what might be possible in an idealised, perfect world, such as that put forward by Rawls. For views such as Rawls promotes are transcendental in the sense that they speculate about a state of perfection, which hardly accords with reality. The identification of 'perfect' justice is, according to Sen, neither necessary nor sufficient in order to understand what is unjust (Boot, 2011). It will actually tell us very little about how to identify and reduce injustices in the here and now. What matters for Sen is comparative justice. Such an approach to social justice is relatively straight-forward to understand since we can all compare justice in different situations without needing some sophisticated theory of justice. A comparative approach also acknowl-edges that different principles of justice can exist, and here Sen offers an interesting illustration of the complexities of deciding what is just.

Three children are quarrelling about a flute. Who should own it? A says she should as she is the only one who can actually play the flute. B, however, is a poor child who has no toys at all in the world, so surely he should have at least have something to play with so why should he not have the flute? At which point we discover that C actually made the flute, so surely she has the greatest right to own it? Deciding ownership of the flute is clearly not straightforward, and any theory of justice must acknowledge that principles can clash. Whatever justice might mean, there seems to be some consensus that it implies equality of some kind, but here again the question is equality of what? Yet even this is not easy. For example, the use of income as a comparative measure of well-being may well be flawed because of the differences in the rates at which people can convert their wealth. In reality, the same income can buy more goods and services in one part of the world than in others.

However it is fairly clear that when we take issues such as famine and disease, we do not need castles in the sky before we can set about determining how to address these issues. We know that the existence of some problems is of itself evidence of injustice and therefore it is incumbent on us to discuss and debate our views about how to 'repair the edifices' in which we currently live. There needs to be open public reasoning about policies that can address injustice, and it is most important to address issues of global justice. Parochialism, meaning the attitude that says that I do not need to concern myself with anyone outside my immediate family or neighbourhood, is not acceptable since this would limit our obligations, making them very narrow indeed.

So for Sen the question of social justice is essentially a global one, for which there needs to be a political approach agreed and debated, that is one that concerns itself with what are apparent injustices in the real world. There can of course be all sorts of debates about how injustice might be addressed, but opting out by confining oneself to one's immediate social circle does not appear, for Sen, to be an option.

In refuting some idealised notion of perfect justice, Sen offers instead an expansion of the notion of justice so as to focus on the development of people's capabilities. This 'capabilities approach' promotes the idea 'that social arrangements should aim to expand people's capabilities, or their freedoms and opportunities to promote or achieve valuable beings and doings' (Banerjee and Canda, 2012: 20).

APPLYING THE THEORIES

Theories that have been summarised thus far represent different positions as regards social justice and these would clearly affect how we would respond to the issues raised by the case study set out at the start of the chapter. So let us apply some of the theories to the case study and see what they reveal.

For the sake of argument we need to assume that the decision to withdraw benefits is one that accords with the law, and so our considerations centres on the extent to which that decision is just, what it says about the law, and what should be the response of a social worker engaged in ethical practice with social work's implicit commitment to promoting social justice.

The theories which are going to be related to practice here are those that are exemplified by Mill, Nozick, Rawls and Sen. As a general typology we can categorise these under four headings: utilitarianism, libertarianism, egalitarianism (or maximin), and capabilities (or comparative) social justice. It is accepted that this typology may appear somewhat crude, or even too generalised, but the broad headings will serve our purposes here and do help to clarify the broad differences between social justice theories. It is also acknowledged that there are other theories of justice and within different schools of thought there are variations. For example utilitarianism includes act utilitarianism, rule utilitarianism, and preference utilitarianism. Nozick is used as an example of someone who believes in minimal state intervention, and generally people who subscribe to similar views are labelled libertarians. Rawls has had a major influence on social work practice with his 'maximin' approach to freedom and equality, while Sen offers a comparative and pragmatic approach that some practitioners might find more appealing.

Utilitarianism

The withdrawal of benefit has clearly made Martha unhappy and at first glance it might be difficult to see how this action could somehow lead to the greatest happiness of the greatest number of people. However the rationale for the changes in regulations that make welfare benefits more difficult to access need to be analysed in this context. This propels us straight into issues of social policy and indeed into economic policy, since ultimately the rationale lies in the political decision-making process that decided dramatic and significant reductions in public expenditure were required. As part of this policy stringent new regulations regarding access to welfare benefits have been drawn up, and a law was passed (Welfare Reform Act 2007) that introduced the so-called 'work capability assessment' that lies at the heart of the case study. The broader justification is the context in which the provision of incapacity benefit was seen to be costing too much and this issue became acute with the economic crisis that began in 2008. Therefore it is in the interests of the population of the UK at large, so utilitarians might argue, for there to be overall reductions in public expenditure and the review of entitlement to benefits is part of this process. So the withdrawal of Martha's allowance in the long term is, supposedly, part of the process that allows economic stability to return and the economy to improve.

There are a whole host of social policy issues that could be explored at this point but we need to focus specifically on the law and role of social workers. If utilitarians are generally sympathetic to the whole notion of social justice, why would they accept implementation of this kind of law that appears to go against the interests of people with disabilities? The answer presumably relates back to the wider overall general rule that says that government is bound to pursue the economic well-being of the country as a whole as a priority, and through doing this the wealth of the country is increased, or at least the economy does not deteriorate. Thus in observance of this general rule, the Welfare Reform Act 2007 could be passed and in individual cases can lead to consequences summarised in the case study. A utilitarian approach might argue that if the social policy argument is accepted, then the social worker's role is to explain to Martha why the changes have been brought about, and then to see what can be done to mitigate the effects of those changes on her personal life. Hopefully she could be dissuaded from pursuing the idea of someone else looking after her children. The law would be seen as just because the law has been passed through democratic process and there is no doubt that the outcome of the assessment was a result of what is now due process. In other words it complied with the law and, as the law was legitimate and in the interests of the majority, it might therefore be construed, from a utilitarian perspective, as just.

Nozick and the Libertarians

If utilitarians would feel obliged to defend the Welfare Reform Act 2007 in the context of an overall requirement to pursue the economic interests of the population as a whole, there is no such obligation for those who follow the thinking of Nozick. Indeed they would probably perceive welfare benefits as no more than charitable provision for people with disabilities. So the notion that this is a legal entitlement jars with the minimalist state approach which Nozick would advocate.

For many social workers perhaps the key issue is that Nozick appears unconcerned with laws that may themselves be manifestly unjust in terms of tolerating huge variations in wealth. The only consideration appears to be that people's possessions were acquired legally. This brings to mind a well-known quotation from Anatole France who in Chapter 7 of *The Red Lily*, written in 1894, wrote

> The law, in its majestic equality, forbids the rich as well as the poor to sleep under bridges, to beg in the streets, and to steal bread.

This somewhat tongue-in-cheek comment underlines the fact that there is a wider context in which the law operates. From a social justice perspective any law that criminalises people begging on the streets could be seen as oppressive. It also raises the broader question of why it is that people feel compelled to sleep under bridges and steal bread. What is the context in which this occurs? Instead of passing a law that criminalises such behaviour surely it would be better to have a social welfare system in which it was not necessary for people to take such action? Yet at the same time, of course, the statement is true. The law itself has to be applied equally to all people so theoretically the law does forbid rich people to steal bread. This of course crystallises a difference between the way in which the law operates where it applies to everyone, and the broader context in which laws can themselves be oppressive.

In a sense Nozick personifies the non-interventionist approach so the social work role in this context would be minimal. There would be no suggestion of challenging the law itself although the social worker might encourage Martha to look for alternative, charitable, sources of funding. Ultimately if she decided to ask someone else to look after her children, that might be what the social worker would do. It is of course difficult to apply Nozick's principles in the context of UK social work since his fundamental philosophy is against the state having an active role in people's lives anyway.

Rawls' Maximin

Unsurprisingly, perhaps, Rawls' theories are very popular in social work circles although allegedly sometimes misrepresented (for a fuller account of this alleged misrepresentation see Banerjee, 2011). It may be that the appeal relates to what can be attained working in real-life situations, and of course his views certainly justify continuous action on other people's behalf. There is a strong element of distributive justice in Rawls which strikes a chord with social workers across the world: the International Federation of Social Workers' definition refers to striving to 'alleviate poverty' and 'liberate vulnerable and oppressed people in order to promote social inclusion' (IFSW and IASSW, 2004). Yet it is clear that there is no desire to overthrow existing systems altogether. Essentially Rawlsian theory is about fairness to all based on principles of co-operation with a specific view of the state's duty to promote social co-operation.

To be more precise, the first principle, the equal liberty principle, guarantees basic political and civil freedoms which can be encapsulated as the right to participate in society (freedom of speech, movement, religion, choice of occupation, right to own property and so on). The second principle includes the notion of equality of opportunity, meaning fair access to education and work for all people with equal ability and talent, whatever their background. The second principle also includes acceptance of difference, for example, people with greater talent and greater responsibility in their jobs should be paid more, but nevertheless there is a requirement that inequalities benefit least advantaged citizens to the greatest extent possible. So it would be acceptable to argue that there should be financial rewards for the most talented as they are responsible for creating employment for others and this means that everyone, including the 'least advantaged', becomes better off. So, taken together, Rawls' two principles of social justice imply acceptance of differential payments according to people's talents and abilities, but also argues for what one might call a 'level playing field'.

What does this then say about the role of law as it relates to social work ethics and social justice? At one level a social worker following Rawls' views would be in favour of encouraging people with disabilities participating in the workforce. This is, after all, a key aspect of social inclusion. Yet there is a danger that the consequences of implementation of the Welfare Reform Act 2007 in this case might lead to the break-up of the family and such a degree of poverty that Martha is unable effectively to participate in society. This would then violate the equal liberty principle. So quite what approach would be taken is debatable but it is worth noting that there would be no objection to a social worker challenging the law itself, as well as the way it is being enforced in this case. The case study raises questions about how this action is congruent with principles of distributive justice.

More generally, if we follow Rawls' thinking, it is possible to designate some areas of law as being of particular relevance to social work. One would be human rights legislation and provision such as, for example, the Human Rights Act 1998 which enshrined the European Convention on Human Rights into UK law by setting the Convention as the yardstick by which to assess court judgments, legislation itself, and decisions by public bodies that employ social workers. Another area would be equal opportunities legislation now consolidated in the Equality Act 2010. As regards the general role of social work, there would presumably be support for the advocacy role of social workers representing the interests of the 'least advantaged', striving to help them improve their position in society, and this might well be the role of the social worker in Martha's case.

Sen and the Capabilities Approach

Having to make assumptions about how to interpret Rawls' theory in practice does highlight a gap. One key limitation is that his theory principally concerned 'working poor citizens' and so he excludes from his framework people who cannot work or who are utterly dependent on others. In contrast, theorists such as Sen with his capabilities approach supports freedoms for all people in a broad sense, promoting protection of the most vulnerable, including older people and children (Banerjee and Canda, 2012).

If we adopt this approach, the scope of relevant law now becomes wider to include all legislation to protect vulnerable people, adults and children, all measures to provide services for those who are in any kind of social need, including Martha in our case study. Our starting point would appear to be what is just, not defined in an absolute sense, but judged simply on the basis of how Martha's position relates to that of others. Here we are not comparing her position with other people with disabilities who have also been subject to work capability assessments; instead we are looking towards an overall assessment of how her position relates to others. Looked at in a broader, comparative, sense, does the legislation that apparently pushes people with disabilities into work appear to be just? In one sense it could be argued that such a move tries to expand people's capabilities, although this conclusion would be more persuasive if the legal measure were to be accompanied by active steps to encourage employers to employ people with disabilities. This last point could feasibly be made in the context of the Equality Acts of 2006 and 2010 which between them established the Equality and Human Rights Commission and provided a statutory remit to promote and monitor human rights, besides protecting, enforcing, and promoting equality across the seven 'protected' grounds of which disability is one (section 4, Equality Act 2010).

This raises all sorts of questions about the social policy that led to the Welfare Reform Act 2007 being passed. Is it just and proportionate in relation to other measures designed to reduce public expenditure on welfare benefits? What are its results in terms of the consequences for people affected by legislation? Is the requirement to work just and fair in the context of high general unemployment and in the context of implied threats to withdraw benefits? This may have a disproportionate effect on the people concerned, impoverishing them in a generally affluent society. Given the broader role of social work implied in the International Federation's definition, Sen appears to be giving social workers permission to challenge the existence of legislation that appears to be, in comparative terms, unjust.

How to interpret Sen's views in relation to the individual concerned is more debatable. An immediate concern might be whether this claimant has been treated fairly compared to other claimants in a similar position, or whether the process by which the decision was made was fair. There would appear to be a strong argument in favour of an advocacy role, and issues of empowerment do come to the fore in terms of tackling the decision made and in encouraging Martha not to give up. Certainly the notion of having to separate from her children seems manifestly unfair and unjust, and it would be difficult to see how, if one adopts Sen's approach, a social worker might acquiesce to this request. In essence that really would be unethical.

CONCLUSION

In this chapter we explored the whole notion of social justice and touched on the relationship between law, social justice and ethics in social work. The principal case study concerned the threatened withdrawal of welfare benefit which was analysed towards the end of the chapter using some of the theories covered in the main part of the chapter when we explored the whole notion of what is social justice. Before presenting theories of social justice, we posed a more general question about what constitutes justice. A brief consideration of this included a profound ethical dilemma, whether to use torture, alongside a real-life case where a criminal court made a decision about a driving offence. This highlighted the fact that in practice courts in Britain adjudicate by using a mix of theoretical approaches to justice. In some cases an absolutist approach is used; in others there is an element of consequentialist considerations, yet in determining sentence there is almost invariably consideration of the character of the offender, reminiscent of a virtue ethics approach.

The main body of this chapter covered social justice theories including those of Aristotle, Hobbes, Smith, Mill, Miller, Nozick, Rawls and Sen. The purpose of this was to provide introductory knowledge of competing views of what constitutes social justice. Subsequent chapters will combine some of the insights from these theories, applying them to different areas of social work using practice or case-law examples. For this purpose theories will be grouped together under the headings of utilitarian, libertarian, maximin (Rawls) and capabilities (Sen). This analysis will begin, perhaps appropriately, with social workers themselves and considers an issue that brings together ethics and justice, namely accountability. To what extent and in what ways are social workers accountable?

3

Accountability, Ethics and the Law

INTRODUCTION AND CHAPTER OVERVIEW

The underlying principle behind codes of ethics that undergird social workers' professional practice is respect for service users and promotion of their interests. This includes the need to protect service users from harm and to advocate for them where necessary, a core social justice principle. The law requires social workers to conduct themselves in a way that commands public confidence and to respect the fundamental rights of service users and carers, including basic human rights enshrined in the European Convention on Human Rights. As was seen in Chapter 2, there are various different theoretical interpretations of what actually constitutes social justice, but many social work practitioners subscribe to a Rawlsian approach that argues powerfully for the formalisation of fundamental human rights. As we also saw in Chapter 2, theorists differ about the extent to which the state, including state agents such as social workers, have a duty to embrace promoting individuals' rights to equality and fair treatment – and, after all, what exactly does the word 'fair' mean?

This chapter therefore begins with a case example of where social workers may encounter a conflict between how they would interpret their role in terms of pursuing social justice, how the employer might perceive that ambition, and how this all relates to ethics, especially the formalised codes of ethics which social workers are required to follow. This case is analysed using the theoretical frameworks outlined in the first two chapters of this book. Following on from this, the second half of the chapter connects accountability to the law itself. Under the heading of accountability and the law, reference will be made to organisational and professional accountability, as well as accountability to the courts and the wider public. A key issue here is that in extreme cases, social workers may be required to be very assertive in promoting service user rights. One real case is included here as it is in the public domain and demonstrates the very real challenges some social workers face in practice. It concerns the gross abuse of trust which was only revealed after a sustained personal campaign by a residential social worker determined to stop the abuse of youngsters in the care system and to pursue justice on their behalf. This leads, in the conclusion to the chapter, to a discussion of expectations made of social workers and the ways in which social workers as professionals may be required to do more than just observe the regulations and requirements of their employers. Likewise employers and professional bodies are entitled to expect social workers to observe ethical principles in all that they do.

This chapter is directly relevant to one specific aspect of the Professional Capabilities Framework (The College of Social Work, 2012): namely values and ethics which requires social workers at various stages in their career to apply social work ethical principles and values to guide professional practice. Naturally reading this chapter will help you engage in critical reflection and analysis, which is another Professional Capabilities Framework expectation, and may also help you operate effectively within your own organisational framework – this falls under the Context and Organisations heading in the Framework.

Exercises integrated into this chapter are designed to promote the attainment and development of the Critical Thinking Skills 2, 3, 4, 7 and 8:

comparing and contrasting different viewpoints and experiences;

relating different views to underlying philosophies or ideologies;

evaluating different perspectives and ideas;

reflection and reviewing, re-evaluating and reformulating your own views.

In addition its content is particularly relevant to Social Work Subject Benchmarks 5.1.2 (5) and 5.1.3 (3–5) (for list see Introduction).

Social work has always had a strong commitment to protecting and promoting the well-being of vulnerable people, adopting an approach that emphasises the importance of building a positive, professional relationship with people who use services as well as with professional colleagues. Social workers must be able to balance the tension between the rights and responsibilities of the people who use services and the legitimate requirements of the wider public (Kline and Preston-Shoot, 2011). For example, where there are issues to do with child protection, criminal justice or mental health, the social worker may have a dual role of protecting service users and protecting the public, and clearly occasionally these will clash. Social workers may also encounter a potential conflict if they perceive their role to act in accordance with ethical codes or principles of social justice as being different from the role which their employer would expect them to fulfil.

Underlying all of this is a broader question concerning what is meant by accountability. Or to be more precise: to whom are social workers accountable? Logically one could argue that, as social workers are employed by someone, they are responsible to that person or agency (Doel and Shardlow, 2005, especially Chapter 11). If social workers are required to subscribe to a code of ethics, as indeed they are, then surely they have a higher level of professional accountability to act in accordance with the code, which in some cases may mean challenging an employer's interpretation of their obligations to provide services (Preston-Shoot, 2011). At the highest level one could argue that social workers are accountable to the law itself, not just through professional registration which includes observing specified codes of conduct, but also in determining how their obligations to the interpretation of the law and advising courts are to be interpreted. For example, if an employer proposes to act in a way which, in the social worker's view, does not fully comply with legislation, does the social worker then at least have an obligation to inform the employer or even to challenge policies concerning interpretation of legislative responsibilities? If social workers are required to give evidence in court in care proceedings, or provide pre-sentence reports in youth justice cases, how should the social worker interpret their obligations to the court?

These debates can sound quite theoretical so perhaps it is best to start with specific examples which can then be related to theories of ethics and justice explored in Chapters 1 and 2.

CASE STUDY 1

Over-enthusiastic, too 'political', or the kind of social worker everyone would like to have?

Anita was an enthusiastic, committed social worker in the field of adult care specialising in disability. She was very unpopular with her managers for she believed that her primary role was to encourage service users to fight for all the services to which they were entitled, to challenge every decision made by agencies (including the local authority itself) regarding access to services, and to complain whenever they felt excluded from the kind of events and activities which other people could enjoy. Her fundamental belief was that disability was a socially constructed concept, and that the disability label risked people being seen as disabled in all aspects of their life and, in short, led to social exclusion. Her managers believed that this led her to be unnecessarily provocative in her dealings with themselves and other agencies, and furthermore this sometimes led her to take risks with people's safety by encouraging service users to believe that they were more capable of living independently than, in fact, they were.

Whether you consider Anita over-enthusiastic, political or idealistic will naturally reflect your personal approach to social work generally. A more fundamental question which the case study raises, and which is relevant to all social work in every sphere, is: to whom is the social worker accountable? In the context in which she works, where do her responsibilities lie? How does all of this relate to the ethical principles that relate to social work, to the whole notion of justice and, of course, to what the law says?

Critical thinking exercise 3.1

In this exercise, you are asked to reflect on the whole issue of accountability. Specifically you are asked to connect Anita's approach to her work to the various ethical theories which were discussed in Chapter 1 and also to the social justice theories outlined in Chapter 2.

It is not the task here to decide whether Anita is right or wrong in her approach to social work, nor is the task to judge the employers. Rather the intention is to match this approach to what ethics, social justice theories and the law say about the way in which the social worker is accountable.

The overall question to be answered is: to what or to whom is Anita accountable? So the specific questions you need to answer are:

1. How can ethical theories be applied to the approach she adopts to her work?
2. How can the different social justice theories be applied?

    Later in the chapter you will also be asked to reflect on the role of the law in accountability, but set this aside just for the moment.

3. How do these relate to what you think the law says about accountability in social work?

These are not easy questions to answer, so it may pay to look back at the theories discussed in previous chapters. It will repay you to do so particularly as we shall be taking forward the analysis in those chapters into discussions in subsequent chapters of how they apply to particular case scenarios or to particular service user groups. As regards the law, you may want to look back at some of the basic social work law texts: for example in, Brammer (2015: Chapter 1), Brayne, Carr and Goosey (2015: Chapter 2), Johns (2014b: Chapter 9).

ACCOUNTABILITY AND ETHICAL THEORIES

In Chapter 1 we explored deontological, utilitarian, virtue-based and feminist (or care) approaches to ethics. So how do these apply to the ethical position of the social worker? Are there any other approaches that might be considered more valuable and relevant in the context of social work?

Deontological

The deontological or Kantian approach looks for absolutes or categorical imperatives (see Chapter 1 for full explanation).

It might be thought that one absolute rule would be that an employee always follows instructions of their employer. Yet if that were to become an absolute, it is clearly conceivable that a social worker might be compromised into acting in a way which contravened the broader commitments to pursue empowerment and independence for social work service users. Ultimately it could lead to a social worker condoning not just poor practice, but practice that was actively oppressive or even abusive (as in the events that led to the Waterhouse Inquiry discussed later in this chapter). So it would be difficult to see how this would be an appropriate absolute rule, although clearly by and large it would seem a sensible basic expectation indicating the course of action that most social workers would adopt on most occasions.

One way round this absolutism would be to argue that sometimes exceptions need to be made but the problem with a categorical rule is that once exceptions are conceded, the categorical ('you must always …') is violated. For example, if a friend suddenly appears on your doorstep desperate for help as they are being pursued by vicious criminal gangsters so you agree to hide them in the attic, what do you do when the gangsters appear on your doorstep asking if your friend is in your house? Kant argued that you would have no option but to answer 'yes', even when telling the truth might cause a great deal of hurt or even murderous consequences. Yet clearly most people would lie in these circumstances. The question then is how to justify the lie. The problem with saying ' you must not lie, except …' is that then there needs to be absolute agreement about what exceptions there should be, and inevitably there is the risk that the list will grow longer and longer. An approach that can accommodate this is to suggest that there is a kind of hierarchy of rules: for example, preserving life might take precedence over lying, thus justifying the exception to the rule.

If we return to the way in which a rational person decides what is the correct action following Kant, the social work practitioner might decide that the correct road to follow is the code laid down by their professional body, rather than instructions issued by an employer. The question (or maxim) they would then have to pose is whether they would be willing for everyone to follow this rule. Would it be acceptable if everyone followed the agreed codes of their respective professions? Clearly it would be perfectly justifiable to answer 'yes' to this question, in which case in certain situations professional codes would take precedence over employer instructions. There are plenty of examples of where this might generally be the case, for example, a doctor obeying the Hippocratic oath and therefore refusing to participate in certain kinds of procedures or actions a health authority might try to require. Another example might be that of a priest who would refuse to divulge what was said to them by way of confession, even if the law supposedly required this in some circumstances. So the social worker might decide that social workers always do what is deemed to be the 'correct' professional action, and this would apply over and above the instructions or expectations of an employer.

Naturally this assumes that there is some particular action that is 'correct' and somehow this will be ascertained by reference to the professional body code of ethics or some similar reference point. In reality this may not be so. Banks (2012: Chapter 4) offers a clear exposition concerning the limitations of codes of ethics in an examination of putting absolute principles into practice. Here she identifies the tension between codes of ethics that are too generalised and open to interpretation, and those which are so prescriptive that they do not appear to allow room for professional judgment. Generally she concludes that professional codes

> comprise mixtures of abstract ethical principles, aspirational ideals, descriptions of practice, prescriptions for action and stimuli for reflection and education … The statements of principles are as much rhetorical devices to demonstrate professional credibility and/or inspire social workers to aim higher. They are also designed to educate (by highlighting areas of potential ethical conflict or concern) as well as to regulate behaviour by offering rules for action. (Banks, 2012: 119–20)

As regards a more general appeal to professional principles and values, this would clearly have merit in offering something outside the narrow confines of the employer-employee relationship, but a difficulty in practice would be that such values are even more generalised than those contained in some codes of ethics, hence the difficulty in seeing how these could be translated into specific rules that must be obeyed at all times. So while using professional codes as absolutes might initially seem attractive, in practice this may prove problematic.

A third way might be to say either that social workers must always do what service users say whatever the circumstances, or else to say that social workers must always do what the law says in terms of interpreting their role. The question then is, would the social worker be satisfied if everyone followed either of these rules? This again might prove problematic.

Following service users' instructions as if they were sacrosanct would be particularly difficult in cases where service users were unable to understand what was in their own best interests or where there were serious concerns about abuse and there was a need to protect them. Many social work cases involving children would clearly fall into this category, but also here might be included vulnerable adults who have lost capacity in relation to certain kinds of decision-making or who are coerced by others into expressing views or requests that are not truly their own. Nevertheless as a general principle it is self-evident that social workers would comply with service users' wishes, but the difficulty here is that we are trying to move beyond general principles to categorical rules which inevitably become intrinsically more challenging.

It is easier to see why simply using the law as a means of deciding how to deal with individual cases might prove inadequate. The very simple reason is that the law does not tell social workers what to do in particular individual circumstances. In a valuable guide to incorporating social work law into practice, Braye and Preston-Shoot (2010) make this case quite emphatically:

> an exclusively legalistic model, where the law is elevated to become the main form of admissible knowledge, is inadequate for the complexities social workers face. It may be challenged for creating an impression that the law offers a clear map for welfare practice when, in fact, it provides a series of maps within statute, regulations, guidance and court decisions, regularly redrawn, sometimes inconsistent, and variable in detail and prescription. (Braye and Preston-Shoot, 2010: 6)

On the basis of all of this it would seem reasonable to conclude that a search for infallible, incontrovertible, unchanging rules to govern social work practice may be a bit of a fool's errand: a desirable objective but one that is not in practice attainable.

Utilitarian

Readers will recall from Chapter 1 that the principal difference between a deonto-logical and a utilitarian approach is that the former is based on a priori principles, whereas utilitarianism focuses very much on the consequences of the actions. So here how we judge Anita's approach to her work would very much depend on how successful she was in achieving certain objectives. Overall did she improve the quality of the lives of service users for whom she was responsible? In each individual case could the consequences be justifiably described as a good outcome? One way of measuring this would be, of course, to ask service users themselves, but note that this is not the same as simply complying with service users' instructions. It implies that there is a more objective evaluation of the overall attainment of the social worker in promoting people's well-being.

In attaining her objectives with individual service users Anita may be obliged to 'tread on a few toes' and indeed she may end up antagonising her own employers to the extent that they decide to dispense with her services altogether. She may feel obliged to fight people's corners for them, but what if this is to the detriment of other people's needs? For example if her articulate and persistent pursuit of resources and services for her service users means that others in greater need are denied those resources, then at a broader level Anita's approach may fail the utilitarian test in that this does not result in the best distribution of the scarce resources for service users generally.

Virtue Ethics

In virtue ethics, what really matters is the character of the agent, in this case the social worker, Anita. Following Aristotle we might ask which personal characteristics she possesses that might persuade people that she is a virtuous person who is pursuing the correct path in this situation. Aristotle's teacher, the Greek philosopher Plato, identified four virtues: wisdom, courage, self-control and justice. For Aristotle justice was the dominant virtue, to be supplemented by a number of personal qualities or virtues such as patience, truthfulness and indifference – in the sense of neutrality and not wishing to pursue one's own ends of publicity and achievement. Applying this to the case study, we might then ask of Anita:

Is she courageous in pursuit of her service users' needs, indifferent to her own selfish desires?

Is she honest, conscientious and loyal?

Is she compassionate?

If she displays all of these attributes one might conclude that her actions are entirely consistent with good sound ethical social work practice but there are a number of questions to pose.

First, although not judging her approach by the consequences as would be the case with a utilitarian approach, we must inevitably be concerned with the issue of meeting service users' needs generally. If her fight on her own service users' and carers' behalf ignores the plight of other service users and carers with whom her team or agency deals, then what does this say about the overall commitment to promoting the rights of people with disabilities? Aristotle argued that what distinguished human beings from other kinds of beings was their ability to reason (rationality) and their membership of a group or community. Thus this raises the question of how she has reasoned out her priorities in relation to the wider community, and how that community is defined.

Second, the related issue of loyalty is also very relevant here since it is equivocal. Loyalty to whom? Clearly the employer might not perceive her as very loyal, perhaps preferring an employee who consistently follows departmental policies and procedures. If the loyalty is to people with disabilities generally then there may be a conflict between promoting the general needs of that service user group and fighting energetically and vigorously on behalf of individual service users. However if loyalty were categorised as applying specifically and only to those individuals who are on Anita's 'caseload' then her loyalty would be beyond dispute, as would her integrity and commitment. Nevertheless the weighing up of priorities in relation to the wider community would still have to be a consideration.

A Care Ethics Approach

One way of resolving this debate about loyalty would be to shift the focus slightly away from general virtues towards an ethic of care, with a sharp focus on the care relationship as the bedrock for sound professional practice in social work. Relationships are central and relationships are key. In this approach it will be easier to evaluate Anita's qualities as a social worker. Do service users value the relationship she has with them and does she demonstrate, through that, that she cares about their situations? In her interactions with them, do they feel cared for?

Given the feminist element to much of the care ethics approach, one could also argue from this perspective that she needs to be aware of broader issues as they relate to policy, politics and the law. Specifically in the kind of context in which she works, does she work positively towards addressing gender imbalances whereby women are expected to care for family members in need, and where the dominant work ethic has translated into clearly oppressive practices focused on people with disabilities?

ACCOUNTABILITY AND SOCIAL JUSTICE THEORIES

This almost seamlessly leads to a consideration of the policy and legal context of social work as demonstrated in this case. There can be no doubting Anita's commitment to her work, with her unswerving dedication to empowering people with disabilities, so what can we say about the underlying philosophy behind her approach to work and the way in which this relates to theories of social justice? Having considered various interpretations of ethics, how does Anita's approach to her work measure up to the social justice theories that we examined in Chapter 2? As in the previous chapter, we are going to divide social justice theories into four groups: those that generally fall under the category of utilitarianism, acknowledging a number of variations such as rule utilitarianism; libertarian theories that stress the importance of individual freedom, such as those put forward by Nozick; the principles established by Rawls, particularly his maximin idea; and the radical challenge to all of this put forward by Sen who stresses capabilities.

Utilitarianism

Highlighted earlier in the book was one utilitarian solution to determining the appropriateness of an approach or action through a series of rules deemed to create the greatest good for that community. Following such rules within the system of rules can be deemed to lead to the greatest 'utility', and that would be the best result for the majority. A general rule that most would accept is that all should be treated equally by the law. More controversial would be a rule that says that in promoting and encouraging equality, it is necessary to devote more resources to one comparatively 'disadvantaged' group than to another, and this would be with the intention of doing more than just ensuring that people were treated equally by the law, but that they became more 'equal'.

Anita's interpretation here is to say that the service users she deals with should have available to them the resources that would enable them to attain the maximum degree of parity with people without disabilities. Furthermore, her role actively promotes the notion that, generally speaking, everyone should be included in society. Inclusiveness in this context might well mean people having the same rights to achieve to their maximum potential, and therefore any barriers that stood in the way of that process need to be broken down or overcome. In this respect services that support people with disabilities and promote their well-being are connected to the notion of removing disadvantage, insomuch as this is possible.

However it needs to be noted that there may not be such generally accepted rules and that we have simply ascribed to Anita's motives an assumption that such rules exist. A utilitarian does not necessarily argue for such rules, but explains the process of evaluating actions by implying that if such rules existed, and could be proven to promote the maximum utility for the whole of society, then they would be valid and worthwhile. Nevertheless as soon as we start unpacking the various elements in this, it becomes clear that we are making a number of assumptions and that there is no specific utilitarian underpinning justification for promoting equality and social inclusion in this way. In fact the evidence is somewhat against this if we go back to the original ideas of Mill (see discussion in Chapter 2). In his famous work *On Liberty* Mill argues forcefully for minimal external control over individuals' lives, which rather cuts across the extensive state intervention that generous provision of social services seems to imply. Thus Mill stresses the civil and political freedoms of the individual, which leads us neatly on to libertarianism.

Libertarianism

The libertarian approach, as exemplified by Nozick (first discussed in Chapter 2), is relatively straightforward to explain. It promotes vigorously the notion of freedom as equating with maximum freedom from state intervention, and denies any real role for the state in promoting people's welfare, relegating state intervention more or less exclusively to defence and law and order.

Setting aside the question of whether social workers should be employees of agencies financed by the state, libertarians would also dispute the notion that powerful advocacy on behalf of people with disabilities is necessary. There would of course be no objection to people with disabilities promoting their own interests or arguing strongly on their own behalf, or indeed others arguing for them, but there would be opposition to any state-sponsored advocacy.

Furthermore there would be fundamental objection to the imposition of equality legislation or provision of services financed by taxpayers. Equalities legislation would be an example of increased state regulation and control over people's rights to choose: the obvious example being the employer's right to choose workers. Service provision would be considered best left to the private market according to most libertarians, who generally subscribe to what is known as neoclassical economics – a strong belief in free market forces and a minimum of regulation.

While libertarians would not necessarily have any argument with Anita's belief that disability was a socially constructed concept, and that this may result in social exclusion, they would strongly refute the idea there was any obligation to do anything about it. It would be anathema for those who adopt a libertarian perspective to have someone whose salary is paid out of public funds employed to advocate for more state support for a particular group. There are a number of reasons why libertarians adopt this approach. There is a perceived danger that such an approach might encourage dependency. Pressing for more resources to be paid for by public funds would inevitably mean higher taxes for others which of itself is perceived as an infringement of liberty. Taking all these measures together there would overall be a decrease in freedom right across the board.

The Maximin Approach (Rawls)

Rawls is sympathetic to the libertarian promotion of freedom or liberty, but argues for the promotion of maximisation of liberty for all, within the wider framework of liberty for all. He would take specific issue with libertarian objections to equality legislation, promoting instead the notion of employment being open to all which implies some kind of equal opportunities policy. As explained in Chapter 2, Rawls accepts in principle the desirability of equalisation of difference, although with conditions. In effect he promotes redistributive policies but not equality just for the sake of it.

The consequence is this view offers a much stronger acceptance of Anita's basic premise that, in fighting for the rights of people with disabilities, she is actively promoting social inclusion and therefore plays a role in redistributing power. To this end it is logical to push for better services and resources for people with disabilities since such provision mitigates the limitations that disabilities necessarily impose and therefore facilitates more effective participation in society generally. It could be argued that her commitment reflects a higher principle which is that of promoting people's rights generally and contributing towards a fairer distribution of resources, and this would be consistent with a Rawlsian approach. So in terms of accountability, we could simply conclude that Anita is accountable to this higher ideal, although this begs the question of how that accountability is to be put into practice and how it is to be judged. Observance of professional codes of ethics could be one answer, although, as we saw earlier in this chapter, there are limitations in judging accountability by reference to codes which run the risk of being either too general, or conversely too specific.

The Capabilities Approach (Sen)

If a Rawlsian approach seems too theoretical or idealised, it may be that the comparative stance of Sen's capabilities approach has more to offer. This starts from the premise that, while one might have difficulty formulating a view as to what constitutes justice in a perfect sense, everyone knows what constitutes injustices and when something is unfair (Sen, 2010). Hence in this case it is transparently obvious that people with disabilities are not in the same position as those without, and therefore what the social worker is doing is developing the capabilities of her service user group to participate in society, in the same way as others do. All she does is centred on promoting their capabilities and their opportunities to achieve something valuable in terms of who they are and what they can do. As we saw from the discussion at the end of Chapter 2, Rawls has difficulty accommodating within his theoretical framework people who are unable to work or who are always dependent on others. No such difficulty presents itself with Sen's capabilities approach which actively promotes the needs of the vulnerable or excluded generally.

As with the Rawlsian approach, we might conclude that this means that Anita is accountable to some kind of higher ideal, and such an ideal might well be made explicit in a professional code of ethics. This code of ethics would then claim precedence over the contractual relationship through which an employee would simply be accountable to their employer. Such an arrangement does exist in relation to the medical profession, in that the Hippocratic oath obliges doctors to abide by certain principles regardless of organisational accountability structures. However currently there is no equivalent in social work or anything that has quite that degree of power, so in practice the issue of accountability distils into various mechanisms whereby accountability is enshrined in law. This can be law that holds social workers to account when they fail to abide by professional codes of conduct, or it may be where expectations are enshrined in statute, or in terms of expectations laid on social workers by courts.

So appropriately at this point we move on from examination of accountability in relation to ethics and social justice principles towards the relationship between social workers as ethical actors and the law itself.

ACCOUNTABILITY AND THE LAW

In Critical thinking exercise 3.1 you were asked to connect accountability to various approaches to ethics and to social justice theories. You are now asked to think about accountability and the law.

Critical thinking exercise 3.2

For this exercise, return to the case study and reflect on the whole issue of accountability. Then consider these two questions:

1. What do you think the law says about social workers' accountability? Which laws or legal processes apply and how?
2. To what or to whom is a social worker legally accountable in their everyday work?

There are several ways in which social workers may be held accountable and to some extent the precise accountability relationship will depend on the agency that employs a social worker, and the context in which it works. For example in an independent agency there may be a direct financial relationship between the social worker and their 'client' and in that sense the accountability crystallises into a direct 'hiring and firing' relationship. However in UK social work this is unusual, although in adult care in particular there exists a wide range of independent sector agencies where lines of accountability to the agency are much more direct than they would be in local authorities.

In statutory agencies, accountability acquires an additional level in the sense that social workers are accountable not just to their employers, but also to the legal mechanisms comprising rules and regulations that may require their employers to act in certain ways. Furthermore social workers are accountable to the courts charged with interpretation of those rules. In addition there are specific instances where social workers are required to set aside the normal levels of employer-employee relationship and hold themselves accountable directly to the courts. We shall now explore these areas in more detail, but note that this is not an exhaustive overview of accountability in social work (for which see Banks, 2004; Braye and Preston-Shoot, 2010: Chapter 6; Welbourne, 2010) but one that focuses on ethics and social justice. This consideration includes specific case examples.

ACCOUNTABILITY TO AGENCIES AND ORGANISATIONS

It would go without saying that employers have the right to expect that their employees who are social workers would discharge their responsibilities competently, conscientiously and in a trustworthy and reliable fashion. Failure to do so could clearly lead to dismissal. In our case study it would be quite unfair and unreasonable for the employer to dismiss Anita on the grounds that they did not like her approach to social work, but she would need to be careful that her actions complied with reasonable instructions from her employers, and that she took note of their concerns about potential risks to service users. In other words she has to balance a number of competing ethical issues:

- loyalty to the employer;
- her personal ethics and values encompassed in her strong commitment to social justice;
- ethical considerations concerning the safety of service users.

More may need to be said about this last point as it has not yet been discussed, and it does touch on major issues concerning risk-taking which are an inherent part of social work practice. Here there is beginning to be explicit acknowledgement of the degree of risk to which service users may be exposed (for a summary of developments of the whole notion of risk see Parton, 2010). For example, in the Final Report of the Munro Review of Child Protection (Munro, 2011: Chapter 2) principle seven of an 'effective child protection system' stated

> Uncertainty and risk are features of child protection work: risk management can only reduce risks, not eliminate them. (Munro, 2011: 23)

Munro went on to say

> Risk management cannot eradicate risk; it can only try to reduce the probability of harm. The big problem for society (and consequently for professionals) is working out a realistic expectation of professionals' ability to predict the future and manage risk of harm to children and young people. (Munro, 2011: paragraph 2.32)

In adult care the issues are very similar. A White Paper (HM Government, 2012: 37) defined high-quality care as including protecting people from 'avoidable harm' but including 'freedom to take risks'. The current policy of personalisation, that is centring services on people's needs and choices with maximum direct service user control and choice over the services, carries an intrinsic element of risk (Carr, 2010). This is acknowledged in government guidance:

> Personalisation is about enabling people to lead the lives that they choose and achieve the outcomes they want in ways that best suit them. It is important in this process to consider risks, and keeping people safe from harm. However, risks need to be weighed up alongside benefits. Risk should not be an excuse to restrict people's lives. (Department of Health, 2010: 5)

In a scoping paper for the Joseph Rowntree Foundation on rights, responsibilities, risks and regulations Glasby (2011: 11) comments:

> Risk is important – but people using services often perceive this in a disempowering way as something that is imposed on them by the system.

> Taking risks is an everyday part of life – and life without risks would be very dull indeed. … Rather than being risk averse, we need to work in a way that enables positive risk-taking – and we need to support practitioners and the organisations that employ them to do this without fearing that we will come down on them like a ton of bricks if things go wrong.

Speaking more broadly about the whole issue of safeguarding and protecting adults, Lord Justice Munby, who has adjudicated on many cases involving consent, capacity and safeguarding, commented at a conference in 2010:

> We must adopt a pragmatic, common sense and robust approach to the identification, evaluation and management of perceived risk. The fact is that all life involves risk … The emphasis must be on sensible risk appraisal, not striving to avoid all risk, whatever the price, … What good is it making someone safer if it merely makes them miserable? (LAG, 2012: 6)

It is worth noting in passing that all of these comments imply a strong ethical stance towards independence of individuals and families together with a powerful promotion of social justice in terms of encouraging maximisation of choice and independence.

Critical thinking exercise 3.3

This is a Reflection point:
What might be the downside of this legal form of approach to social justice? What about those who cannot articulate their own needs, or do not have the capacity to understand about risk?
We will return to this topic in Chapter 8.

The test of accountability is what happens when something goes wrong. In child care cases responsibility for investigating serious cases is sometimes taken out of the hands of social work agencies, as in the case of Serious Case Reviews. These are constituted under Local Safeguarding Children Board Regulations (section 13 Children Act 2004) as outlined in *Working Together* (HM Government, 2013). In some cases, government ministers themselves take direct action as in the case of baby Peter Connelly which follows. A brief consideration of this case demonstrates how these procedures can give rise to challenging questions about accountability and justice.

CASE STUDY 2

The Peter Connelly case and accountability

In 2007 Peter Connelly (aged 17 months) was killed. After the conviction of the mother and her boyfriend, the Secretary of State ordered an independent investigation by the Office for Standards in Education, the inspection body for education and children's services. This was required to complete its investigation in a truncated period, concluding that there were serious flaws in the child safeguarding procedures in the London Borough of Haringey. As a consequence, the Secretary of State immediately ordered the local authority to dismiss the Head of Children's Services, Sharon Shoesmith, who did not have a background of social work. Shoesmith subsequently appealed to the courts eventually winning her case for unfair dismissal, on the grounds that she had not been afforded an opportunity to defend herself (*R (Shoesmith) v OFSTED and others*, 2011).

So in this case, and in a very real way, someone was held to account for their overall responsibility for the case. Shoesmith was not personally dealing with the matter. Indeed, she might have known nothing about the case whatsoever, but she was the person ultimately responsible. However, the point at issue here was that she was never allowed to explain this to the council who were 'required' to dismiss her on the grounds of negligence and failure in her duty of care to the children for whom the local authority was responsible. In the case of the two social workers directly involved in the case, they lost their initial appeals against dismissal since their cases had been considered by the authority and they had not been summarily dismissed without a full consideration of the circumstances. However, as they were both social workers they were also referred to the professional regulatory body, which at that time was the General Social Care Council.

This leads us appropriately then to consider next accountability to professional bodies.

ACCOUNTABILITY TO PROFESSIONAL REGULATORS

Since implementation of the Care Standards Act 2000, in addition to social workers being accountable to their employers, they are also accountable to the professional body charged with overseeing registration of social workers. These procedures are in line with other professions such as nursing, medicine and teaching. In the baby Peter Connelly case the social workers were not only dismissed by the local authority but also referred to the General Social Care Council conduct committee who decided against striking each social worker off the register permanently. Instead they were both suspended from the register for a specified period. The conduct committee explained its decision by taking the whole context of their work into consideration, not only in relation to this particular case but also as regards the organisation's lack of staff and excessive demands made on their workers. Subsequently there was a marked increase in the number of referrals to the General Social Care Council's conduct committee (General Social Care Council, 2012: 51).

The grounds for referring social workers to the conduct committee would have to relate to a stipulated code of conduct. This is not the same as a code of ethics as promoted by professional bodies. Following the abolition of the General Social Care Council in 2012, responsibility for conduct committees and overall procedures for registration of social workers transferred to the Health and Care Professions Council. This body lays down Standards of Proficiency which set out what registrant social workers must be able to do.

The Health and Care Professions Council Standards of Practice for Social Workers in England includes 15 sets of standards which social workers are committed to attaining at the point of qualification and registration, and must then uphold throughout their professional working lives. Breach of them can result in a range of sanctions ranging from admonishment right through to permanent removal from the register, and a record of these are held on the Health and Care Professions Council website. The Standards particularly relevant to ethics and social justice in practice are as follows:

Health and Care Professions Council Standards of Practice for Social Workers in England (2012)

2 be able to practise within the legal and ethical boundaries of their profession

2.1 understand current legislation applicable to the work of their profession

2.5 be able to manage competing or conflicting interests

2.6 be able to exercise authority as a social worker within the appropriate legal and ethical frameworks

2.7 understand the need to respect and uphold the rights, dignity, values and autonomy of every service user and carer

2.8 recognise that relationships with service users and carers should be based on respect and honesty

3.1 understand the need to maintain high standards of personal and professional conduct

3.4 be able to establish and maintain personal and professional boundaries

5.3 be aware of the impact of their own values on practice with different groups of service users and carers

13.4 understand in relation to social work practice:

... the development and application of relevant law and social policy;

... the impact of injustice, social inequalities, policies and other issues which affect the demand for social work services;

... concepts of participation, advocacy and empowerment.

While high-profile cases hit the headlines, many important cases do not. The outcomes of 'conduct' cases, as they are called, are available to the public on the relevant website. For example, in Northern Ireland one social worker was struck off the register in 2012 for falsifying reports by stating she had been to see clients when she had not, and also by submitting false mileage claims for those fictitious journeys (there are parallels here with our newly qualified social worker in Chapter 1). In another, a social worker was struck off for failing to inform the Council of convictions for drink-driving and driving while disqualified (Northern Ireland Social Care Council, online). In one case in Wales, a learning disabilities social worker was made subject to a two-year suspension order with conditions for failures to protect vulnerable service users (Care Council for Wales, online). For an overview of cases considered by the General Social Care Council when it had responsibility for conduct hearings for social workers in England see McLaughlin (2010).

Critical thinking exercise 3.4

Reflection point:
    For what kinds of actions do you think social workers should be removed from the professional register and effectively be debarred from practice?

ACCOUNTABILITY TO THE COURTS AS INTERPRETERS OF THE LAW

In certain circumstances, social workers may find themselves being called upon to explain agency decisions, or indeed their own decisions, in a court of law. This may be part of a judicial review or, more commonly, in proceedings involving children such as care proceedings under Part IV of the Children Act 1989. The next chapter examines a specific example where courts commented quite extensively on the legitimacy and ethics of the social work approach adopted. The case concerned care proceedings where there was a history of domestic violence (*EH v London Borough of Greenwich*, 2010).

In other cases, courts have commented on the way local authorities themselves have interpreted the law. In community care law, one of the key cases often cited is the Gloucestershire and Barry case (*R v Gloucestershire County Council ex parte Barry*, 1997) in which the courts declared unlawful the withdrawal of services without a new assessment (under section 47 of the National Health Service and Community Care Act 1990, the legislation that then applied) where services were already being provided under various community care provisions. In other words, once a local authority has declared a certain level of need following assessment, and undertaken to provide certain kinds of services as a consequence, it could not review the level of service provision without reviewing the assessment.

In Chapter 9 reference will be made to cases where courts have been particularly critical of actions taken by social workers which, in the opinion of judges, demonstrate a lack of knowledge of the law itself. In one, judges virtually accused social workers of taking actions in order to circumvent the law (*London Borough of Hillingdon v Neary and others*, 2011). In another case (not covered in this book) judges were so appalled by the ignorance of the Mental Capacity Act 2005 demonstrated by one local authority's social workers that they insisted on naming the authority in order to expose what the court considered to be the failings of its senior management (*G v E and A Local Authority*, 2010). It is clear that courts are not afraid to take social workers and their employers to task where they consider that they have failed to comply with legal requirements. If nothing else, this underlines the importance of social workers knowing about the law, and certainly serves to demonstrate that accountability is a concept that has real meaning in practice.

ACCOUNTABILITY TO THE COURTS AS ADVISERS AND REPORTERS

In some branches of social work, practitioners are regularly called upon to report to the courts. For example, social workers who are members of Youth Offending Teams will be called upon to compile pre-sentence reports for the courts on young people who have broken the law. In this setting, social workers are regarded as experts who will be able to advise a court on appropriate sentence or combination of measures that will reflect the seriousness of the offence committed and will also fit the offender in terms of trying to ensure that they do not reoffend. There are strong parallels between this role and the role played by the probation service in relation to adults, which in Scotland is also the role fulfilled by social workers.

Social workers are also quite likely to become directly involved in legal proceedings that involve children in need of protection. In care proceedings, brought under Part IV of the Children Act 1989, the social worker with principal responsibility for the case is likely to be the key witness in court. Here it is important to understand that the first duty of the social worker is to the court, as it is in youth justice cases, and on occasion there may be a divergence between their professional view and that of the local authority that employs them. In that case, the social worker's duty is to be honest about their opinion even if 'this may mean expressing a personal view which conflicts with the agency stance' (Brammer, 2015: 81). The obligation to tell the court the truth is an absolute; a Kantian position if ever there was one.

Likewise, where social workers act as guardians in child care cases, their duty is first and foremost to the courts with an absolute obligation to be truthful. Guardians are now employed by an independent agency, CAFCASS (Children and Family Court Advisory and Support Services), whose duties include giving advice to courts about Children Act 1989 and adoption applications (section 12 Criminal Justice and Courts Services Act 2000). Yet where they are appointed (generally under section 41 Children Act 1989) they are responsible to courts for what they say and do in terms of writing reports and instructing solicitors on behalf of children.

Critical thinking exercise 3.5

Reflection point:
   Where and when might tensions arise between the social worker's obligation to
their employers and their duties to the courts?

ACCOUNTABILITY TO THE WIDER PUBLIC INTEREST

Between 1974 and 1990 widespread and systematic sexual abuse of young people, predominately boys, occurred in a number of local authority and independent sector residential homes in North Wales. Subsequently there was a public inquiry (Corby, Doig and Roberts, 2001; Department of Health, 2000b) which is usually referred to as the Waterhouse Inquiry, named after the High Court judge who chaired it.

Such public inquiries may be ordered by the Secretary of State where there is very serious concern about social work practice under various laws (Tribunal and Enquiries Act 1992, Local Authority Social Services Act 1970, Children Act 2004). It is a procedure that is sometimes put into place when there is a great deal of public interest in a particular social work related issue, and is a very real demonstration of accountability to the public who can, if they wish, attend the inquiry hearings.

The Waterhouse Inquiry followed on from an investigation carried out by the local authority principally responsible for the homes, Clwyd County Council, which had demonstrated that a very powerful and widespread paedophile ring had operated in the area, and this included senior care staff and possibly police officers and politicians. It is not proposed to explore this particular case in detail – the Waterhouse Inquiry Report is 893 pages long – but to highlight a couple of issues that emerge from it that raise fundamental questions about ethics in the operation of law concerning investigation of serious malpractice.

The first issue emerged in late 2012, when it became clear that the Waterhouse Inquiry Report had not actually heard a considerable amount of evidence that could have been available to it. Consequently opportunities to connect the abuse to other paedophile rings and to prevent subsequent abuse had, it is alleged, been lost; this was important and relevant in the light of discoveries about the abusive behaviour of a number of high-profile celebrities. There were a number of reasons for this, and a further inquiry, the Macur Inquiry, was instigated in November 2012 to investigate this. One major concern was that the internal inquiry conducted by Clwyd County Council had indeed uncovered some of these connections, and had clear evidence of specific incidents of abuse, yet this report could not be published. The Waterhouse Inquiry Report itself made the following comment:

The misfortune was that, in the view of leading lawyers who were instructed to advise Clwyd County Council, the report could not be published … because publication would probably constitute a fundamental breach of the Council's contract of insurance, entitling the insurers to refuse to indemnify the Council in respect of outstanding and potential claims against the Council by children formerly in its care who alleged that they had been abused while in care. (Department of Health, 2000b: paragraph 2.03)

In other words, the insurance company, who covered the local authority for claims against it for malpractice and breaches of duty, had effectively gagged the report for fear that there would be a deluge of claims against the local authority which it would have been obliged to pay.

The second issue that emerged from the Waterhouse Inquiry Report concerns whistleblowing. Given the vulnerability of the young people concerned, you may be wondering how the case first came to attention. Many people believe that this was a result of the sustained and determined efforts of a residential social worker, Alison Taylor, who had been employed as an officer in charge of a children's home in Bangor and in that capacity had made complaints about a number of colleagues. As no action had been taken by the local authority, she approached local politicians and a police investigation commenced which did not result in any prosecutions. Subsequently, Taylor was herself suspended by the local authority since the Chair of the Social Services Committee had concluded:

that she is a most unfit person to be in charge of a children's home, and that she is a blatant trouble maker, with a most devious personality. (Department of Health, 2000b: paragraph 2.17)

Subsequently, she was dismissed from her post and began a long campaign that involved contact with politicians and the Welsh Office, the latter dismissing her complaints having asked her former employer for their views of her – an action heavily criticised in the Waterhouse Inquiry Report (Department of Health, 2000b: paragraph 49.68). Eventually her personal campaign succeeded in having the Waterhouse Inquiry itself established but, even so, her actions continued to create controversy. In 2005 a book was published by Richard Webster entitled *The Secret of Bryn Estyn: The Making of a Modern Witch Hunt* (Webster, 2009) which alleges that the Waterhouse Inquiry Report was itself the result of a lot of public hysteria, that innocent people had been imprisoned on the basis of allegations of serious abuse that could not really be substantiated, and it cast aspersions on the integrity of people who made the allegations, making what one reviewer called 'unsubstantiated comments about her emotional stability and motives' (Corby, 2006).

Critical thinking exercise 3.6

Reflection point:
  Is whistleblowing really worth it?

In the light of what we know about this case and others, this seems a valid question to ask, but it goes back to social workers' commitment to service users, which is where this chapter started. An overriding concern for people's well-being should surely prevail against the protective self-interest of an organisation or even the social worker themselves; this appears to be an absolute, reminiscent of Kant, which governs some social workers' perspectives.

Dismissing people who bring to public attention issues of abuse and malpractice is an obvious ploy for an employer, anxious to undermine such allegations, to adopt. It is for this reason that legal protection for whistleblowers was introduced in the Public Interest and Disclosure Act 1998. In relation to social work, the most relevant provision is section 1 concerning disclosures in good faith where an employer is failing to comply with legal obligations or where the health or safety of an individual is being endangered. Raising such complaints should not result in detriment to the individual, and subsequent action by the employer against a whistleblower could result in an appeal to an employment tribunal (section 3 Public Interest and Disclosure Act 1998).

CONCLUSION

This chapter has covered a very broad area, examining the way in which ethics, law and social justice intersect in the context of social work accountability. To whom are social workers responsible? That question has been a theme right through the chapter, beginning with our case study of the enthusiastic, committed social worker whose approach to her work sometimes brought her into conflict with her managers. In the second part of the chapter we connected accountability to ethical approaches: deontological, utilitarian, virtue ethics and care ethics. In the third part, we connected accountability to social justice theories using utilitarianism, libertarianism, Rawls and Sen approaches to analyse different interpretations of the social worker role. The fourth and final part of the chapter consisted of an overview of accountability and the law in relation to organisations, professional regulators, the courts and the wider public interest.

The intention of the chapter was to help readers reflect on their ethical and legal responsibilities in social work. Inevitably the emphasis was very much on social workers themselves, and the fact that they are accountable in a broader sense than just being responsible to their own organisations or employers. Certainly employers, professional bodies and the courts will expect social workers to observe ethical principles in all that they do, but likewise social workers as professionals may be required to do more than just observe the regulations and requirements of their employers. Here there may be a conflict between the social worker's own personal values and expectations of employers, as was evident in the case study. There may be issues for readers of this book where their own personal views, which could derive from cultural or religious beliefs, might potentially bring them into conflict with what organisations and professional bodies might expect. Those issues need to be explored openly in discussions with other social workers, students, tutors and practice educators, and it has to be acknowledged that sometimes accommodation needs to be found between one's personal viewpoint and professional expectations. Furthermore, for individual social workers there may some-times be a conflict between their own personal values and the formalised codes of ethics to which they are officially committed, or between what they see as ethical practice and the law.

It needs to be acknowledged, so important are ethical issues in social work, that inevitably a book like this can only really indicate issues for further consideration, which is why this chapter introduced some points for reflection. Necessarily there can be no definitive answers.

At this point, the book now moves on to consider the intersection of law, ethics and social work in specific practice contexts, paying particular attention to the way in which the courts have seen themselves as being involved in the process. As part of this there will be consideration of decisions in certain key cases. This will provide some clues as to the way in which courts decide how to act in those demanding and difficult cases where there are no clear-cut answers. In turn this may help to provide some kind of guidance for social work practice for the future.

4

Protecting Children or
Supporting Parents?

INTRODUCTION AND CHAPTER OVERVIEW

This is the first of a series of chapters in this book that focus on the interconnections between ethics and law in one specific area of social work practice. The intention in Chapters 4–9 is to bring forward the theoretical insights from preceding chapters and apply them to social work practice, especially when particular issues emerge. Quite often these will be in contentious cases that have had to be determined by the courts. For example, there may have been an application for judicial review in an adult care case or an appeal against a decision made by magistrates or County Court judges in care proceedings cases. In one or two cases, appeals have gone right through the UK appeals system through to the European Court.

All the chapters in this part of the book follow a similar pattern, with some slight deviation from this in Chapter 6.

- There is an overview of the legal context that will apply to the case study chosen for the chapter, with a summary of any important legal knowledge necessary in order to understand the issues raised by the case.
- This is followed by the case example or case examples. Cases will be of particular relevance to the law–ethics dimension which the book seeks to explore.
- There is an explanation of the specific relevant legal issues.
- This is then followed by an analysis of how these connect to social work ethics.
- Wherever possible there will also be reference to the competing theoretical perspectives explored in the earlier part of the book, in particular theories relating to social justice.
- In some instances, where the example has particular complexities it will be divided up into sections or phases, in which case there will be an analysis of specific legal issues, ethics and social justice in relation to each phase.
- There will then be an exploration of the kinds of issues that arise in connecting law and ethics to social work practice in this particular area of social work practice.

As there is some commonality between these chapters in terms of their aims, the connections between them and the formal requirements of social work education and practice will only be set out in this chapter.

This set of chapters are all directly relevant to one specific aspect of the Professional Capabilities Framework (The College of Social Work, 2012) namely values and ethics. In addition, they will also be of some relevance to the elements of the Framework that relate to justice, knowledge and critical reflection. Under the justice heading, there is the expectation that social workers will advance human rights and promote social justice. In terms of knowledge, social workers are expected to apply knowledge of law. As regards critical reflection, social workers are expected to be able to apply analysis to inform and provide a rationale for professional decision-making.

Exercises integrated into this set of chapters are designed to promote the attainment and development of Critical Thinking Skills 1, 2, 3, 4, 7 and 8:

demonstrating understanding and application of theoretical ideas;

comparing and contrasting different viewpoints and experiences;

relating different views to underlying philosophies or ideologies;

evaluating different perspectives and ideas;

reflection;

reviewing, re-evaluating and reformulating your own views.

Furthermore all of the chapters connect into Social Work Subject Benchmarks 5.1.1 (6), 5.1.2 (3) and (5), 5.1.3 (2)–(5) and 5.1.4 (5)–(6) (for list see Introduction).

This chapter explores one of the most challenging dilemmas in social work practice: how to balance the protection of children with support to parents. In the vast majority of cases it can be taken as read that providing support to parents has the benefit of promoting the upbringing of children in their own families, which conforms exactly to the requirements of the Children Act 1989. However in a very small percentage of cases needs of children must be addressed separately from those of their parents, yet the law requires practitioners to work in partnership with parents even in those cases, and to avoid legal action such as care proceedings unless it is absolutely necessary. How should practitioners interpret these requirements? What does the law say? Some recent cases have particularly brought this issue into the limelight when parents appear to be able deliberately to deceive professionals in order to carry out acts of calculated cruelty – most especially demonstrated in the horrific case of Daniel Pelka reported in the autumn of 2013 (Coventry Safeguarding Children Board, 2013). This is one area or practice where social workers most definitely need to be very clear about their objectives and ethical principles, about how to balance ethics, social work principles and justice within the operation of the law.

The case study in this chapter highlights some of the dilemmas that emerge when the local authority decides it can no longer work in collaboration with parents, and indeed is met with an element of alleged duplicity. The case, which is real, came to court in 2010 as a result of an application by a local authority for a care order on the grounds that it was unable to protect children without removing them from their home and keeping them in its care. There was clear evidence of a child being deliberately injured by the father, yet the local authority appeared not to support attempts by the child's mother to take herself and the children to a refuge where they would be safe from further injury. As a consequence the court made some criticisms of the local authority in a way that highlights a number of ethical issues.

So this is an invaluable case example for our purposes here, well worth exploring for the connections with ethics and social justice theories. The chapter begins, though, with an explanation of the legal context, enumerating the relevant laws and statutory guidance. Necessarily this is somewhat cursory, and for full information about the legal background students should refer to the standard social work law texts (Brammer, 2015; Brayne, Carr and Goosey, 2015; Johns, 2014b). The case study then follows, with a discussion about the broader legal contexts and how this case fits with existing assumptions about the relationship between parents and children and social work law. This brings us to consider other relevant cases prior to the more substantive discussion in this chapter which focuses on ethics and social justice. The case study will be analysed by reference to the various approaches to ethics that we considered in Chapter 1. It will also be analysed by reference to the social justice theories that were examined in Chapter 2. This mode of analysis will be adopted now in all subsequent chapters in order to connect the case study, law and ethics to principles of social work practice. Finally the chapter will reflect on the challenges the case poses for social work practice, given the interpretation of law that the courts appear to be adopting and the principles of ethical practice that seem to be most pertinent to the case.

The heading of this chapter is deliberately tendentious in the sense that it implies there is a choice to be made between protecting children and supporting parents. Experienced social workers will immediately counter this by stating that it is possible, indeed commonplace, to do both. Indeed if you look at the relevant statutory requirements, set out in the next section, you will see that this is expected.

SOCIAL WORK LAW CONTEXT; RELEVANT LAW AND STATUTORY GUIDANCE

Section 17 Children Act 1989 requires local authorities to 'safeguard and promote the welfare of children in their area who are in need' and 'promote the upbringing of such children by their families by providing a range and level of services appropriate to those children's needs'.

Section 47 Children Act 1989 mandates local authorities to investigate where there is reasonable cause to suspect a child in its area is suffering, or likely to suffer, 'significant harm'. To this end there is a requirement for them to make enquiries in collaboration with other authorities, such as the police, health services and schools.

Section 18 Children Act 2004 requires children's services directorates to decide whether in any particular case it is necessary to apply for a court order, especially if refused access to children, and they must determine whether they have sufficient information to make decisions about such cases, deciding when to review those cases if they decide not to apply for an order.

Under section 31 Children Act 1989 a local authority may apply to the court for an order which places a child in the care of the local authority, or alternatively under its supervision. In order for the order to be granted the case must meet certain threshold criteria which are:

that the child concerned is suffering, or is likely to suffer, significant harm

that the harm, or likelihood of harm is attributable to (i) the care given to the child, or likely to be given, … not being what it would be reasonable to expect parents to give … (ii) the child being beyond parental control

Where the court is satisfied that the case meets the grounds for a care order, it may in addition make a placement order under section 21 Adoption and Children Act 2002. A placement order means that the child will be placed for adoption and such an order may be made without parental consent if the court is satisfied that this consent should be dispensed with (we will return to this issue in Chapter 5). In all such cases, the overriding consideration must be the child's welfare which is the 'paramount' consideration as stated in section 1 Children Act 1989 and section 1 Adoption and Children Act 2002. In order to determine whether a particular case meets this paramountcy principle, before making any order in relation to a child, courts and therefore social workers who report to it, must consider what is known as the 'welfare checklist'. This checklist includes the following:

(a) the ascertainable wishes and feelings of the child;

(b) the child's physical, emotional and educational needs;

(c) the likely effect of any change in the child's circumstances;

(d) age, sex, background and any characteristics the court considers relevant;

(e) any harm the child has suffered or is at risk of suffering;

(f) how capable each parent is of meeting the child's needs;

(g) the range of powers available to the court.

The key principles set out by the Department of Health (1989) with regard to supporting families are:

children should usually be brought up in their own family;

local authorities, working in conjunction with voluntary agencies, should aim to support families offering a range of services appropriate to children's needs;

services are best delivered by working in partnership with parents;

parents should express their wishes and feelings and participate in decision-making as should children, commensurate with their ability to understand.

Article 8 of the European Convention on Human Rights centres on the right to family life. The state is only allowed to interfere in family life where legislation allows and where it is necessary

> in the interests of national security, public safety or the economic well-being of the country, for the prevention of disorder or crime, for the protection of health or morals, or for the protection of the rights and freedoms of others.

Courts and local authorities are obliged to abide by what the Article says and how it affects interpretation of the law and decisions in particular cases by virtue of the Human Rights Act 1998 (sections 3 and 6).

In short, the implication is that the majority of work with families should be undertaken in co-operation with them and in only a small minority of cases, and in exceptional circumstances, should social workers directly intervene by taking unilateral decisions that would invariably entail court proceedings. Even so there is a duty to take steps to avoid the necessity to ask the court for a care order, and all efforts should be made to address the child's needs by other means. This would, of course, include placing the child with extended family members, or else it might be feasible to take some other action in order to protect the child from someone who poses a risk to them. Only in the most extreme cases should children be placed outside of their own families permanently.

CASE STUDY

Where to draw the line – Phase 1

EH v Greenwich London Borough Council and others [2010] 2 FLR 661

PHASE 1

The case concerned two children. This was an appeal against a care order made under care proceedings, and a placement order made at the same time as the care order. At the care proceedings hearing, the judge decided that the father had deliberately fractured the arm of a five-month-old child. The father had lied about this, and was considered to be a threat to the child as he was inclined to be violent. The judge decided that the mother must have been aware of what had happened. There was considerable delay in taking the child to hospital, and both parents lied about what had occurred.

The mother left the father and went to live in the refuge. The local authority did not assist this, nor did it make plans for the children to be rehabilitated to her despite the fact that there was some evidence of good parenting. Instead it informed her that the plan was for care orders followed by adoption.

The guardian and two experts recommended the return of the children to the mother's care. The local authority opposed this, preferring adoption on

(Continued)

(Continued)

the basis that there was too great a risk that the parents' relationship would continue. To demonstrate this the local authority pointed out that the father had been seen near the contact centre at the time of the mother's contact, that he had her telephone number, and that they had both been seen together by the social worker in a shopping centre two days before the hearing. The mother denied this, but could not produce any supporting counter-evidence. Because of this, the experts concluded that there appeared to be an element of duplicity and therefore could no longer recommend that the children should be returned home.

Critical thinking exercise 4.1

In what ways do you think the court might decide that the local authority action did not comply with the law?

We shall consider the answers to these questions before going on to look at what happened next in the case.

Legal Considerations

One obvious way in which the local authority failed to observe the letter of the law relates to the way they interpreted, or rather failed to interpret, section 17 Children Act 1989. There were clearly steps that they could have taken to try to keep the children living with parents or relatives. More generally, there was a failure to observe the principles of partnership working that underpin the provision of services aspects of the Children Act 1989 (essentially Part III of the Act).

In terms of the application for care proceedings, one could suggest a number of ways in which the local authority might have adopted other courses of action to prevent having to apply for a care order. It does not matter for the moment what those courses of action might be and whether they would have been appropriate in this case, since it is more important to note a number of requirements that compel the local authority to pursue care proceedings only as a very last resort. First, the whole tenor of the Children Act 1989 is provision of a range of services intended to support families where children are in need, all with parental agreement and taking into account the child's wishes and feelings (section 53 Children Act 2004). Second, where parents are unable to care for children themselves in their own homes even with support, the local authority is expected to offer accommodation assuming that there are no other family members who are able or suitable to provide alternative care (section 20 Children Act 1989).

In order to ascertain whether the local authority in this case did comply with legal requirements, more information may be needed as to what they did at the preparatory stage in examining alternative options. These requirements are not in the legislation itself but are in statutory guidance such as the Children Act 1989 Guidance and Regulations of which there are several volumes, one of which applies to court orders (Department for Children, Schools and Families, 2008; Welsh Assembly Government, 2008). Such guidance is obligatory under the terms of section 7 Local Authority Social Services Act 1970. This guidance sets out a number of steps local authorities must take prior to initiating care proceedings, including exploring alternative care solutions for the child. A legal gateway planning meeting is to be called to consider whether the threshold criteria are met and what further action the local authority ought to take to prevent it from having to proceed with court action. Following this, a Letter Before Proceedings formally notifies parents of the intention to start proceedings, but also sets out the local authority's concerns and what steps the parents need to take in order to avoid the case going to court. To this end, a pre-proceedings meeting is to be arranged that sets out what support is on offer from the local authority and this then could include a care plan, a child protection plan or a child in need plan.

With regard to the care proceedings themselves, local authorities need to be careful that they are meeting all the statutory criteria which relate to the principles as well as the specific threshold criteria set out in section 31 Children Act 1989. An overriding principle is that care proceedings must conform to the requirements of Article 8 of the European Convention on Human Rights (see below). A specific requirement in section 1 Children Act 1989 is that any proceedings must be consistent with the paramountcy principle, as it is known, namely that in making any court order the court must regard the child's welfare as the paramount consideration. So the local authority must ensure that separating the child from both mother and father is in their best interests, indeed is in their paramount interests. The threshold criteria set out in section 31 (see above) consist of two elements: harm or likelihood of harm; proof that the harm is attributable to a reason connected to the parents. One of these reasons is that the care which parents are giving or will give is not what one would expect of 'reasonable' parents. However one could justifiably ask in this case why the mother's plan to separate from a violent partner and take children to a refuge would not be perfectly reasonable.

What appears to have happened is that there was subsequently contact between mother and father, and this appears to have incensed the professionals dealing with the case to such an extent that they changed their views, and persuaded the judge to make care and placement orders. This was the point at which there was an application to the Court of Appeal, which was concerned about the lack of attempts to understand this apparently duplicitous behaviour and also to avoid care orders, as we shall see in the next phase of the case study. However before going on with the case study we need to explore some of the ethical and social justice dimensions.

Connections to Ethics

Critical thinking exercise 4.2

How would you analyse the actions of the social workers involved in this case in relation to ethics?

Not surprisingly it is difficult to categorise people's ethical actions as either exclusively principle driven (deontological) or determined on the basis of utility (utilitarian). In this case there is an overriding imperative, from which few would dissent, which is that children should be protected from harm. There also appears to be a rule that the professionals have adopted, namely that it is always wrong for people to tell lies, at least in this context. Or, from a virtue ethics perspective, is it that the professionals are indicating that the mother's actions demonstrate that she is not the kind of person who should be trusted to care for own children? An examination of the legislation reveals that there are elements of all these. The deontological principle – children's safety comes first – is clearly enshrined in section 1 Children Act 1989. Yet in determining individual cases, courts are obliged to consider whether the threshold criteria are met by judging the 'reasonableness' of parents' care. This can be hugely problematic in practice, and has unsurprisingly given rise to a number of challenges, but from an ethical standpoint the key question is: how does one judge reasonableness? To give but one instance of the complexity of this: suppose parents have learning disabilities, and provide care which is consistent with the standards of care that other parents with learning disabilities offer their children, but for whatever reason falls short of what a parent who does not have a learning disability might offer. Are parents to be judged in comparison with other similar parents, or with some mythical 'average' parent? There is no obvious answer to this dilemma, but this does underline the importance of incorporating ethical considerations in applying the law.

Let us look at the whole issue of care proceedings from a wider perspective by considering the utilitarian approach. Why, ethically, should the state intervene in family life? The answer presumably is because to do so in this context serves the interest of the greatest number of people. It is in the interest of the majority of society to protect children and if necessary to remove them from families where they appear to be at risk of harm. One might then ask why? To which there are all sorts of answers ranging from the fact that it makes people feel more comfortable to know that children are protected to the fact that future generations need children to be well looked after. You may well have thought of others, but note that utilitarian arguments do not start from absolute principles or imperatives, rather they look to the consequences of the actions. In the long term will the consequences for society of intervening be better than the consequences of leaving things as they are?

Competing Perspectives: Social Justice and Ethics

Critical thinking exercise 4.3

How would you analyse the actions of the social workers involved in this case in relation to social justice? Are there any tensions between ethics and social justice?

Some of the tensions between competing perspectives in social justice can be seen played out in the way in which child protection legislation is formulated. The fundamental challenge that the Children Act 1989 addresses is the balance between the state (here represented by local authority social workers) and the family, and also between parents and children. A libertarian view of this would be to lay a great weight on the relative autonomy of the family, arguing very powerfully for minimal state intervention in family life, only conceding that such intervention is necessary where there is serious abuse and no possible resolution without coercion. To some extent this approach is reflected in the qualification or rider to Article 8 of the European Convention on Human Rights that concedes that the state is entitled to intervene, but only to the extent that there are certain specific threats (listed above) including the 'protection of the rights and freedoms of others'. A utilitarian approach would argue perhaps for a wider degree of state intervention, but the question then is: to what extent should the state intervene, what is the desirable consequence of intervention, and would such a consequence accord with the greatest utility? A more positive view of state intervention will be put forward by Rawls and Sen who would presumably argue that child care legislation is an instrument for promoting social justice. In the case of Rawls, the system of child care and family support would be seen as a means of redressing social disadvantage, and to that end the principle that the child's welfare is paramount and on occasion may override parental rights would be eminently defensible.

There are a variety of other ways of linking child protection cases to social justice and it is not proposed to examine all of these here. Suffice it to say that thinking philosophically, and reflecting on the broader intent of legislation and practice in social policy terms, is important and is greatly facilitated by a study of both social policy and social justice theories. In terms of understanding the development of child care legislation, it is useful to study the context and background in which the legislation was originally formulated, since this often clarifies some of the debates and ethical considerations. A major driving force behind the introduction of the Children Act 1989 was events in Cleveland in the late 1980s. Cleveland centred on a controversy that arose when diagnoses of child sexual abuse resulted in a substantial number of children being compulsorily removed from their homes and subject to extensive periods in public care before the courts could consider their cases. The formal investigation that resulted in the Butler-Sloss Inquiry (DHSS, 1988) concluded that the law needed to be much clearer in setting out the relationship between the state and the family, in this case represented by local authority social workers and parents of children where there were child protection issues. The courts needed to play a much more active role in demarcating the boundaries. Social work practice needed to be more stringently regulated, not because practitioners were incompetent or over-zealous, but because the boundaries between the state and the individual family needed to be very clearly marked out. Where it became clear that parents were not always acting in their own child's best interest, for example by failing to protect them from harm, then it needed an independent body, in this case courts, to declare that this was so. Even then, the principle undergirding the Act would be that ways of addressing the child's needs should be sought within the extended family and only as a last resort should the child be committed to the care of the state, in the form of the local authority.

From this short analysis it is clear that much of this reflects a particular view of the relationship between the state and the family, one that is reflected in the European Convention on Human Rights and is supported by certain views of social justice. For further reading on this, including consideration of other aspects of practice covered by the Cleveland Inquiry such as partnership working see Rai and Stringer (2010).

CASE STUDY

Where to draw the line – Phase 2

EH v Greenwich London Borough Council and others [2010] 2 FLR 661

PHASE 2

The Appeal Court criticised the judge's line of reasoning and the local authority's actions.

The judge ought to have considered why the mother might have lied about seeing the father.

The judge should have explicitly addressed Article 8 of the European Convention on Human Rights. 'When making a Draconian order, such as a placement order, the judge was required to balance each factor within the welfare checklist in order to justify his conclusions and to determine whether the final outcome was appropriate. ... [He] must show how this extreme interference with family life was both necessary and proportionate.'

As far as the social workers' actions were concerned, the court declared that it was important to offer the non-abusive parent support at any early stage. 'It was very poor social work abruptly to deny help to a mother who needed and was asking for help to break free from an abusive relationship, without explanation. The conduct of the authority in this case had been entirely inimical to the ethos of the Children Act 1989, ...The local authority formed a view far too early that their care plan should be to place the children away from the parents. ... [and] had plainly pre-judged the issue.'

The appeals were therefore allowed. The care and placement orders were set aside, and the case remitted to the judge for a fresh final hearing.

Connecting Law, Ethics and Social Justice

The Appeal Court's decision provides a valuable study of how the law, ethics and social justice principles need to be connected. In this particular case the Appeal Court obviously took a particular view on this.

Critical thinking exercise 4.4

1. Categorise which elements of this case relate to:

   a) interpretation of the law
   b) ethics
   c) social justice.

2. Which of these is the most important for its implications for social work practice?

The answer to the first question appears immediately below so if you want to try the exercise first, stop reading and complete the exercise now. The second question is clearly a matter of opinion, but will be addressed in the discussion towards the end of the chapter.

One approach to answering the first question might be to list the elements of the decision in the order in which they were presented and connect them to law, ethics and social justice. If you were to do it this way you might end up with the following list:

1. The judge should have considered why the mother lied.
2. The judge should have considered European Convention on Human Rights Article 8.
3. Denying help to this mother was poor social work.
4. The local authority had acted contrary to the spirit of Children Act 1989.
5. The local authority had pre-judged the case.

Looking at the analysis in this way underlines the way in which law, ethics and social justice interrelate. It is difficult to categorise any particular one of these points as exclusively legal, ethical or relating to social justice. However you could broadly say that points 1 and 3 relate to ethics, 2 and 4 to the law, while point 5 mainly concerns social justice. Nevertheless, while two specifically referred to the law in both there is reference to the context of how it is to be interpreted with regard to other principles, and these principles essentially relate to ethics and social justice. A closer examination may help us to understand this more fully.

1. Lying of itself does not appear to be something that would automatically condemn someone to lose their children, even lying to court-appointed investigators or to the court itself. It is not therefore an absolute, as might be implied in Kantian approaches to ethics. It is relative to the situation in which someone finds them-selves and in this particular case there are a number of reasons why a woman might

feel coerced into not being completely truthful. From a social justice perspective an analysis of power would be important, suggesting an imbalance between her relative lack of power and the overbearing power of her male partner. So the context of the action needs to be considered.

2. Article 8 of the European Convention on Human Rights makes it clear that permanent separation of children from their own parents would be regarded as a clear breach of fundamental human rights if the parents have not consented to this. The circumstances in which such an action can be contemplated have to meet the exceptions criteria in Article 8 (for which see above). In this case the most relevant appears to be that such action is necessary 'for the protection of the rights and freedoms of others', in this case, presumably, the children. What the court is saying effectively is that, as this is such an extreme measure, it needs to be satisfied that every other avenue has been explored, and that there really is a compelling case for overriding parents' fundamental human rights. It has to be 'necessary' and 'proportionate'. Specifically in relation to UK statutes, the judge had not really connected the reasons for making a placement order with the principles in section 1 of both the Children Act 1989 and Adoption and Children Act 2002. These enshrine the 'paramountcy' principle but section 1(3) Children Act 1989 makes it clear that before making an order the court must consider what is known as the 'welfare checklist' (a truncated version of the list that appeared on page 74 above). The court should really have explicitly addressed that list.

3. It is difficult to see why the local authority was resistant to assisting the mother to find alternative accommodation where she felt safe from the abuse. One can only surmise that there was some reason why the social workers in the case did not fully trust her, or felt that she would not comply with any arrangements made, but the court expressed strong disapproval of this. It is interesting to note that the court referred to ethical principles it thought should undergird social work, since it could also have referred to the failure to attempt actions that would have avoided the necessity of the care proceedings. Such actions would have been required by the statutory guidance that then applied: the Children Act 1989 Guidance and Regulations (Department for Children, Schools and Families, 2008; Welsh Assembly Government, 2008), Preparation for Care and Supervision Proceedings (Ministry of Justice, 2009) and the Public Law Outline (Ministry of Justice, 2010).

4. The spirit of the Children Act 1989 is made quite explicit in various sections of the Act, and in the accompanying guidance such as that relating to court proceedings (currently Department for Education, 2014b). From this it is clear that local authorities really ought to do everything within their power to avoid bringing care proceedings, including naturally offering accommodation under section 20 Children Act 1989. Such measures invariably require the co-operation of parents, so the range of options where parents do not co-operate is necessarily somewhat limited. Even so the local authority ought to consider a range of resources that might be of assistance in a particular case, including members of

the extended family. Essentially the whole ethos of the Children Act 1989 is to provide support to children and their families, to take preventative action to avoid the necessity of bringing legal proceedings, and to promote the potential for children to be brought up by family members in situations where their parents are unable to do so.

5. The local authority could be accused of prejudging the case by assuming that the range of options was more limited than they actually were. Certainly the guardian's initial opinion appeared to be that, with support, the local authority could keep the children living with their mother and take steps to ensure that she and they were no longer at risk of abuse by the father. To make a deliberate decision not to pursue a particular course of action runs the risk of being accused of failing to take steps that might avoid extreme measures. Naturally one might have doubts about certain courses of action, but the essential message here is that such action at least needs to be attempted before a local authority can embark on care proceedings with a request to a court for a care order. Use of the term 'prejudging' implies that the local authority's actions are considered to be contrary to the principles of natural justice. In social justice terms one could argue that it paid insufficient regard to the needs of someone who was vulnerable, and the local authority did not take steps to promote the citizenship rights of that person themselves.

CASE STUDY

Where to draw the line – Phase 3

EH v Greenwich London Borough Council and others [2010] 2 FLR 661

PHASE 3

The case was remitted back to the first judge who reconsidered the case, concluding that care orders and placement orders were the best course of action, which in effect meant the children could be placed for adoption immediately, whatever the views of the parents.

After the Court of Appeal case (Phase 2 above) a number events occurred that heavily influenced the final decision:

- The parents accepted that they had been seeing each other regularly and had lied about this.
- The mother accepted that she had persistently lied right through the assessment period.
- The mother had lied to a judge in order to get an injunction.
- The mother had lied at the Court of Appeal hearing.

(Continued)

(Continued)

Significantly, in the course of the judgment a number of declarations were made by the judge concerning the approach to be adopted in cases such as this. In summary form these were:

- The children should be brought up by both of their natural parents, or at least one of them, if at all possible.
- The parental role of the mother and father should only be displaced for very strong reasons, grounded in the welfare of the children. The right of the children and of the parents to have a family life together is a strong one, as Article 8 of the European Convention makes clear.
- The claims of others to care for the children should only be considered if the rights of natural parents have to be forfeited because they are unable properly and safely to care for their children.
- If the parents' applications are rejected then consideration will be given to the offer from other family members to care for the children.
- Only if they are rejected should non-family members be considered.
- The least interventionist approach should be adopted.
- Adoption is a last resort, as being the most interventionist approach.
- A placement order should only be made if such an order is positively required in the interests of the children.
- Irritation with the continued lying of the mother and the father must play no part in consideration of what is in the best interests of the children.
- Judgments must be, and must exclusively be, child-centred.

Critical thinking exercise 4.5

1. How does the ultimate decision in this case reflect different approaches to ethics?
2. How does it relate to social justice theories?
3. How do they connect?

It is not easy to answer these questions, since there are elements of different ethical approaches in all of the judge's reasoning.

Interestingly, one kind of reasoning which the judge seems to be explicitly rejecting is values ethics, at least values ethics in the sense of deciding that the parents are 'bad' parents because they are 'liars'. Deciding what to do on the basis of irritation or annoyance with someone's character is not acceptable – presumably this lay behind the Appeal Court's decision. One could justifiably look at the consequences of persistent lying in terms of the potential impact it would have on working relationships, and conclude that it would have serious repercussions for the future well-being of children, but that would be a utilitarian argument, for it looks to potential consequences.

However, that line of reasoning does not appear in this phase of the case study, which appears on the surface to be a series of categorical imperatives, yet with some counting for more than others. These merit closer examination since the question then arises as to how to choose between apparently competing imperatives. Chapter 3 identified the problem of resolving moral choices by simply adding exceptions to rules, for how and why then is one exception to be preferred to another? One alternative deontological approach was suggested by Ross (Pojman, 2002: 137) who argued for a distinction between different kinds of rules: prima facie (at first glance) rules and conditional rules. Prima facie duties must be followed unless there are overriding obligations; they are obeyed unless a higher duty exists. Prima facie duties are:

- fidelity: to act in accordance with promises and compensate for past wrongful acts;
- gratitude: paying debts such as services performed;
- justice: promotion of equal portion of pleasure and happiness;
- beneficence: act to promote the well-being of others;
- self-improvement: act to improve myself (in, for example, education, behaviour);
- non–malificence: refrain from doing harm.

One simple example is the duty 'never to take a human life'. This is clearly a prima facie duty, but it may need to be outweighed by other considerations, and might become 'never take a human life except in self-defence'. Interestingly the European Convention on Human Rights Article 5 virtually states this and then lists a number of other exceptions.

So in the Greenwich case above, one categorical imperative appears to be that children should always be brought up by their own parents, but this obviously has to yield to the principle that children need to be safe. In legal terminology this becomes the principle that children should always be brought up by their own parents except where the welfare of the children requires that principle to be violated. One could then argue that the overriding imperative is that children's needs come first, and that is categorical, but then that would not be quite correct. The paramountcy principle, as in section 1 Children Act 1989, declares that this only actually comes into play where courts are involved in making decisions, and, as is made clear from the judge's line of reasoning above, then only after the potential for parents continuing to care for their own children has been fully considered.

To what extent are these principles based on rule utilitarianism? The declaration that children should normally be brought up by their own parents could be seen as a rule devised on the basis that, considering what is in the best overall interests of the majority, it is always better for society to expect parents to care for their own children. This would be overridden in cases where there is clear evidence that parents are unable to offer appropriate care, but note that this decision will be based on an assessment of children's future needs and the consequences of parental behaviour continuing in the way that it has done in the past. So the rule would now become that, looking at potential consequences, it would be acceptable for a court to compel parents to give their child up for adoption. The legal means of achieving it will be a placement order.

When trying to reconcile parents' rights and children's welfare, the rule appears to be that in the last analysis it is a child's needs that decide the case. This, one could argue, reflects the overall interests of society where it is best for children to be cared for outside their families, rather than to risk a situation where children may be abused or harmed within them. As a means of achieving this, adoption is acceptable as it is the course of action that most readily achieves this ambition by preventing any future action by parents that might undermine this.

Relating the decision made in this case to social justice theories may be more straight-forward, given the references to the need to be 'least interventionist'. This has strong echoes of a libertarian approach to the relationship between the state and the family, one that argues for absolute minimum state intervention. To some extent this approach is reflected in the Children Act 1989 which is founded on the principle of parental responsibility, services to support parents in caring for their children, and making it very clear that care orders and placement orders (strictly speaking placement orders come under the Adoption and Children Act 2002) are very much a last resort. In this sense the Children Act 1989 is not so much an Act about children, but an Act about parental rights. Its drive is strongly against compulsory intervention in families, a principle that is firmly reinforced by Article 8 of the European Convention on Human Rights.

This particular approach to social justice connects to ethics through the princi-ples that determine the way in which decisions are made. These principles appear to be categorical imperatives, but these imperatives sometimes clash with each other. Therefore in effect the libertarian approach to social justice has determined that when the principle of family upbringing (right to family life) is set against the principle of the paramountcy of children's needs, courts need to make decisions on the basis of a hierarchy of rules, or prima facie duties, as Ross would call them.

The first rule is the state should not intervene in family life except where absolutely necessary, only being justified where there is incontrovertible evidence of some kind of inadequacy of care for children. The second rule is that, even if there is some kind of inadequacy, children should be cared for by relatives rather than the state. The third, however, is that if the state does need to intervene then it will do so by siding entirely with children's needs, if necessary overriding parental objections to adoption. This is in effect a formula for deciding between applications of different rules, and it can be seen that the operation of these rules reflects an evaluation of how to determine between competing considerations, looking at potential consequences for children and also the way in which it is in the overall interests of society to ensure that, in extremis, children can be removed from potentially harmful family situations.

CHALLENGES FOR SOCIAL WORK PRACTICE

So, on the basis of all these considerations, what can be said about the challenges for social work practice?

In essence, this case is about juggling social work responsibilities and duties to chil-dren with obligations to support parents. It is very much about competing sets of rights, and the extent to which social workers are obligated to try to promote the well-being of children by working in partnership with parents. In this case, you may well have been surprised or even shocked by the apparent reluctance of the local authority to assist a mother who had clearly been subjected to domestic violence. The courts were very critical of this, and spelt out ways in which they thought the social work approach was not only wrong in principle, but wrong in law in terms of obligations under section 17 Children Act 1989. So one challenge for social work is to ensure that everything is done to enable parents to avoid potential harm to their children, facilitating access to the resources necessary to empower them to do this.

The second challenge, as in all such cases, is to know where to draw the line. Ultimately, in this case the court sided with the local authority view that the children should be subject to care orders and placed for adoption. The court drew the line at the extent to which parents were being untruthful about what was happening, and implicitly judged that this would have serious consequences for the potential for social workers to engage with them. Therefore it would also have serious consequences for the well-being of their children, detrimental to the extent of causing potential significant harm. In practice, deciding where to draw the line is a perpetual challenge, debated daily by social workers up and down the country.

Exploring and analysing different approaches to ethics and social justice helps practitioners to know where to draw that line. In this respect there are a number of other key legal cases where this has been an issue. Here are just a couple of examples, with more to follow in later chapters:

- The key influence on the formulation of the Children Act 1989 was the Cleveland Inquiry in 1987 (DHSS, 1988) which addressed the whole issue of balancing parental rights and children's rights, acknowledging the complexity of the work and the dangers of social workers being condemned for whatever decision they take. The inquiry followed concern about a social services department intervening too readily in cases where allegations were made of possible sexual abuse. There was well-substantiated criticism of the procedures that then existed, but crucially the Cleveland case is relevant here as it acknowledged the incredibly demanding task for social workers of achieving the correct balance between intervention and non-intervention in family life: the risks that they would be 'damned if they do, and damned if they don't'.

- Almost as influential was a decision in a case that eventually reached the European Court in 2001, often referred to as the Bedfordshire case (*Z and others v the United Kingdom*, 2001). In this case there was no doubt that the local authority had delayed intervening in the lives of children for too long, since it had failed to investigate properly complaints made by various people, resisted taking any form of action to protect the children, including delaying putting the matter before the courts. Initially the courts in the UK refused to hold the local authority to account on the grounds that this might trigger a large number of claims for compensation, but the European Court overruled this, arguing that the children had a justified claim that they had suffered inhuman treatment (a breach of Article 3 of the European

Convention on Human Rights) and that it was wrong to deny them any effective remedy for this. This represents a strong assertion of the rights of children independent of their parents, and also underlines the accountability of social workers employed by public authorities.

CONCLUSION

This chapter centred on an actual case where the courts had to consider where to draw the line between the obligation to support parents and the need to protect children. The case highlighted a number of important ethical and social justice issues:

- the obligation of social workers to support parents who are trying to extricate themselves from abusive relationships;
- the duty to promote the principle that children should be brought up by their own parents;
- the extent to which deception should influence decisions made in the case;
- the exact point at which parents' views on consent can be overridden in order to meet the welfare needs of children.

The case raised some fundamental issues about the relationship between the state and families, and about the whole issue of applying principles to cases such as this. Ultimately the way the case was decided reflected a number of different approaches to ethics and social justice, but a consideration of these supplemented by reference to other examples and case law, may help clarify social workers' thinking about decisions that need to be made in child safeguarding.

In passing, a number of comments were made about how the various approaches to ethics connects to aspects of social justice, and this theme will be explored further in each of the subsequent chapters in this book. One major issue already hinted at in this case study is that of adoption, which forms the focus for the next chapter.

5

Whose Future? The Ethics of Compulsory Adoption Law

INTRODUCTION AND CHAPTER OVERVIEW

This is the second chapter in this book that explores interconnections between ethics and law in a specific area of social work practice. Here the focus is on adoption. Ethical theories and approaches to justice will be matched to the law and practice in adoption through the lens of one specific case which has been through the court system.

As with the previous chapter, the analysis starts with an overview of the legal context that applies to the case study selected, with a summary of relevant law. This is followed by the case example itself and an explanation of the specific legal issues that have arisen in this particular case. The discussion then turns to an analysis of how these might connect, first, to social work ethics and, second, to theories of social justice. The chapter concludes with an exploration of the kinds of issues that arise in connecting law and ethics to social work practice in adoption.

The introduction to the previous chapter set out how the discussion in these practice-related chapters relate to the Professional Capabilities Framework (The College of Social Work, 2012) and the QAA Subject Benchmark Statements for Social Work (QAA, 2008). It also explained how this set of chapters is designed to promote the attainment and development of Critical Thinking Skills (for complete list see Introduction to Chapter 4).

Adoption is an important area of social work practice. There can be few decisions of greater significance in people's lives than to sever breaks with one family and start afresh with a new set of parents. There can also be no doubt that it has enormous personal impact. The Ministerial Forewords to two recent government policy documents on adoption both include personal experiences: one from a Secretary of State who was himself adopted as a baby and the other from a Minister who had two adopted brothers (Department for Education, 2012, 2013). It is also an area of social work practice that is emotive and attracts intense public scrutiny.

The traditional historical view of adoption has been of women who might have been ostracised by the rest of society because of attitudes towards illegitimacy and were effectively compelled to give children up for adoption to childless couples with a higher social status; what some commentators referred to as relinquishment baby adoptions (Simmonds, 2012: 175). Until the development of effective contraception and the abortion legalisation of 1967, such adoptions constituted the majority, with arrangements made for 'unmarried mothers' to give birth in homes away from the rest of society, where doubtless they felt under moral and social pressure to relinquish the care of their child. Given the social stigma and lack of financial and social support in many cases, the pressures were inevitably overwhelming.

Nowadays baby adoptions are comparatively rare, constituting only a small minority; in 2012, only 60 babies were adopted (Department for Education, 2012: 3). In that year, a total of 5,206 adoption orders were made by courts in England and Wales. Seventy-four per cent of adopted children were between the ages of one and four years – this compares with 18 per cent of children in public care being in this age group (BAAF, 2013: online). Unfortunately statistics do not differentiate between children adopted by relatives, usually step-parents, children adopted from abroad, and children adopted from the care system.

It is this last group that has attracted most attention from politicians, since these are children who have been accommodated at the request of parents who are no longer able to provide for them at all, or else more usually have been committed to care by a court following a finding that they have been 'significantly harmed'. Recent figures show a significant increase in adoptions in this group, with a 26 per cent increase recorded in the 2014 number compared to 2013, a 58 per cent increase compared to 2010 (Department for Education, 2014a: 13). This can be traced back to initiatives from 2000 onwards, beginning with a prime ministerial review of adoption that led to the publication of a government White Paper (Department of Health, 2000a). Initially this had a significant impact on the numbers of children in public care placed for adoption but its success tailed off despite the introduction of new legislation in the form of the Adoption and Children Act 2002 (Simmonds, 2012: 184–5). Attempts have now been made (Department for Education, 2012, 2013) to revitalise efforts to provide perma-nent substitute care for some of the 68,110 children who are in public care (BAAF, 2013: online). Cynics might, of course, suggest that such moves may be motivated to some extent by a desire to reduce public expenditure on children in public care, and there is certainly some controversy in professional circles about whether increasing the number of adoption placements necessarily increases the well-being of children, given the risk of adoption breakdowns in the teenage years (Kirton, 2013). However, research suggests that actual breakdown rates compare favourably with those for chil-dren fostered long term (Beckett et al., 2014; Biehal et al., 2010; Sinclair et al., 2007; Triseliotis, 2002).

The most contentious aspects of adoption work is the potential to ask courts to override parental consent in circumstances where it is in the best interest of the child. Recently one judge commented:

It has been observed that with the abolition of capital punishment the decision to make an adoption order, which extinguishes the entire legal relationship between a natural parent and a child and vests all legal rights and duties in the adopter, is one of the most momentous that a court is called on to make. (Z: Adoption: Scottish Child Placed in England: Convention Compliance, 2012)

Not surprisingly such 'compulsory adoptions', as they are known, raise significant ethical and practice issues, and from a legal point of view beg the question of how this relates to the requirements of Article 8 of the European Convention on Human Rights concerning rights to family life (Welbourne, 2002). It is these issues that form the main focus of this chapter.

The case study in this chapter highlights this fundamental issue of the nature of the relationship between the state and parents where it is clear that parents are unable to meet the long-term needs of the children. For here the debate moves beyond consideration of the point at which the state intervenes in family life to an even more basic issue, namely at what point do parents lose the right to have a say in the future of their own children? Is it ever right to divest parents of the rights to have a say in their child being placed with strangers for the rest of their lives? Conversely would it be right to stop a child having an opportunity for a new life in circumstances where it simply will not be feasible to have continuity or permanence in their family of origin?

The case in question went through various stages of appeal and was finally heard by the Supreme Court in 2013. Initially there was an application for a care order which was contested by the parents, and when it became clear that there was little prospect of the child being returned to the parents or any plan for rehabilitation to be feasible, the local authority declared its intention to ask the court for the child to be placed for adoption against parental wishes. The judges had to consider whether persistent parental obstructiveness meant that there was no real prospect of improvements in the quality of the child's experience; if that were to be the case, then should the path be cleared for the child to be placed for adoption? The Supreme Court was not unanimous, and some interesting comments were made which reflect different interpretations of the law and ethics relevant to social work practice. For these reasons, this case example offers potential for debating practice as it relates to theories of ethics and social justice.

As with the previous chapter, as a prelude to the case there is a section that explains the legal context and sets out the relevant law. A comprehensive overview of adoption law may be found in Brammer (2015: Chapter 11) and Brayne, Carr and Goosey (2015: Chapter 9). There is also a more concise summary of the law and policy relating to permanence in Seymour and Seymour (2013). This section is followed by the case study itself which leads into a discussion of reasons why there was so much disagreement about the underlying principles. This naturally leads to an analysis of ethics and social justice theories, all of which raise fundamental question concerning priorities, and how needs of parents and children can be balanced. Clearly this is of considerable relevance to social work practice and the chapter concludes with some reflections on how, in the light of what the law says and what has been learned about ethical theories, it is possible to formulate a sensitive approach to working with children and families in a context where permanent substitute care outside the family of origin is a desirable outcome.

SOCIAL WORK LAW CONTEXT: RELEVANT LAW AND STATUTORY GUIDANCE

Adoption changes relationships and identity, extinguishing all extant parental relationships and substituting new ones with the adopters. It is for life, not for the duration of an order, and cannot be revoked. Adoption affects inheritance and other laws regarding families so that effectively there is no legal difference between an adopted child and a 'natural' child of adoptive parents.

There are two principal kinds of adoption: those that are 'private' in the sense of being within a family or individual context, and those which concern children in 'public' care. It does not of course mean that the public will know about such children for it is still an undergirding principle that adoption proceedings are held behind closed doors and access to documentation very tightly and rigorously controlled to ensure complete confidentiality. It is important to remember that the various duties under the Children Act 1989 outlined in the previous chapter still apply to cases where social workers may be considering adoption for a child in public care. So a social worker would need to be very strongly convinced that adoption was the only effective way of promoting the child's welfare, since it appears to contradict the section 17 requirement to encourage children to be brought up by their families by providing support services appropriate to their needs. However it is recognised that in some cases this is not feasible, hence adoption ought to be considered as part of all long-term planning for looked-after children.

The law regarding adoption, however, applies to both kinds of adoption, although there exist certain legal steps that apply only to adoptions involving children in public care, specifically placement orders (section 21 Adoption and Children Act 2002) which 'free' children subject to care orders for adoption where a return home does not appear to be a viable prospect. Consent to an adoption order is a very serious matter and adoptions have to be ratified by a court process, even if full consent is given right the way through. A fundamental principle is that the parent or parents giving up children for adoption (including biological parents who may not have parental responsibility) should consent to do so, although there is an equally important principle that the adoption should be in the child's best interests.

Indeed that is where the principal law regulating adoption, the Adoption and Children Act 2002, starts since section 1 (2) of the Act declares that the 'paramount consideration of the court or adoption agency must be the child's welfare, throughout his life'. To that end section 1 contains subsections that include a no-delay principle, a requirement to have regard to the welfare checklist that includes the child's wishes and feelings, their specific needs, background characteristics, effects of ceasing to be a member of the family of origin, harm they may have suffered, and wider relationships. In arranging placements, adoption agencies must give 'due consideration to the child's religious persuasion, racial origin and cultural and linguistic background' (section 1 (5) Adoption and Children At 2002). Subsection 6 requires consideration of other powers and what might be termed a 'minimum intervention' principle, important in the context of ensuring an adoption order is a 'proportionate' response in order to comply with Article 8 of the European Convention on Human Rights (right to family life).

Details of the laws and regulations concerning adoption are outside the scope of this book, but suffice it to say that these are very strict in terms of procedures that need to be complied with in order to satisfy the court that the prospective adopters are suitable, and there has been a thorough investigation of the appropriateness of the placement which includes an independent element. There are also precise rules about who can apply, the meaning and effect of adoption, and how adopted people can obtain information about their families of origin. Further information on all of these aspects can be found in a number of social work law and family law texts such as Brammer (2015: Chapter 11); Brayne, Carr and Goosey (2015: Chapter 9); Burton (2012: Chapter 22); Standley and Davies (2013: Chapter 15).

Mention has already been made of the major issue of parental consent to adoption, which in some countries, such as Germany, is a prerequisite before an adoption order can be made. However in England and Wales it is possible in some circumstances to go ahead with an adoption, or placement for adoption, even if one or both parents object. Dispensing with consent is covered in section 52 Adoption and Children Act 2002 which allows adoption without consent where

- a parent cannot be found or is incapable of giving consent, or
- the welfare of the child requires consent to be dispensed with.

Parents here means a parent with parental responsibility so would exclude an unmarried father who does not have parental responsibility, although in practice courts often take their views into account. The paramountcy principle applies when courts are considering dispensing with consent and, significantly, apply to applications for placement orders as well as full adoption orders. This last point is important in situations where local authorities have concluded that the best long-term plans for a child subject to a care order lie in placement for adoption (placement orders can only be made for children already subject to care orders). For obvious reasons it would be highly undesirable to place the child for adoption with prospective adopters in circumstances where it was clear that parents would oppose this, since if the court declined to make an adoption order in the circumstances, the child would be left in limbo. To avoid this the law sensibly allows the whole issue of parental consent to be decided in advance of placement. The mechanism for achieving this, the placement order, if granted to a local authority gives them the right to make arrangements for the child to be placed for adoption and, if successfully placed, there will then be an application for a full adoption order considered solely on the basis of the suitability of the prospective adopters, consent having already been dealt with by the court. The placement order lasts until the child is adopted, attains the age of 18, marries, or is revoked by the court (section 21 Adoption and Children Act 2002).

It is quite apparent from the way in which the law is formulated that there is recognition that there may be conflicting interests that need to be resolved. Parental rights may clash with the child's rights to a secure and stable future; overriding parental rights may appear to clash with the more general human rights to family life enshrined in the European Convention on Human Rights. Balancing these rights has posed some acute dilemmas for the courts and, as these reflect fundamental debates about ethics and practice, this chapter focuses on an important case that was heard, in 2012, by the Appeal Court and, in 2013, by the Supreme Court.

CASE STUDY

Likelihood of harm leads to placement for compulsory adoption

B (a child) [2013]

This case concerned a two-year-old girl, referred to as A. Her mother was described in the judgment as having had 'immense difficulties in her early life' and as a consequence of abuse by her step-father was now a 'very damaged individual with multiple psychological problems, which included severe somatisation disorder, compulsive lying and deception of others, complicated by possible dissociation and self-deception'. After time in a refuge she met E, A's father, who had an extensive criminal record, having spent 15 years of his life in prison.

As soon as A was born, the local authority decided that they would seek a foster care placement for her, with supervised contact with the parents. So they drew up a care plan that included asking the court for an order that they could place A for adoption.

The care proceedings case was not based on any actual harm that A had suffered, but on the likelihood of her being harmed due to the risk which each parent posed to her, including their strong antagonism to professionals, including deliberate attempts to mislead them. Specifically the local authority said that as a result of mother's problems it was likely that A's emotional, educational and social development would be impaired. E, the father, did not understand that the mother was a risk to the child, nor did he understand that she could be untruthful, was therefore unable to protect the child being unable to communicate openly and honestly with professionals. Despite all of this they appeared to be devoted to their daughter, as is evidenced by spending the maximum allowed $1\frac{1}{2}$ hours five days a week with her after her admission to care.

The parents, not surprisingly, contested the care proceedings arguing that the child should be either with them jointly or with the father.

As result of expert evidence, the judge concluded that a safeguarding package was necessary, and found that the parents did not have the capacity to relate to professionals in a way that would keep their child safe. Accordingly the judge endorsed the local authority's care plan, making a care order and declaring that adoption was the only viable option for this child. The parents appealed against this decision.

There were two grounds to the appeal: one related to the degree of significant harm and its likelihood; the second related to the response of the courts in that declaring adoption to be the way forward was disproportionate and therefore contrary to Article 8 of the European Convention on Human Rights which relates to rights to family life.

The appeal by the parents was dismissed.

In explaining why it was dismissed the court made a number of observations and clarifications of its reasons:

- Decisions about children had to be made in the context of the family's cultural social and religious circumstances and only if there was a degree of an acceptable risk should there be state intervention.
- State intervention can only be justified if the reasons were significant enough to justify it, that is that there were circumstances which indicated that protective measures were necessary. The court had to balance protecting children in relation to their health or development with the objective of reuniting the family as soon as circumstances permitted. The action had to be proportionate but it was not necessary for local authorities to wait for the 'inevitable' to happen before they could intervene to protect children; there had to be a balance.
- In this case, there was clear evidence that it was not going to be viable to rely on professionals being able to oversee the family, and so the judge in the original hearing had been entitled to conclude that it was unsafe to allow the child to return to the parents and that permanent substitute care needed to be arranged. The judge had to look for a proportionate response and was entitled to decide there was no 'halfway house' and no obvious route whereby the child could safely be returned to the parents.
- In the light to the needs of the child, the need for a permanent placement was urgent so planning for adoption was the best course of action.

The case was subsequently taken on appeal to the Supreme Court where the decision of the original trial judge and the Appeal Court was confirmed.

In their conclusion, the (majority of the) Supreme Court declared that, while family courts regularly had to make allowance for the negative attitude of parents towards social workers involved in care proceedings, in this particular case the level of antagonism and obstruction was 'of a different order'. Had this not been the case, then the original judge might have allowed time to test out the degree of the parents' co-operation, but given the evidence before the court, there appeared to be no alternative but to conclude that adoption was the right course of action and that this was 'proportionate' in terms of the European Convention on Human Rights.

The Supreme Court decision effectively meant the end of the road for the parents, as the next stage would be for the child to be placed for adoption. Assuming the court agreed that the prospective adopters would be suitable, an adoption order would almost certainly be made. Thus the effect of a placement order is to debar the parents from objecting to the adoption order unless there are significant changes in their situation, and even if this is the case, they initially have to make application to the court for permission to challenge the placement order. A recent case *(B-S (Children) (Adoption: Application of Threshold Criteria)*, 2013) has confirmed that an application for permission to challenge an adoption order is a two-stage process:

a) the court has to be satisfied that there has been a change in circumstances (section 47(7) Adoption and Children Act 2002); if not, the application must fail;

if there has been a change in circumstances the court then has to consider the paramount interests of the child (section 1 Adoption and Children Act 2002) in determining whether or not to grant permission, also taking into account the parents' ultimate prospects of success if leave to oppose were to be given.

Unsurprisingly this has proved to be a very high hurdle to jump, although in *B-S* the court did emphasise that courts should discount the idea that giving leave to oppose might have an adverse effect on prospective adopters, and courts must allow the parents the chance to demonstrate that there had been a significant change.

All of this adds up to a major ethical issue, one where the law interprets the clash of rights of parents and child in a particular way. When social workers advise courts that a child has been 'significantly harmed' and that restoration of the child to parental care is not a viable prospect, the courts can and will override the parents' rights to object to adoption, and will order that children be placed with new parents. Remember that an adoption order, once made, is for life and is irrevocable. An adopted child becomes the child of the 'new' family with the same rights as any other child of that family. Their natural parents cease legally to be their parents and lose all their rights as parents.

Connections to Ethics

Critical thinking exercise 5.1

How does the decision to deprive parents of all their legal rights in some circumstances connect to ethical theory? Specifically how would compulsory adoption be viewed by those who subscribe to:

- deontological, principle-based theories
- utilitarian ideas such as those of Mill
- virtue ethics
- care ethics?

Deontological

Applying compulsory adoption to deontological or principle-based theories is not easy, but a few moments' reflection may suggest that there are some absolutes which appear to be enshrined into the law and social work practice. The key principle, categorical imperative or prima facie duty appears to be the 'paramountcy of the child's welfare' (for discussion of these deontological terms look back at Chapter 4, the discussion of Phase 3 of the case study). This is made explicit several times in the legislation;

specifically in section 1 Children Act 1989, and section 1 Adoption and Children Act 2002. However, as an absolute this will not quite work, at least not on its own.

For the question Kant would pose is: if this were to be a rule, would we be willing for this rule to be applied in all places and at all times, as a universal rule? So if, for example, the only issue to decide in potential adoption cases is whether the new potential family were better able to meet the child's welfare needs than the existing family, then surely there would be thousands of cases where this could be argued, and consequently hundreds if not thousands of adoption orders. Just consider parents who are struggling to bring up children because they are not financially well off, or because they are not experienced enough to cope with children's challenging behaviour, and offset that against wealthy parents with oodles of experience who are well able to offer a 'better' home. If paramountcy of the child's welfare were to be the only rule, then it would be difficult to resist applications in these circumstances. Clearly this is unthinkable, for it violates the principle of parental rights and is akin to social engineering. Essentially what courts and social workers must do in all cases which involve compulsory adoption is balance the paramountcy of the child's welfare with the rights of parents to look after their own children which is enshrined both in UK law and the European Convention on Human Rights.

So a better rule might be that in cases where there are serious doubts that parents are not able to offer children a home that meets certain essential requirements (and these could be stipulated in legislation) then those parents lose their rights to determine what is in the interests of their children, and this right transfers to social workers and the courts who will plan for the child's future on the basis of what is in their ultimate long-term interests. So the rule might in effect be: where courts are required to balance the welfare of the child with the rights of parents they must first find reason for overriding rights of parents and then, and only then, can they look to what is in the long-term interests of the child. In other words, ultimately the child's needs in those situations trump those of the parents. This is more or less what the law actually says, with case-law decisions, such as the one above, that demonstrate determination to afford parents every opportunity to manage care whenever this is feasible, but only in the last resort to divest parents of parental rights and make alternative plans for children. A compulsory adoption is an official declaration to this effect.

Yet where exactly to draw the line remains problematic. The decision in B (a child) (2013) was by a majority. There was one dissenting judge, Lady Hale, who made some general comments about the role of the courts and the state in cases involving permanent removal of children from their parents:

> This case raises some profound questions about the scope of courts' powers to take away children from their birth families when what is feared is, not physical abuse or neglect, but emotional or psychological harm. We are all frail human beings, with our fair share of unattractive character traits, which sometimes manifest themselves in bad behaviours which may be copied by our children. But the state does not and cannot take away the children of all the people who commit

crimes, who abuse alcohol or drugs, who suffer from physical or mental illnesses or disabilities, or who espouse anti-social political or religious beliefs. ... How is the law to distinguish between emotional or psychological harm, which warrants the compulsory intervention of the state, and the normal and natural tendency of children to grow up to be and behave like their parents? (B *(a child)*, 2013, paragraph 144)

She clearly had reservations about the decision to grant a compulsory adoption order in this case. In deontological terms, she is expressing reservations about the desirability of a rule that allows courts to override parental objections to adoption in circumstances where there is allegedly potential for emotional or psychological harm.

One interesting facet of the categorical imperative approach is that it enshrines the principle that human beings are never to be treated as a means to an end but should always be ends in themselves. So the political desire to increase the number of adoptions, for whatever reason, should surely always be subservient to the welfare interests of children. The desire to bring happiness to prospective adopters should never be a consideration if it means treating children as a means to creating that happiness. One could also argue here that the desire not to take risks where parents are demonstrably unco-operative with social work and health-care agencies has meant that those parents have lost their right to future involvement in their children's lives. Does this mean that they have been treated as a means to an end, the end being professionals' peace of mind? This is not a cynical question, but one that challenges social workers and lawyers to think out exactly why they consider this action to be justified. Naturally the welfare of the child is a desirable objective, but when children's needs conflict with parental rights there is a massive dilemma, as Lady Hale's comments indicate.

Utilitarian Theories

Utilitarians focus on consequences, in this case good consequences for as many people as possible. Thus it is conceivable that society will declare that the greatest happiness for the greatest number is achieved by having laws that allow for compulsory adoption. Note that in this view the rights of the parents count for less, since the overriding goal has to be to provide for the best outcome for children. This utilitarian view might accept the paramountcy principle without the riders, in other words without the prerequisites that parents' rights have to be considered first. All that might be said is that if it can be demonstrated that the long-term consequences would yield good results for the child, then that would be in itself sufficient justification.

The problem is, of course, that it is sometimes difficult to judge whether the end result will truly be better. There is, after all, a price to be paid for severing ties between parents and children and who knows whether this will truly lead to an eventual good outcome. It is rather like looking into a crystal ball.

Chapter 3 considered one branch of utilitarianism, generally considered to have originated in Mill's thinking, which is known as rule utilitarianism. This looks at the long-term general interests of society in order to decide what kind of rules should operate, and here one could argue that compulsory adoption is ultimately in the best long-term interests of society as a whole. Note that this is quite different from a deontological approach, although it may seem on the surface to be similar since it talks about rules and principles. The difference is that a deontological approach starts from devising principles which it then applies, whereas rule utilitarians start with the desirable consequences and then work back to calculate the rules that would lead to those consequences. So in this case a rule utilitarian would be able to justify a rule that said that if certain degrees of risk can be proven, and parental co-operation has been tested and found wanting, and there are no other viable alternatives, then the court can consider dispensing with consent to adoption. All of this will be in the context of the overall aim which is to serve the interests of society by preventing children growing up with a potential for criminality, anti-authoritarian attitudes and with their skills and talents less developed than might otherwise have been the case. As to the reservations expressed by Lady Hale in the quotation above, a rule utilitarian might counter these by arguing that implementation of their rule is more likely to have desirable consequences and therefore is justified.

Virtue Ethics

Virtue ethics does not concern itself so much with rules and principles as it does with the nature and characteristics of people involved. Thus in the case of compulsory adoption what might really come to the fore is the quality and characteristics of the parents, and in effect the role model they offer their children. So the issue for consideration is whether the parents have enough of the desirable characteristics of parents to be allowed to look after their children. If they do not, presumably then it is appropriate for them to lose their parental rights and for the child to be brought up by someone else.

Although the legal system is understandably much dominated by rules, antecedents, agreed principles and interpretation, it is noteworthy that in the case study in this chapter (and also in Chapter 4) courts set much store on the characteristics of the parents. In Chapter 4, persistent lying ultimately condemned the parents to the loss of their children. In the case study in this chapter, the County Court judge, together with courts at a higher level, listed the negative characteristics of the parents: 'the wider concerns related to the mass of evidence that each of the parents was fundamentally dishonest, manipulative and antagonistic towards professionals' (B (a child), 2013, paragraph 19).

The court then went on to declare that the character of the parents is a relevant consideration if, but only if, it affects the quality of their parenting. So in this sense a virtue ethics approach is justifiable since virtue ethics concludes that the qualities of a person's character become manifest in actions. As will also be seen in these extracts from the judgments, in the case of children the court may be concerned that undesirable qualities will be handed on to the next generation.

The other element of virtue ethics is the quality and characteristics of social workers and others engaged in providing for the children's well-being. It may not however be sufficient just to say that the professionals display desirable characteristics such as compassion, commitment, honesty, integrity and so on. In the context of compulsory adoption, it is not the personal attributes of professionals that is under consideration but their professional qualities and competencies. This may extend to being objective about what the issues are, being able to conduct a fair assessment, and being able to use evidence rather than intuition or feelings as a sound means of justifying decisions.

A summary of the judgment in *B-S (Children) (Adoption: Application of Threshold Criteria)* (2013) contains a message that needs to be taken to heart by all social workers working in this field. Good practice, the Adoption and Children Act 2002 and the European Convention on Human Rights, all demand that a care plan involving compulsory adoption should be properly analytical since it:

> ...had to address all the options which were realistically possible and had to contain an analysis of the arguments for and against each option. What was required was evidence of the lack of alternative options for the children and an analysis of the evidence that was accepted by the court sufficient to drive it to the conclusion that nothing short of adoption was appropriate for the children. In addition, what was needed was an assessment of the benefits and detriments of each option for placement and, in particular, the nature and extent of the risk of harm involved in each of the options, and there was a need to take into account the negatives, as well as the positives, of any plan to place a child away from its natural family. Further, there was a particular need for analysis of the pros and cons and a fully reasoned recommendation. (*B-S*, 2013, paragraph 1)

So for the courts, a good social worker is one who can present fair balance sheets of positive and negative factors drawing conclusions that are evidence-based and not simply assertions or general statements of good intent.

Care Ethics Approach

Thus far in the examination of the case study, the emphasis has been on analysis of the factors that contribute (or fail to contribute) towards the child's well-being, to some extent overshadowed by an emphasis on parental shortcomings. An ethic of care approach would insist on greater moral significance being accorded to the characteristics of relationships. In the law reports little is said about the relationships between social workers and the parents or child, except insofar as there are detailed factual accounts of lack of co-operation with professionals, and parents' general allegedly anti-authoritarian attitudes.

This may in turn lead to a reassertion of the importance of justice, not legal-technical justice, but in the wider sense of being fair to the parents who, after all, showed significant commitment to the child, putting considerable effort into making a success of the contact which they were allowed, displaying a warm and loving relationship with her, and generally demonstrating they were devoted to her (*B (a child)*, 2013, paragraph 16). There is, naturally, a countervailing imperative of being fair to the child by not exposing her to risk of abuse or harm.

It is interesting that in her commentary on the case, Lady Hale adopts an approach which has echoes of this concern with relationships:

> Every child is an individual, with her own character and personality. Many children are remarkably resilient. They do not all inherit their parents' less attractive characters or copy their less attractive behaviours. Indeed some will consciously reject them. They have many other positive influences in their lives which can help them to resist the negative, whether it is their schools, their friends, or other people around them. How confident do we have to be that a child will indeed suffer harm because of her parents' character and behaviour before we separate them for good? (B *(a child)*, 2013, paragraph 144)

While such a relationship-based approach may not ultimately lead to a different conclusion, it is important to note the difference of emphasis. An ethic of care approach insists on more attention being paid to the quality of relationships, in effect arguing that social work is essentially relationship-based. It cannot proceed simply on the basis of formal expectations in terms of supervision, instruction and checking, but must be firmly grounded in sound effective relationships between social workers and service users. If such a relationship were to exist, this would offer the best opportunities for progress, although in this case there appears to be clear evidence that, for whatever reason, parents were disinclined to try and respond to the overtures made to them – although one would still want to know exactly why they were so resistant.

Critical thinking exercise 5.2

These questions are for reflection on the basis of what you now know about the B *(a child)* (2013) case above, and considerations of the different ethical approaches to the case:

1. Whose interests should come first: those of the child or the parents?
2. Is it ever right to break the parental bond in the way in which adoption implies?
3. Whose interests are being served by compulsory adoption? Those of the child? The adopters? The professionals?
4. To what extent should the characteristics of parents be taken into consideration in making judgments about compulsory adoptions?

CONNECTIONS TO SOCIAL JUSTICE THEORIES

The typology adopted here will follow the pattern outlined in Chapter 2, which distinguished the works of Mill, Nozick, Rawls and Sen under four headings: utilitarianism, libertarianism, egalitarianism (or maximin), and capabilities (or comparative) social justice.

> ## Critical thinking exercise 5.3
>
> How does the case study (*B (a child)*, 2013) relate to these four headings of social justice?

Utilitarian Social Justice

Chapter 2 included a summary of Mill's basic view that social justice contributes to 'general utility' or the greatest benefit to society and distinguishes six areas which would be covered by the concept of justice.

The first of these is legal rights. Applying this to the *B (a child)* case study is straightforward, although there is clearly no easy way of reconciling competing rights. For in the case we could argue that the parents have legal rights, as does the child. Both sets of rights are underpinned by specific legislation and agreed international protocols: the Children Act 1989, Adoption and Children Act 2002, European Convention on Human Rights and UN Convention on the Rights of the Child. Ultimately it could be argued that the overarching legal obligation is the duty to promote the paramountcy of the child's welfare but this then conflicts with the second area, moral rights, whereby laws might be considered unjust if they infringe somebody's right. In this case the rights to parent one's own child is clearly infringed in a major way. Next comes 'requital of desert' (returning good for good and evil for evil) which hardly applies in this case if judicial process is followed, although members of the public who hear about this case might well conclude that these are not the kind of people they would want to have as parents of a child. So a layperson might consider that parental refusals to co-operate and displays of general anti-authority attitudes are justly punished by losing their child. This however is hardly the kind of line of reasoning one would want to follow in social work. Rather what matters to a social worker are the fourth and fifth principles: keeping promises, and impartiality. The fact that the parents are unable in the case to keep promises is usually problematic, yet professionals who are employed in public office must remain neutral and unbiased. Judgmentalism must not be part of their way of thinking, and it is certainly worth noting the comments of the court in the *B-S (children)* (2013) case concerning the lack of analysis in social workers' reports, which tend generally to be a series of assertions (see above). The final area of social justice is equality which is both aggregative and distributive. One could argue that by placing the child for adoption this contributes to the total amount of happiness, but this line of argument tends to relate better to distribution of resources rather than addressing ethical principles and concerns.

Libertarianism

Libertarianism was related in Chapter 4 to the principle of least intrusive intervention in families which is clearly underpinned by the Children Act 1989. This strongly asserts the principle of parental responsibility, and argues for a secondary or minimal role for local authorities. Keeping families operating as independent units is essential. In a number of legal judgments on care orders and compulsory adoption arrangements judges have frequently referred to these as 'last resort' options, in other words only available when everything else has failed. All of this appears to follow the lines of minimising state intervention, but obviously in extreme cases the state is very much involved in the judicial process, in the social work task of selecting and preparing a new home, and in overseeing the child's progress.

Egalitarianism Rawlsian Theory

For Rawls, social justice is essentially about distribution and ensuring there is equal access to rights and opportunities. This develops ultimately into Rawls' 'maximin' rule of game theory whereby everyone has equal rights with the greatest range of liberties compatible with liberty for all, yet any inequalities should be to the greatest benefit of the least advantaged. It has to be said that in application to practice, Rawls' theories fit best to distribution of wealth and equal opportunities policies, although one could apply them in the sense of trying to minimise disadvantages for children by ensuring that the state affords opportunities for growth and development they would not otherwise have.

Comparative or Capabilities Approach to Social Justice

As was seen in Chapter 2, what matters for Sen is comparative justice: justice in different situations. So in this case, there are elements of comparisons made with other cases and these would be relevant as a valid approach to social justice. At the same time the concern expressed by the court for the welfare of the child chime with the 'capabilities approach' that promotes the idea that justice involves making arrangements to expand people's capabilities, freedom of opportunity or potential for achieving in their lives; hence the debate which Lady Hale conducted with herself about whether the extreme measure of a compulsory adoption will truly lead to that end. For even if it does, there may be considerable cost, namely violating the natural fairness of allowing parents to care for their own children.

CONNECTING SOCIAL JUSTICE AND THE LAW

In terms of social justice the fundamental issue is how to balance parental rights with rights of children. It is tempting to conclude that in a compulsory adoption the interests of the child may also be the same as the interests of the prospective adopters, so therefore this might lead to a win–win situation, yet this would be erroneous. For it violates the principle of parental rights and it is no surprise that libertarians such as Nozick would be fundamentally opposed to any notion of forced adoption. Yet adoption could be seen as means of offering a new start and therefore a means of ensuring that an otherwise disadvantaged child gets a better start in life.

The key question remains: how to set about determining whether compulsory adoption should be allowed and, if so, how and in what circumstances. Theories of ethics and social justice will not answer these questions but they will guide processes whereby outcomes are determined.

A deontological approach seems to argue for a hierarchy of rules that may be helpful in at least determining sequencing of questions to ask, as in the processes suggested in the legal judgment.

The problem with a utilitarian approach is that it is only really possible to determine what would be the correct course of action by looking at the consequences, and these consequences would at the time of making the decision be unknown and unknowable.

So in practice much may be made of the character and qualities of the parents and of the professionals involved in the case. Yet this may not be entirely just. Courts appear to be advocating an approach based on an objective analysis of strengths and weaknesses of different courses of action. Thus justice is conceived as being the application of clear principles to factual evidence, rather than interpretations of what may be just by making judgments on who parents are. In this context, compulsory adoption decisions ought to be made on the basis of what parents have done or failed to do, rather than who they are and what kind of people they are.

CHALLENGES FOR SOCIAL WORK PRACTICE

The analysis in this case reflects some formidable challenges for social work practice.

Fundamentally, this case is about determining the point at which there is no purpose trying to work with parents in order to improve their children's future. Instead parents are to be compelled to give their children up permanently so that they can be looked after in a new family. Just as the case study examined in Chapter 4 was about reconciling competing sets of rights, so too is this case study, yet in an even more extreme sense for there is no clear evidence here of any actual harm having been caused to the child. In essence, the case is all about prognostications about what will happen in the future, much of it based on the history of the parents: serious mental health issues, long criminal records, refusal to engage with professionals, antagonism towards those who are trying to help them, and anti-authority attitudes.

In some ways, this case is quite shocking from a justice perspective for it is not based on factual evidence of events that have occurred, but focuses on the propensity for things going wrong in the future. At the same time inaction would be appalling if it was 100 per cent certain that the child was to be harmed. Yet we never can be 100 per cent certain, and even if there is a fair chance that this child's development would not be as sound as other children's, the nagging underlying question still remains: what rights in these circumstances do courts and social workers have to decide that a set of parents lose all their rights in relation to their own children? It was clear that at least one judge had major reservations about this.

As with the case discussed in Chapter 4, much of the court's debates concerned where to draw the line. At what point should they determine that parental attitudes dictated that there was no prospect for change, and therefore the potential likelihood for 'significant harm' was proven as is required by section 31 Children Act 1989? Relating this case to theories of ethics and social justice may help to elucidate where the line should be drawn, although it also raises sharp questions about whether the action taken can be truly justified.

Such considerations have been made in other similar cases where courts have concluded that the finality of adoption is the only solution:

- In *P (children) (adoption: parental consent)* (2008) the court had to consider whether it could make a placement order where a local authority, acting as an adoption agency, could not be absolutely confident that it would be able to place the child for adoption. Long-term fostering might have to be considered as an alternative. Despite this, the court decided that it could still go ahead and make the order. The court had no objection in principle in appropriate cases to 'dual planning' (preparing both for adoption and for potential return of children to parents simultaneously). Dual or parallel planning was a permissible use of powers given to local authorities and adoption agencies under the Children Act 1989 and the Adoption and Children Act 2002.
- *J (Children)* (2012) was an appeal against a judge's decision to make a placement order in respect of an eight-year-old boy who was subject to severe abuse (his hand was deliberately burned as a punishment). The appeal was founded on the submission that the proposed compulsory adoption would breach Article 8 of the European Convention on Human Rights, and the judge ought to have decided that long-term fostering should be considered as a better alternative. The Appeal Court rejected this. The judge had considered that compulsory adoption would be a significant interference in the human rights of the parents, but considered that in the circumstances it was a 'proportionate, reasonable and a necessary response'. Article 8 was therefore not breached. Furthermore, the judge urged parallel planning, since she had determined that the delay was contrary to the child's interests and so the local authority were right to consider both adoption and long-term fostering at the same time.
- In *N (A Child) (placement order: alternative option to adoption)* (2013) the Court of Appeal allowed an appeal from a mother against a placement order that would have led to compulsory adoption. During the application for the placement order, it became clear that there was an offer from the child's grandmother to care for him but the initial judge decided that the local authority would need to make further investigations in order to clarify whether this was a viable option. Nevertheless the judge made a placement order. The Court of Appeal said this was wrong in principle, and specifically unlawful since the court had to declare that the welfare throughout the child's life required adoption (section 52 (1)(b) Adoption and Children Act 2002).

CONCLUSION

This chapter concerned compulsory adoption, the most extreme safeguarding measure available, where courts order that a child can be placed for adoption despite the objections of one or both parents. These parental objections can be overruled on the grounds that 'the welfare of the child requires the consent to be dispensed with' (section 52 (1) (b) Adoption and Children Act 2002). The case study concerned the grounds of 'likelihood of harm' (section 31 Children Act 1989) in a case where no actual harm had occurred. The court had decided to find the likelihood grounds proved, and had endorsed the local authority care plan to have a care order and placement order to which the parents strenuously objected. Parents lost their appeal against this. The Supreme Court decision was explained, with the decision-making process related to different ethical and social justice theories.

Such cases raise fundamental questions about the role of the state, social work intervention in families, and the way in which practitioners reflect on the ethics of their practice. In passing, reference was made to another case in which the court complained of social work submissions being little more than assertions, and directed that in future they wanted fully analytical professional assessments which were evidence-based. Clearer thinking about ethics and social justice will surely aid this process.

The next chapter moves on to the area of youth justice, which offers considerable potential for relating in greater depth theories of ethics and social justice to human behaviour and the court process.

6

Youth Justice

INTRODUCTION AND CHAPTER OVERVIEW

This third chapter exploring interconnections between ethics, law and social work practice focuses on youth justice. Naturally the spotlight will be turned here towards theories and approaches to justice which include the field often referred to as criminal justice. Yet issues of social justice are also relevant as are ethical theories that underpin different approaches to work with young offenders.

Unlike the previous chapter, this chapter on youth justice does not start by analysing the current social work law context. Instead it begins by asking some fundamental questions about what justice means and specifically why people should obey the law in the first place. What does youth justice actually mean? What is the purpose of sentencing young offenders? Some theories and perspectives that are specific to justice are introduced here. The discussion then moves on to the background to contemporary social work law. There is then a more detailed analysis of the social policy developments that have taken place over time: scrutinising different formulations of law is essential to aid understanding of how social work practice itself has changed. For it has to be acknowledged that the field of youth justice is particularly contentious, subject to significant shifts in politics and social policy, with both social workers and young people themselves caught up in these changes.

The chapter then moves on to consider a case study based on real-life events although obviously the participants have been anonymised. Readers are then invited to speculate as to what the outcome for the three young men would be under different legal regimes, reflecting the different approaches to youth justice. This facilitates an analysis of current law in an ethical and practice context, enabling the chapter to conclude with an identification of the kinds of challenges that arise for social workers currently engaged in the field of youth justice.

The Introduction to Chapter 4 set out how the discussions in these practice-related chapters link to the Professional Capabilities Framework and Subject Benchmark Statements for Social Work. The Introduction to Chapter 4 also explained how practice-related chapters promote the attainment and development of Critical Thinking Skills.

Youth justice is a fascinating area of social work practice since it is so closely allied to shifts in social policy and has changed dramatically since the heyday of the so-called 'welfare' approach to youth justice that prevailed in the early 1970s. It is unique for two reasons. First, in England and Wales practice nearly always takes place within an inter-professional setting since youth justice social workers are invariably members of multi-disciplinary teams, generally called Youth Offending Teams, which have a key role in preventing offences being committed by young people, writing reports on offenders, implementing various court orders, and supervising offenders on their discharge from custody. This means that while social workers may be employed by local authorities, they are ultimately responsible to the courts for the work that they carry out with young offenders, so there is a kind of dual level of accountability. The second reason for the uniqueness relates to different approaches to youth justice in the four countries that comprise the United Kingdom. In England and Wales social workers do not work in the adult criminal justice system, which is the prerogative of the probation service. However, in Scotland and Northern Ireland, they do: social workers are potentially involved in the entire criminal justice system, including work with adults and adult mentally disordered offenders. The reason for this is partly historical and partly legal since the Scottish system in particular is based on quite distinct legal principles which, in the case of young offenders, has led to the evolution of a different system of adjudication in cases involving young people, with children's hearings rather than youth courts. Readers who are unfamiliar with the background to the Scottish children's hearings systems will find plenty of information on the Internet (look for Children's Hearings Scotland) or for the broader social policy context and comparisons of systems see Muncie (2011) or McGhee et al. (2012).

WHAT IS YOUTH JUSTICE?

Few textbooks on youth justice challenge the way the word justice is used in the context of contemporary social work practice. Most start with an assumption that readers are aware that the term youth justice applies to young people getting into trouble with the police, and the ways in which the criminal justice 'system' applies to people under the age of 18. While it is true that this is how the term is used in England and Wales, it may be worth pausing for a moment to consider that youth justice could mean, for example, ensuring that young people receive their fair distribution of resources, social goods, and opportunities, that they are generally treated fairly in the political, economic and social systems. Such a definition would not, of course, concern itself solely with young people as the perpetrators of crime; indeed, its focus would be quite different. It would equate youth justice with social justice whereas youth justice is in reality solely concerned with sanctioning the behaviour of young people – which may tell us something about perceptions of young people as threats to social order and about overall social attitudes towards them.

Nevertheless the fact remains that the term youth justice is now generally used as meaning a specific branch of criminal justice, adapted to apply to young people. The form of this adaptation has changed over time, and there is a substantial sociological and social policy literature on the shifts in youth justice policy, reflecting different ways in which young people are perceived in society (for a useful overview of this see Smith, 2014: Chapter 7). One recurring theme is that fear of young people's behaviour is long-standing.

'What is happening to our young people? They disrespect their elders. They disobey their parents. They ignore the law. They riot in the streets inflamed with wild notions. Their morals are decaying. What is to become of them?'

Astonishingly, this statement (attributed to Plato) was made 2,400 years ago and virtually every generation since has joined in the chorus to such an extent that there is now a word to describe this fear of young people, ephebiphobia. There is a range of literature attesting to how young people can be vilified, with labels such as 'hooligan' (Pearson, 1983) and their behaviour exaggerated out of all proportion, so contributing to what Cohen (1972) describes as a 'moral panic'. The question then that arises is whether the existence of youth crime plays a particular role in society and is necessary as part of social structures, indeed that youth justice as such is socially constructed (Muncie, 1999). This literature points to the much broader context within which youth justice policies operate, and although outside the scope of a book that focuses on the relationship between ethics and the application of social work law, it is important to acknowledge this wider dimension.

However, it would be perfectly appropriate to pause for a moment and ask a radical ethical question at this juncture: should young people obey the law? If so, to what extent should the law always be obeyed? Is it ever justifiable to 'break' the law?

Not surprisingly, there are competing answers to this question. As examples of these different views and as a prelude to a broader consideration of ethics and social work practice in youth justice, it may be useful to return to the thinking of Rawls, and specifically his interpretation of the notion of justice.

In Chapter 2 there was a discussion of Rawls' thinking in relation to fairness and the distribution of wealth or social justice, but Rawls has also addressed the question of why people should obey the law (Rawls 1993, 1999). Rawls says it is reasonable to expect people to obey the law providing that there is agreement that the law is legitimate. This means that the law must not represent the partial views of some people who hold specific values – that, for example, might relate to one particular religion – but they must be agreed through the political processes that citizens in a pluralistic society would agree to endorse. In other words, there is a social contract (for a fuller explanation of how this is to be envisaged see the discussion of Rawls in Chapter 2). Once the means of formulating laws are seen as legitimate, it then becomes incumbent upon individuals to obey them, in other words, effectively to agree to restrict their own liberty. Specifically Rawls argues that an individual cannot be released from the obligation to follow the rule of law since everyone enjoys the benefits of a society in which individuals have agreed to observe the laws. Or, to put it another way, on the basis of a social contract it is necessary for everyone to agree on the rules of behaviour and, having done so, it is unfair to the rest of society if someone tries to gain an advantage by acting otherwise. In this sense, it is unacceptable to disobey the law.

At the other extreme, radical thinkers such as Kropotkin, a Russian revolutionary whom some would label an anarchist, argues that the disobedience of the law never requires justification. Instead the question ought to be: why should people obey the law at all? Why does the law need to exist? Or rather why do so many laws need to exist? After all if we abolished property then there would be no such thing as theft. Laws protect the privileges of the few and overall the law is useless and would best be abolished. So get rid of all laws which are fundamentally unfair. Demolish prisons, do away with all law enforcing agencies, do away with all laws about 'penalties and misdemeanours' (Palmer, 2005).

Between these two views Palmer (2005) suggests looking at the ideas of Thoreau, who argues that the key concept that should influence behaviour is justice rather than legality. The question Thoreau poses is whether it is right to obey unjust laws, and if not, should attempts be made to amend them and obey them until such amendments take place, or could they legitimately be disobeyed in the meantime. Surely, he argues, the only real obligation is to do what is right and just, and in determining what this is, there is an important role for conscience. What is right may not always be what is lawful. There can be undue respect for the law.

These differences of views about the fundamental approach to law and criminal justice are important although clearly they do not directly affect social work practice with young people, which of necessity must take the criminal law as a given. Yet the operation of the law can pose major challenges for social workers regarding values and ethics. Indeed one textbook on youth justice comments:

'the discord between social work ethics and legal principles is perhaps no more keenly felt than in work with juvenile suspects and lawbreakers. (Pickford and Dugmore, 2012: 2)

This discord will be explored in this chapter in a number of different ways.

We begin by exploring different approaches to offences committed by young people (until the 1990s this meant under 17s but now means under 18s). The first distinction concerns interpretation of offences: does a commission of an offence indicate that the young person is 'bad' and needs to be punished or corrected for their misdemeanour, or is it that the offence demonstrates some shortcoming or inadequacy in their upbringing or education that needs to be 'corrected'? The second distinction concerns response to offences which moves us into the competing ethical and philosophical views of the purpose of formal responses to these offences – what in the court system is referred to as sentencing. This then leads to an analysis of what happens when these different approaches have been played out in practice, for youth justice is a particularly interesting field in that historically different approaches have held sway at different periods of time. So in the 1960s, for example, there was a strong movement towards what is known as the 'welfare' approach, which was sharply reversed in the 1980s and has been subsequently reinforced by greater emphasis on the 'justice' approach right up until the present day. This analysis is important as it enables us to explore further the ethical challenges to practice to which Pickford and Dugmore were referring.

DEPRIVED OR DEPRAVED: COMPETING EXPLANATIONS OF YOUTH OFFENDING

The debate about the concept of justice highlights the fundamental distinction between social justice, which creates the conditions necessary for people's participation in society, and justice more narrowly defined simply as obedience to the existing law. In this debate, there is a divergence of view that centres around the whole notion of what was fair and just for young people. In essence, the welfare approach argues that justice takes into account the background and personal circumstances of the offender, for it seems unjust to punish offenders for deficiencies or inadequacies that are beyond their control. Thus the offender's needs preoccupy the court's considerations, thereby permitting 'medicalisation' of behaviour with the use of terms such as 'treatment', 'prevention', 'symptoms', 'diagnosis', 'maladjustment' and 'deviance' (Box, 1980: 113). Conversely, the justice approach argues that any court sentence must fit with the severity of the offence committed, and the offenders' background per se cannot mitigate the offence.

For simplicity these approaches can be categorised under two umbrella headings: approaches that are welfare or treatment oriented, and those that are justice or punishment oriented: 'welfare versus justice'.

Critical thinking exercise 6.1
Welfare and justice models compared

Set out below is a commonly used framework for analysing youth justice policy: the welfare and justice models. As the distinction between welfare and justice is explored, try to think how these relate to:

- ethical theories and
- other assumptions about criminal justice and young people.

Table 6.1   Welfare and justice models

	Welfare	Justice
Offences are	Products of offenders' adverse environment	Consequences of offenders' choices and rational decisions
Social, economic and personal circumstances are	Very relevant	Irrelevant

(Continued)

(Continued)

	Welfare	Justice
Offenders are	Not totally responsible for their actions	Responsible for their actions in proportion to their age and are held accountable for them
Offenders and non-offenders should be dealt with	In the same system, since need for care is made manifest in offences	By separate tribunals in isolation from consideration of other needs
The prime consideration is	The needs of the offender	The seriousness of the offence
Strict rules of procedure	Need not be followed, informality is necessary to determine needs	Must be followed in accordance with the law
Underlying principle is	Response should fit need of offender	Consistency important, punishment must be proportionate to offence
Voluntary outcomes are	Preferable, but even if imposed, 'care' not to be regarded as punishment	Not acceptable, courts determine outcomes
Outcomes are influenced by	Social work or medical professionals with expert interpretation highly valued	Legal considerations only
Offender's welfare is	Paramount	Irrelevant
Focus is on	Needs	Deeds

You may have found relating these approaches to youth justice to the ethical theories outlined in this book quite challenging. This is partly due to the fact that, inevitably, when policy and practice become reality, practitioners and policymakers do not always make explicit the ethical base from which they are working. Indeed policy may not be consistent with any one particular approach.

Deontological Approaches

An initial application of Kantian theory would suggest that the law should be taken as absolute, and anyone who breaks the law should be punished. In other words, this is a pure justice approach. However it needs to be recognised that Kant does allow for individuals to have reasons for breaking the law, providing these are the outcomes of a rational process. There is an allowance for a higher order of right and wrong that can stand above what the law actually says – hence it was possible to put on trial and execute Gestapo commanders after the Second World War despite the fact that German law at that time apparently permitted their actions. The question the individual needs to ask is whether their view of what was right and wrong could be universalised. In some cases this may mean the law itself is challenged, and indeed might be changed. One of the most famous examples in Britain is the 1932 mass trespass of Kinder Scout which challenged the right of landowners to stop hikers walking in the Peak District, and eventually led to the creation of a national park and a 'right to roam' law.

Utilitarian Theory

Utilitarian theory is, of course, concerned with consequences. If young people disobey the law what response to this has the best outcome? If a welfare approach to youth justice is adopted, will the consequences of this overall be better for society than a justice approach? In order to determine this, a utilitarian would certainly be interested in the consequences in terms of reoffending. In some cases the welfare approach might prove more effective in addressing the causes of the offence; in others a retributive approach could be justified on the basis that it would deter other potential offenders and therefore have the best overall consequence. Note that the law itself is not challenged; what is debatable is the best means of enforcing it. There is no particular predisposition to argue in favour of either welfare or justice – it all depends on what works.

Virtue Ethics and Ethics of Care

Virtue ethics focuses on the quality and character of individuals within an overall concern to enable people to lead a good life. It is concerned with those qualities that lead to human flourishing both in an individual sense and as a means to another end which might be regarded as the flourishing and the welfare of society as a whole. Virtue ethics has proved particularly attractive to feminist thinkers who believe that deontological (Kantian) theory, based on duty and right, represents a male approach to morality. Thus a deontological approach may not pay proper attention to qualities such as care and compassion which are important, not only in their own right, but also as they apply to women in particular. It is immediately obvious how virtue ethics therefore might generally be much more sympathetic to the welfare approach to youth justice, and indeed might also concern itself with differential treatment of young men and young women in the youth justice system – an issue often highlighted in standard texts on youth justice (for example, Smith, 2014: 151–6).

How do these competing approaches then relate to what courts should do about offences committed by young people. In other words, what do they say about the purpose of sentencing?

What to Do About Young Offenders? The Ethics of Sentencing

Critical thinking exercise 6.2   The purpose of sentencing

The table below sets out three approaches to sentencing. It uses the labels often attached to different approaches to sentencing: retribution (offenders getting their just deserts), deterrence (deterring the individual and others in order to prevent crime) and rehabilitation (or reform of the individual who has committed the crime).

When you read through this table consider how these apply to the different approaches to ethics as outlined in the previous section – deontological, utilitarian, and virtue ethics. You may want to consider possible objections to these approaches and it may also be worthwhile reflecting on what would be the implications for policy and practice.

Naturally these approaches to sentencing apply to adults as well as young people but when exploring these different approaches try to focus on what they would mean for young people.

Table 6.2   The ethics of sentencing: what is its purpose?

	Retribution	Deterrence and prevention	Rehabilitation or reform
More specifically	Court should impose a punishment: it is what the offender deserves because of what they have done, should be imposed even if no good consequences might come of it	Court should be concerned with the consequences of sentences and whether sentences serve to increase society's general security and happiness	Court should concern itself with reasons for behaviour and measures that can be taken to control such behaviour in the future
General principle	Deserts	Whatever works	Reform
Punishment is	Necessary since guilt alone justifies it	An instrumental good, prevents others committing crime	Not what it is about, rather sentences are about treatment
Aim of sentence	To make an important pronouncement that what the offender did is wrong and to apply a punishment that is a proportionate response to what they did	Apply some kind of deterrent in order to stop others committing crime or else remove individuals who threaten the general happiness and security of others	Aim is to control individual's tendency to engage in offending behaviour through education or therapy or even conditioning
Sentence is	Backward looking	Forward looking	Mixture

	Retribution	Deterrence and prevention	Rehabilitation or reform
Offenders are	To be punished for what they have done	To be deterred from further crime	To be reformed
The prime consideration is	Reinforcing the law	Consequences for society	Reforming the criminal
Strict rules of procedure	Must be observed	Should be observed unless it is better for society not to	Should be flexible enough to accommodate assessment of need
Outcomes are influenced by	Need to make a point	Consequences of sentence imposed	Potential success in reforming offender
Offender's welfare is	Totally irrelevant	Usually irrelevant	Very relevant as it is a predictor of likely success of reform

It is tempting to jump to the conclusion that the measures outlined in the first column could simply be labelled a reflection of the Kantian or deontological approach, and indeed generally they are, but as explained earlier, individuals may consciously choose to break the law using overriding principles which in our view transcend the requirements of the law. So in this sense a deontological approach allows for the possibility of a duty to obey at a higher principle that is above the law. The principal objection to this approach is that it may just appease a primitive and almost barbaric desire for revenge. In the context of youth justice, it may be particularly harsh if the young person concerned did not really fully understand why their actions were wrong or what a consequence of those actions might be.

The second approach is interesting in the sense that it allows for a variety of possibilities of actions to be taken, so long as they deter that particular offender from committing that crime, and also deter other people. The assumption is that in deterring offences, court sentences contribute to promoting the greater harmony of society. In some ways this is the most flexible approach but it could also be the most punitive. For example, segregation from the rest of society for the rest of someone's life might be what the majority of society wants, yet it could be out of all proportion to the nature of the offence committed. Furthermore, it does not necessarily matter if someone is proven to be guilty since sentencing an innocent person could still meet the utility principle.

The third approach, being offender rather than offence focused, is one that would lend itself most closely to virtue ethics. The assumption here is that by committing an offence the young person demonstrates lack of desirable personal qualities and therefore the sentence of the court ought to be able to correct that so as to mould a more virtuous and valuable citizen. In many ways, this could be seen as a much more positive approach to youth justice but there is a danger that, in ignoring the just deserts argument, the reformative action adopted by the courts could involve measures that appear to be disproportionate to the offender themselves. It might even ride roughshod over consent and threaten the integrity of the individual.

The implications for policy and practice can be examined very readily by exploring shifts in youth justice policy over the last 50 years, so in the next section there is a brief summary of changes in legislation that reflect different emphases on retribution, deterrence and reform.

SOCIAL WORK LAW CONTEXT: CHARTING THE SHIFTS IN YOUTH JUSTICE POLICY

Children and Young Persons Act 1969

For many years, young offenders were treated in the same way as adults, with little allowance made for age except for a long-standing rule that children under the age of eight could not be prosecuted. Different systems for responding to youth crime began to develop in the middle of the nineteenth century and in 1908 separate courts were introduced for dealing with young offenders. For most youngsters who were considered to be in need of some kind of custody, the Children and Young Persons Act 1933 introduced approved schools with an emphasis on education. These were always under the aegis of the Home Office, which was then responsible for the entire criminal justice system. They were available to the courts as a sentence, although not exclusively for proven crimes, since it was also possible to ask the courts to commit children to them who were 'beyond control' of their parents. This welfare aspect provided an element of confusion, since the regimes were primarily intended as a punishment for offenders. The system was brought into disrepute by three notorious incidents. In 1947, a major breakout at Standon Farm School resulted in the death of a member of staff and a review of the system whereby boys' periods of detention could be determined solely by the Headmaster. In 1959, there was open rebellion at Carlton School in Bedfordshire. Finally in 1967 a member of staff 'blew the whistle' on the severity of punishments at one approved school, Court Lees, and this resulted in an official inquiry and, shortly afterwards, the abolition of the whole 'approved school' system.

During the 1960s, a number of official reports had been published that were increasingly hostile to the prevailing punitive, retributive approach to youth justice (Home Office, 1960, 1965, 1968). At the same time, social work had gained greater prominence and there was a growing chorus for 'reform' with the demand that more attention be paid to the background of young offenders, with a system that tried to address the kind of environmental circumstances that led to young people committing offences.

This is exactly the approach adopted in the Children and Young Persons Act 1969. This Act took away courts' powers to send young offenders into custody, but instead insisted that in some cases young offenders could be placed under supervision of social workers (or probation officers), or in other cases committed to the care of a local authority, who then had the power to decide at what kind of establishment a young person should be placed and what measures to adopt in order to 'reform' them. The severity of the offence did not necessarily connect to the severity of the outcome; instead the fact that the young person had committed an offence was deemed to be a demonstration that the young person was in need of some kind of re-education or reform which the local authority was best placed to offer. For our purposes, this approach encapsulates an almost pure application of the rehabilitation or reform approach outlined above.

Criminal Justice Act 1982

Predicated on a strong belief that offences committed by young people demonstrated welfare needs best met by referral to social workers, the Children and Young Persons Act 1969 was clearly vulnerable to the shift away from a belief in state intervention generally, coupled with the firm reassertion of individual responsibility, and that is exactly what happened. Significantly, the 1969 Act was never fully implemented. Its intention to remove all custodial options from the courts was never realised, partly because of a change in government shortly after it was passed but also because a 'magisterial revolt' effectively undermined it, as did the actions of the police and others involved in its implementation (Thorpe, 1983). This resulted in successful demands that courts retain the power to send young offenders into custody and, as confidence in social workers' ability to 'reform' young offenders diminished, so the use of custody increased: from 3,200 offenders sentenced to custody in 1971 to 7,700 in 1981 (Muncie, 1999: 265–6). Public opinion, persuaded by a growing 'problem' of lawlessness, influenced major changes in policy in the period 1979 to 1981. There was a strong push towards the removal of social work from youth justice altogether, a move supported by commentators who alleged that innovative reformative practices in the 1970s simply had the effect of 'up-tariffing': young people convicted of minor offences found themselves committed to care, propelling second and serious offenders immediately into custody (Haines and Drakeford, 1998). This was reinforced by the alleged unpredictability of a system that appeared to penalise young people for their backgrounds, rather than for what they had actually done (Morris and Giller, 1983).

Furthermore, critics successfully argued that the unfettered powers of the courts ignored due processes, trammelling the legal rights of the young person. There was evidence of class and racial discrimination. Rehabilitation was perceived as being used to justify unnecessary and significant intrusion in the lives of children. There was a desire to hold parents accountable for the actions of errant youth (Haines and Drakeford, 1998: 153). This accorded with a broader emphasis on individual responsibility. It can also be argued that during this period there was a major shift of emphasis towards a reassertion of the need for social control, discipline and generally a more authoritarian approach to young people (Muncie, 1999).

The passing of the Criminal Justice Act 1982 marked a turning point, with a reassertion of the 'justice' model and the return of the distinction between the 'deprived' and the 'depraved'. Essentially the Act reintroduced a tariff system whereby sentences were connected directly to the seriousness of the offence. Statutory tests had to be fulfilled before young offenders were committed to custody. No longer were young people to be sentenced according to their welfare 'needs', but were to be judged and sentenced according to their 'deeds' (Haines and Drakeford, 1998). In some ways this justice model, as it was called, was an inversion of the welfare ideals that undergirded its predecessor, the Children and Young Persons Act 1969, focusing instead on: offending, not the offender; responsibility for actions, not concern with family background and social explanations; equality of punishment, not individual treatment; and determinate sanctions rather than indeterminate rehabilitation.

One ironic consequence of this Act was that in the following decade the percentage of 14 to 18 year olds committed to custody for offences decreased significantly from 13,500 in 1983 to 3,300 in 1993 (Muncie, 1999: 281). Thus the predominance of the welfare reform approach in the 1970s appears to have had the unintended consequence of sending a far greater proportion of offenders to custody, while the prevailing justice and retribution ideology of the 1980s resulted in the opposite effect.

Crime and Disorder Act 1998

The change of government in 1997 heralded a shift in youth justice policy in which prevention supposedly became prominent ('tough on crime, tough on the causes of crime'). Specific preventative measures included the work of the Social Exclusion Unit and Connexions, Sure Start schemes, neighbourhood renewal, truancy sweeps, summer activities schemes, the Youth Inclusion Programme, child safety orders, parenting orders and the Intensive Supervision and Surveillance Programme (for summary see Smith, 2014: Chapter 2, also see Pickford and Dugmore, 2012). However, policy shifted in another sense: while it emphasised prevention in a general way it broke sharply with the focus on the needs of the offender as exemplified by the 1969 Act. Goldson (1999: 9) quotes politicians of the time who stated explicitly that the welfare needs of the offender could not be allowed to outweigh the need of the community to be protected from their behaviour.

The Crime and Disorder Act 1998 established Youth Offending Teams and local inter-agency partnerships to oversee and 'manage' youth crime. The Act also created Anti-Social Behaviour Orders intended to prevent individual offences or acts of anti-social behaviour. Commentators have labelled this Act as an example of the then government's corporatist, micro-management approach to youth justice (Smith, 2014: Chapter 3) since the Act took away discretion from decision-makers and imposed a detailed and specific graduated system of measures: for example, only a specific number of warnings or reprimands to be issued. Thus the Act 'represented an intensification of the processes of criminalisation and punitive actions against young people' (Smith, 2014: 39).

Subsequently the Youth Justice and Criminal Evidence Act 1999 introduced referral orders. The Criminal Justice and Police Act 2001 allowed courts to make security requirements for holding young people accused of crimes, the Anti-Social Behaviour Act 2003 and the Criminal Justice Act 2003 extended Anti-Social Behaviour Orders and created a further range of requirements that could be imposed on children and young people.

Criminal Justice and Immigration Act 2008

The Criminal Justice and Immigration Act 2008 in many ways represents the apotheosis of the micro-management approach in the sense that it consolidated a whole raft of measures to 'address' offending behaviour. The contrast between this Act and the Children and Young Persons Act 1969 could not be more stark. The 1969 Act, in its original form, allowed courts only three measures, or sentences, to impose on young people themselves: conditional discharges, supervision orders, or care orders. The Criminal Justice and Immigration Act 2008 has 18 possible requirements (for complete list and further details see Johns, 2014b: 127–9).

Legal Aid, Sentencing and Punishment of Offenders Act 2012

Initially the government that came to power in 2010 declared itself committed to a reduction in the degree of intervention in young people's lives implied by the combination of Anti-Social Behaviour Orders and Youth Rehabilitation Orders under the Criminal Justice and Immigration Act 2008. This was reinforced by rhetoric that appeared to argue for a more welfare-oriented approach to youth justice generally, although hinting at the introduction of 'payments by results' (Smith, 2014: 64–70). What emerged in the Legal Aid, Sentencing and Punishment of Offenders Act 2012 was greater discretion in the courts' application of tariffs, encouragement of informal responses to youth offending, yet accompanied by harsher approaches to certain kinds of crimes (mandatory custodial sentences for knife crimes, for example). Alongside an emphasis on restorative justice, the more recent changes move policy back to more of a mixed approach. The pendulum has effectively swung from, using the distinctions outlined in Table 6.1, a strong 'welfare' approach in 1969, to ultimate 'justice' in 2008 and now slightly back towards the middle ground.

This brings the discussion up-to-date and sets the scene for the next stage of our analysis connecting law to ethical theory and social work law practice.

CASE STUDY

Three 14-year-old boys who were friends from the same school, but lived in different parts of a small town, found they shared the same interests and met together regularly in each other's houses, mostly on Saturdays. Their principal interest was war games and, as they were all academically quite able, they moved into developing and designing their own. One day, they fell into discussing covert operations and strategies for finding out secrets. The conversation took place in the house in which one of them, Jamie, lived with his parents.

Jamie then mentioned something that had puzzled him for a long time: he wondered what was kept in the room above the corner shop which was next door to his house, since he could just see that room through his bedroom window, and

(Continued)

(Continued)

what he saw intrigued him. He thought it might be a base for secret agents. The group then decided to find out, which they did by an ingenious combination of using listening devices and fire-escapes. They soon ascertained that the room was used as a store-room for the shop and that no one lived there. Overwhelmed with curiosity, they managed to find a back way using fire-escapes to break into the room and were amazed to discover, not secret agents, but several boxes of their favourite sweets and chocolate. Filling their pockets to capacity they returned to base and spent the rest of the afternoon in chocolate paradise!

Every subsequent visit to Jamie's house from then on included a chocolate raid until one day the inevitable happened, and they were discovered. The police were called and they found themselves being processed through the youth justice system.

Jamie's parents were distraught and ashamed by what he had done. They constantly, from then onwards, reminded him of the disgrace he had brought on them and stopped him from associating with his two mates outside school. David lived with his dad, who was furious with him and punished him severely telling him this was no way for a teacher's son to behave. Mikey's parents thought it was all quite amusing, although his mum was bitterly disappointed that her son was so mean he had not shared any of the chocolate with her!

Subsequently ...

What happens subsequently depends on how youth justice law operates and the ethical theories that underpin it. So what follows are some hypothetical scenarios for consideration, although each quite strongly reflects different approaches to youth justice in different eras or different places.

So let us assume that we start with a blank sheet of paper and can sit down to design a youth justice system based on certain agreed principles. In the first scenario, the assumption is that youth offenders need re-education; the second scenario assumes they need treatment; the third assumes they need punishment; the fourth rehabilitation.

This exercise will facilitate analysis and reflection on what is meant by 'justice' and will enable us to predict certain consequences of their application.

Critical thinking exercise 6.3
Young offenders need re-education

In this scenario, the prevailing social policy is that of assuming that the causes of offending behaviour lie primarily in factors connected to the offender's background and environment. It may be that parents have failed successfully to teach the difference between right and wrong, or else that there is overwhelming neighbourhood or peer pressure to engage in criminal behaviour. Offenders are 'deprived' rather than 'depraved'. This approach therefore firmly falls under the welfare label above, and is consistent with the approach of the Children and Young Persons Act 1969.

If this were the approach to youth justice, what sort of outcomes would you expect for the three young men in the case study and what role would social workers play in this scenario?

One might be tempted to conclude that all these young men need is re-education as to how to use these inquisitive skills more appropriately (and legally)! However there would be some effort made to try to understand what they had been taught about acceptable and unacceptable behaviour, and a crucial part of this would emphatically be the responses of the respective parents. Here Mikey might be particularly unfortunate since courts would take a dim view of the parental bemusement and consequently he might find himself committed to some kind of institution where he would be offered 'appropriate' role models. Conversely, the response of Jamie's parents might be considered, of itself, sufficient; likewise with David's dad, although here the court might want to know how the punishment might actually help him to learn to differentiate right from wrong. Indeed there are a number of ways in which courts could interpret the educational needs of each boy, and doubtless in their decision-making would be strongly guided by both school reports and a social work analysis of their learning needs.

For our purposes, what is especially noteworthy is the degree of attention the courts would pay to each young man's individual needs. The actual offence plays a secondary role, although clearly its commission indicates, presumably, some kind of 'faulty' learning. Hence the outcomes might be different according to different assessments of educational needs and evaluations of parental responses. Social workers would play an important advisory role and may also be involved in devising the re-education schemes the courts might require.

How does this relate to deontological, utilitarian and virtue ethics approaches?

If there is general agreement or, to be more precise it is a categorical imperative, that it is wrong to steal, then that principle is non-negotiable. The absolute priority would be to ensure that the law is obeyed. However, in this system the means to achieve this rests on another absolute principle which is that the needs of the offender are paramount. The challenge is that these two principles might collide. If compliance with the law is the overriding principle then the second principle (meeting an offender's needs) would then be judged by its success in attaining the first objective (obedience of the law). However if the law were to state that the offender's needs come first, then further offences would have to be tolerated. So this approach might not quite accord with a strict deontological view.

Utilitarians would argue that the needs of the majority are served by arrangements whereby the greatest good can be achieved. The problem then is: if the greatest good is attained by stopping offenders offending, there is only justification for a system that attaints that goal successfully and the needs of the offender might be deemed irrelevant if an educational outcome failed to attain that objective. However if it works, it works, and utilitarians would be satisfied if that were to be the case.

A virtue ethics approach would pay attention to the character of each young man, ask questions about what kind of people were their parents, and to what kind of regime or role models they might respond. The relationship the families had established with youth justice professionals would be considered important. The extent to which courts would deem it necessary to intervene in their lives would depend to a very great extent on an assessment of the key people involved in these offences, and motivation for committing the offence would naturally be a major consideration.

In all these respects, it can be seen that the re-educational approach envisaged here fits most closely with virtue ethics.

Critical thinking exercise 6.4
Young offenders need treatment

In this scenario, the prevailing social policy is that of assuming that offending behaviour demonstrates that the young person needs social, psychological or medical treatment. The causes of offending behaviour lie within the offender themselves since by committing offences they are acting out some kind of emotional turmoil, or are engaging in faulty thinking or are unable to perceive the consequences of their actions. In short, offenders could be regarded as both deprived and depraved, yet the general approach still falls under the welfare label above as it is primarily offender focused.

If this were the approach to youth justice, what sort of outcomes would you expect for the three young men in the case study and what role would social workers play in this scenario?

This approach relies on thorough assessment of the offender's background as an assumed causative factor in explaining the offence, and the measures adopted to address this would be primarily therapeutic. It is difficult to overstate the degree of intrusiveness this might necessitate since full information would be required about early childhood experiences, upbringing, self-perception and a range of other factors relevant to psychodynamic interpretations. For example, does the enthusiasm for chocolate that impelled the individual boys to agree to act illegally demonstrate a craving for affection or satisfy some other emotional need? If so, what would be the best means of addressing this? Alternatively, does the social background explain the behaviour? Was there a lack of facilities for young people that meant that they became bored and consequently redirected their energy to criminal behaviour?

Whatever the explanation, the role of social workers is central and crucial in understanding it, interpreting it to the court and addressing it through measures that the court would endorse. Note again that, being offender focused, the interpretations and recommendations to the court might vary significantly between the individual young men.

As with the educational approach, the difficulty for a deontological approach is that there might be a clash of principles: the first being that the law should be obeyed and the second that the needs of the offender are paramount. There would need to be some decision about prioritisation of these but if, as is likely, the overriding principle is respect for principles of ownership of property, then it is difficult to reconcile this with a strict deontological view.

A utilitarian view would tolerate this approach to youth justice providing it works, for reasons explained in discussion of the educational approach.

There is some fit here with the virtue ethics approach since this approach does concern itself with a full assessment of individual nature (for a fuller explanation see earlier discussion on virtue ethics and the re-educational approach). An ethics of care approach could also fit in the sense that, in order to bring about significant change for these young men, a strong supportive and transformative relationship needs to be established between them, professionals engaged in their care, and their families.

However we might here want to include views put forward by Rawls who argued that a youth justice system based on needs of offenders could be seen as a means of redressing social disadvantage, and to that end the principle that the offence is a trigger for state intervention that may enhance the offender's well-being and compensate for some kind of deficit in upbringing would be eminently defensible.

Critical thinking exercise 6.5
Young offenders need punishment

In this scenario, youth justice policy concerns itself with the nature of offences committed by young people and laws are devised to stipulate the outcomes for actions that are deemed criminal. It is solely the nature of the offence that counts and reasons for its commission are largely irrelevant. Once guilt is determined, the outcome is calculated by reference to a tariff, with all considerations centring on the seriousness of the offence. This is the quintessential 'justice' approach to youth justice, an approach strongly reasserted by the Criminal Justice Act 1982.

If this were the approach to youth justice, what sort of outcomes would you expect for the three young men in the case study and what role would social workers play in this scenario?

This approach concentrates on the seriousness of the offence, the impact of it, the degree of culpability of those who committed it, the need to send a marker to indicate that the offence itself merits some kind of sanction. This accords with the retributive approach outlined earlier, and is as close as it is possible to conceive of an approach that follows deontological thinking. There is only a very limited role for social workers in this approach, one that confines them to the assessment of the offender's motives and a role in the implementation of certain sentences, such as supervision orders.

Whether it is a utilitarian approach depends ultimately on its success, assuming the overall aim is to prevent the commission of further offences as a means of enhancing the greatest utility for the majority. This may serve to alert us to one of the limitations of utilitarian approaches which is they may not help to inform which path is more ethical unless we can be reasonably sure of the consequences of adopting that approach. The focus is on outcomes, consequences and results, yet no court can be sure as to what the outcome of particular sentences might be. It could be argued that, in itself, a retributive or 'justice' approach might be best as it is the one that might command greatest public approval. Yet popularity of certain kinds of sentences does not guarantee success in reducing offending – it might simply make people feel better, but would not necessarily achieve its objective. One classic example of this is the popularity of the death sentence at the time when its abolition was being mooted. A major argument in favour of abolition was the lack of effectiveness of capital sentences in reducing the murder rate, yet a majority 'believed' in it, nevertheless.

An offence-based approach to sentencing pays scant attention to the needs of the offender. In that sense, it has no relation to a virtue ethics or ethics of care approach. Although courts do pay some attention to the motives and past behaviour of the offender in determining what sentence to pass, this is for the purpose of assessing degrees of culpability. The principal objective of sentencing remains to apportion punishment in accordance with the severity of the crime, and the degree of the offender's responsibility for committing it.

The justice model does, of course, have its critics. Since the overriding concern is with the offence itself, some would argue that the model deliberately ignores the causes of crime, especially issues of social disadvantage. Placing importance on punishment can lead to a form of injustice for young offenders if it assumes they all start with equal awareness of what is right and wrong, and have all enjoyed the same opportunities to be guided into acceptable behaviour. One does not have to be a social worker to realise that this is far from the truth.

Critical thinking exercise 6.6
Youth offenders need rehabilitation

In this scenario, youth justice policy concerns itself with the nature of offences committed by young people and their effects. Laws are devised to address the consequences of actions. It is both the nature of the offence and its consequences for the victims (individuals, organisations or society generally) that matter. Once responsibility for the offence is assessed, the outcome is determined by reference to the effects of the crime on others and the ways in which this can be addressed. What can the offender do to put right the wrong they have done? Although there is some attention paid to the offender's need to restore or rehabilitate, nevertheless this is still primarily a justice approach to youth justice, with echoes of this approach being discernible in the Criminal Justice and Immigration Act 2008, and associated legislation.

> If this were the approach to youth justice, what sort of outcomes would you expect for the three young men in the case study and what role would social workers play in this scenario?

This is a classic blended approach to youth justice so includes elements of all the ethical approaches that have been discussed in this book. The 'justice' element accords with a deontological approach (more or less). The restorative element has hints of both virtue ethics and ethics of care approaches (the quality of character of the offender, together with the potential for successful rehabilitation with social workers and others acting as intermediaries and facilitators of reconciliation, being important issues), yet overall the intention to be concerned with the eventual consequences of the mixture of options available in, say, youth rehabilitation orders, argues for labelling this a utilitarian approach.

Social workers play a significant, but not determinant, role in this approach. Clearly they are important in assessment of some aspects, such as assessing the potential suitability of restorative strategies, implementing sentences that address social factors that explain the behaviour, and in seeking to address it through work with families and the community affected by the crime. It is comparatively easy to see what social workers' roles would be by examining what social workers currently actually do in Youth Offending Teams (for which see Pickford and Dugmore, 2012: Chapter 5).

CHALLENGES FOR SOCIAL WORK PRACTITIONERS

So, on the basis of all these considerations, what can be said about the challenges for social workers?

Let us start to answer that question by learning a lesson from history, for the case study above relates to events that occurred when the Children and Young Persons Act 1969 was in force, when the youth justice system was offender, rather than offence, related.

Subsequently ...

At the subsequent court hearing, which all parents attended, Jamie was fined, David was given a conditional discharge, and Mikey committed to the care of the local authority under a care order so that he could be 'sent to an institution where he would be well away from the nonchalant attitude displayed by his parents' as the magistrate described it in court.

This created huge resentment. The parents were dumbfounded as they could not understand how the court could take three different courses of action in relation to what was, basically, the same offence. There was considerable sympathy for Mikey's parents, who were distraught at the thought of their son being 'put away'. They believed the court's actions were totally out of proportion to what their son had done. As for the young men themselves, they had different reactions. David was pleased to have 'got away with it' and could not quite believe his luck. Jamie did not quite see why he should have to pay a fine while David did not, especially as he knew his parents would be constantly reminding him of this and the misfortunes he had brought on them; they would also find it very difficult to pay a fine. Mikey himself was stunned. He was unable to take in what had happened. When eventually he came to realise what the court order meant, he was absolutely furious. He believed he was being discriminated against. He believed he was being punished for his mother's attitude. There was absolutely no way he was going to co-operate. He was going to run away from any home where he was placed.

Whatever you may think about the action taken by the court, and it does not take a great imagination to think through the consequences for Mikey in particular, the point here is that this approach to youth justice makes no sense whatsoever in terms of those people who experience it, the young people themselves and their parents. It is inevitable, surely, that they will expect outcomes to have some regard to what they themselves have done, not to something such as parental attitude or social background. So one immediate challenge for social work practice is to consider what sense the youth justice system makes to the young people who are caught up in it.

At a deeper level, the challenge for social work practice is to reflect on what justice actually means in this context, and specifically justice for whom. It is tempting to see young people just as young offenders and concentrate solely on the offence. In many ways the youth justice system encourages practitioners to do just that. However one core social work value is to respect individuals and to work with them in a way that is empowering rather than disempowering. Encouraging people to take responsibility for their actions is consistent with this, but this is only likely to gain a positive response in a context in which young people understand that what is happening to them is fair and proportionate. Restorative justice clearly has a role to play here since it is comparatively easy to understand how trying to put right what has been done wrong is an appropriate course of action.

Fundamentally, youth justice raises profound questions about the nature of justice and the ethical theories that underpin it. This gets to the heart of assumptions about what lies behind unacceptable behaviour. Is it the result of incorrect thinking, the poor outcome of rational decision-making processes? Is it the inevitable corollary of certain kinds of social background, meaning that, if young people come from certain areas or housing estates, they are bound to behave in a certain kind of way? Is the youth justice system trying to distinguish between inherently 'good' people who have made a mistake and those who are essentially lacking in virtue, for whom more extreme measures need to be considered? What assumptions have you made?

CONCLUSION

This chapter concerned youth justice, a topic that raises fundamental questions about the nature of justice and assumptions about human behaviour. After reflecting on what constitutes justice, the chapter then explored competing approaches to addressing offences committed by young people. The distinction was drawn between the 'welfare' and 'justice' approaches, which was analysed in terms of implications for court sentences. This was then related to the ethical theories explored throughout the book. Perhaps unsurprisingly, it soon became clear that the no single approach to justice equates exactly and directly to one specific ethical theory, although there are some clear parallels between certain kinds of approaches and virtue ethics.

A significant part of this chapter is given over to an exposition of different legal approaches adopted over the last 50 years or so. This began with the welfare approach embodied in the Children and Young Persons Act 1969, which gave way to a system geared more towards the tariff-based approach of the Criminal Justice Act 1982. More recent developments have included the rise in popularity of Anti-Social Behaviour Orders under the Crime and Disorder Act 1998, and the wide menu of sentences available to courts under the Criminal Justice and Immigration Act 2008. The most recent developments have included the Legal Aid, Sentencing and Punishment of Offenders Act 2012, bringing in what might be called a more blended approach to youth justice that tries to place some emphasis on restorative justice.

The chapter then focused on a case study in which readers were invited to relate the different sentencing responses to competing ethical theories. Finally, what actually happened in the case was revealed, raising the whole issue of how youth justice feels on the receiving end, and the implications of this for social work practitioners in terms of considering what constitutes justice, what assumptions practitioners might make about causes of behaviour, and how all of this might relate to values and ethics.

The next chapter moves into a rather different area of social work practice, namely community care. Specifically the focus will be on a case decided by the Supreme Court that raises fundamental questions about how ethics can relate to the law, and how social work decisions can be compromised when there are financial issues at stake. This proved to be particularly poignant in the case study since financial considerations appeared to impel a local authority to act in a way which might have resulted in a fundamental breach of someone's dignity and therefore their human rights.

7

Community Care and the Ethics of Resource Allocation

INTRODUCTION AND CHAPTER OVERVIEW

This is the fourth chapter in this book exploring interconnections between ethics and law in one specific area of social work practice. The discussion now turns towards adult care and specifically ethics, law and practice in relation to community care legislation, rationing resources, personalisation and empowerment. A number of ethical dilemmas arise from, for example, the need to maximise individual rights to choice and dignity, and the overriding (and sometimes overwhelming) fact that social care budgets are constrained and therefore resources have to be allocated in as fair a way as possible.

The discussion in this chapter starts with an overview of the legal context that applies to adult care generally, with a summary of relevant law. This is followed by the case example itself and an explanation of the specific legal issues that have arisen in this particular case. The discussion then turns to an analysis of how these might connect, first, to different approaches to ethics and, second, to theories of social justice. The chapter concludes with an exploration of the kinds of issues arising when connecting law and ethics to adult care social work in the community care context. The format followed is similar to that of Chapter 5.

The Introduction to Chapter 4 set out how the discussion in these practice-related chapters relate to the Professional Capabilities Framework (The College of Social Work, 2012) and the QAA Subject Benchmark Statements for Social Work (QAA, 2008). It also explained how this set of chapters is designed to promote the attainment and development of Critical Thinking Skills.

Community care, popularly referred to as social care (although that is in fact a broader term), in practice refers to arrangements made to support adults living in the community who need some kind of support services to enable them to continue to do so. Adults here means anyone aged 18 or over, although in practice the majority of those who use community care services are in the 80+ age group or else have some kind of disability. Strangely, community care as a term incorporates residential care although most people would probably regard that as being outside the 'community'. Nevertheless, legally, community care refers to all care that takes place outside hospital and includes all forms of care except that which is primarily medical. As practitioners will be aware, the distinction between 'medical' and 'social' care really matters since in England and Wales service users are obliged to pay for social care while medical care is free at the point of delivery.

Operationally, there is an important dividing line between assessment and provision of services. Since implementation of the Griffiths Report (Griffiths, 1988) by the National Health Service and Community Care Act 1990, local authorities have been required to ensure that those who assess community care needs do so as objectively as possible. This means without having one eye to actual resources, since that would inevitably mean matching the person to the resource rather than designing a care package, a package that accurately sets out what someone needs as a first stage prior to deciding then how those needs can best be met. The final stage for a local authority is to decide the extent to which the local authority is itself going to meet those needs, the assessment having been concluded.

The policy underpinning the introduction of the National Health Service and Community Care Act 1990 included offering service users and carers greater choice through the introduction of a market-based 'mixed economy' of social care providers. Subsequently this principle has been reaffirmed in government policy (Department of Health, 2005, 2006; HM Government, 2007) and extended through legislative changes, most recently the Care Act 2014. In all of this, personalisation was taken to mean 'starting with the person as an individual with strengths, preferences and aspirations and putting them at the centre of the process of identifying their needs and making choices about how and when they are supported to live their lives' (Carr, 2010: 3). An intrinsic part of personalisation is the encouragement of the use of personal budgets and direct payments whereby individual service users and carers take responsibility for deciding exactly what services to purchase, having been allocated a sum of money by local authorities on the basis of assessed needs (SCIE, 2010). Services should enable and foster this approach to placing the individual at the centre, and later policy documents (HM Government, 2010, 2012) set out how this should be achieved.

In practice, there have been a number of cases where the inevitable rationing of community care resources has been challenged in court. In the celebrated Gloucester case (*R v Gloucestershire County Council ex parte Barry*, 1997) it was established that, once need has been declared and services provided at one level, services could not be peremptorily withdrawn without a reassessment of need. However, when needs were re-assessed, the local authority was entitled to take into account its own resources available to meet that need. In the case study that forms the focus of this chapter, the Supreme Court was asked to adjudicate on how a local authority sought to provide for someone's needs to be met when the local authority wished to change the existing arrangement, presumably in order to reduce their community care expenditure, although that was never explicitly declared as a driving factor.

The case study raises fundamental questions about human dignity and the extent to which services should respect this in order both to meet need and to share funds among all service users and carers. It highlights the conflict between a number of competing principles: the desire to empower individuals and encourage them to make their own choice, the drive to make budgets balance and minimise public expenditure, the wish to be fair in the distribution of resources, and the need to offer services that not only promote independence but also maintain people's self-respect and dignity.

As happened in the case study covered in Chapter 5, the Supreme Court was not unanimous in its verdict, and once again telling judicial comments were made on law and ethics relevant to social work practice. Underlying this is a fundamental debate about whether the principles are absolute determinants of practice or guidelines for good practice that generally ought to be observed.

As a prelude to the case there is a section that explains the legal context and sets out the relevant law as it operated at the time of the Supreme Court case. A comprehensive overview of community care law may be found in Brammer (2015: Chapter 14) and Brayne, Carr and Goosey (2015: Chapters 11–13). There is also a more concise summary of the law in Johns (2014b: Chapter 5). All incorporate references to the Care Act 2014, which in future will be the cornerstone legislation in this area. This section is followed by the case study itself with an exposition of the underlying debate about principles and ethics. This then leads to consideration of how ethics can apply to an area where budgets have to be balanced in the demographic context of an increasingly ageing population. The debates covered in this chapter are relevant to everyday social work practice where difficult decisions have to be made regarding resource allocation, yet where there is an imperative to show due regard to people's fundamental rights as human beings.

SOCIAL WORK LAW CONTEXT: RELEVANT LAW AND STATUTORY GUIDANCE

Until the full implementation of the Care Act 2014, and its Welsh equivalent the Social Services and Well-being (Wales) Act 2014, adult social care law could best be described as a hotchpotch of laws covering community care assessments, the kinds of services local authorities could provide, and carers' rights. The Care Act 2014 and its Welsh equivalent consolidated many of these, but the interpretation of legislation that concerns us here has not changed in principle, namely that assessment is the first stage of determining the extent to which someone should be provided with services. What changes with the Care Act 2014, and the Social Services and Well-being (Wales) Act 2014, is the emphasis on prevention and promotion of well-being. The Acts also extend the entitlements of carers, and local authorities have the duty to provide information and advice proactively, to facilitate a diverse market for social care through commissioning, to work towards integration with the health service providers, and to encourage person–centred planning through increased use of advocacy. The Acts reform financial arrangements and in particular require personal budgets to be offered once an assessment has been made. There is also, for the first time, a statutory duty to investigate safeguarding cases.

At the time when the events described in the case study occurred, the primary legislation governing community care assessments was the National Health Service and Community Care Act 1990, specifically section 47 of that Act that laid on local authorities a duty to carry out an assessment of need for services for anyone for whom local authorities 'may provide or arrange for the provision of community care services' where that person appears to need such services. Having conducted an assessment, the local authority had to decide whether those needs 'call for the provision by them of any such services'. What services were actually provided depended on a number of factors, as we shall see in the case study, but naturally also depended on what services could be provided by law. In this regard, legislation included a whole welter of regulations, guidance and circulars issued by central government (for a summary table see Johns, 2014b: 86–7 or Brayne, Carr and Goosey, 2015: Chapter 12).

The Care Act 2014 (section 9) and Social Services and Well-being (Wales) Act 2014 (section 19) obligations to conduct an assessment are actually very similar to those contained in the National Health Service and Community Care Act 1990 although the more recent legislation has a stronger emphasis on involvement of service users and carers in that assessment.

For the purpose of analysing ethical considerations, the primary focus here is on what happens as the result of an assessment. How can resources be distributed equitably? By what principles should it be decided whether services are appropriate for one particular service user? For many years, the official guidance was contained in a document entitled *Fair Access to Care Services* (Department of Health, 2003) which laid down national eligibility criteria by which local authorities were meant to assess needs. In practice this devolved into four categories: critical, substantial, moderate or low. However the guidance did not state how exactly services were to be provided. Nor do the new regulations introduced by the Care Act 2014 and Social Services and Well-being (Wales) Act 2014. All the newer legislation states is that local authorities must determine whether any needs meet national eligibility criteria.

So the consideration in this case study of how exactly local authorities actually meet needs, and the extent to which they can respond to individual perceptions of appropriate service provision, is still very relevant. The concern with how resources can be distributed fairly necessarily overshadows all decisions regarding provision of services. If a great deal is spent on one service user, inevitably this reduces what can then be spent on others. If budgets are allocated on a year-by-year basis and must not be overspent, then there is a finite amount to share between those in need, so an equitable way of determining how to allocate resources is a major consideration, and this is precisely where ethics, law and social work decision-making intersect.

CASE STUDY

Reassessment leads to allegations of imposed indignity

R (on the application of McDonald) v Royal Borough of Kensington and Chelsea [2011]

A former professional ballerina, who had suffered a stroke in 1999, broke her hip in 2006. Following various falls resulting in an extended period in hospital, the local authority provided a package of care as a result of assessing her needs. This included ten hours per night care as result of the assessed need for assistance with toileting, and with needs that also arose as result of a bladder condition. The purpose of the care was to assist Ms McDonald to use a commode. The care package was assessed at £703 per week.

In 2008, the care package was revised and it was declared that it would be preferable for Ms McDonald to use incontinence pads. This would avoid the necessity of employing a night-time carer and reduce costs by £20,000 per annum. There were other arguments put forward by the local authority in favour of using incontinence pads, but these were strongly challenged as covert justifications for reducing costs. Ms McDonald's major objection to the local authority's plan was that it was an affront to her dignity, forcing her to be incontinent, whereas with a night-time carer she was enabled to use a commode, remain continent and therefore retained some aspect of self-respect and semi-independence.

As the local authority went ahead with its plan, there was no legal alternative but to challenge this through judicial review.

There were a number of other considerations in the various courts as the case proceeded, centring on what exactly had been written down in the various care plans, but what concerns us here fundamentally is the final deliberations conducted in the Supreme Court. These focused on whether, legally, the reviews of the case were technically reassessments, whether the decision to provide incontinence pads breached Article 8 of the European Convention on Human Rights, and whether they were compliant with the requirements of the Disability Discrimination Act 1995 (now incorporated in the Equality Act 2010). Essentially, however, the question turned on whether what the Royal Borough of Kensington and Chelsea expected Ms McDonald to do respected her fundamental rights and, naturally, this raises a question of what exactly those rights are and how rights are to be balanced in the context where resources are finite.

At the Supreme Court there was a majority decision in favour of the local authority. This decision was largely ratified by a subsequent European Court decision reviewing the case in 2014 (*McDonald v United Kingdom*, 2014).

The essence of the majority reasoning was that the community care assessment acknowledged the toileting need and then sought to provide for that need in a way that seemed appropriate to the local authority – which, unsurprisingly, was the less expensive way. There was no need, therefore, by implication, to enter into a lengthy debate about rights and dignity since there was a wide margin of appreciation in relation to interpretation of Article 8 of the European Convention on Human Rights, and also her dignity had been respected since she had been consulted right through the assessment and reassessment processes. There was much debate among the judges who formed the majority about the technicalities of the reassessment process, but these are not really relevant to the fundamental argument here which concerns the interpretation of ethical principles in a judicial context. Nevertheless, there was some acknowledgement that the reassessment might not have been a true reassessment of need as such, but a reinterpretation of need in order to accommodate the need to reduce expenditure. As one judge put it:

> Ms McDonald's needs were precisely the same as they had been when they were originally assessed. The change had come about not because there had been any authentic re-evaluation of what the appellant's needs were but because it was felt necessary to adjust how those would be expressed in order to avoid undesired financial consequences. And one, somewhat absolutist, way of approaching the case is to say that the appellant is not incontinent. Incontinence pads are provided for use by those who are. She needs help to move and she needs to move during the night. Her needs are therefore related to her difficulty with mobility, not to a problem with incontinence. (Lord Kerr in judgment in this case para 39)

Moreover one judge, Lady Hale, did maintain that the issues of dignity should be at the forefront of all considerations and that therefore there were compelling arguments for finding against the local authority. She did not concern herself with technicalities about care plans and reassessments. Rather, for her, the issue was whether it was right for the local authority to insist on providing incontinence pads for someone who is not in fact incontinent, but simply needed help to get to the toilet two or three times a night. She maintained that there needed to be a rational answer to the question of what action should be taken to meet needs that had been identified. In this case she was of the opinion that the local authority decisions were irrational for two reasons. First, if incontinence pads were to be provided instead of assistance with mobility, this would logically end up in a situation where she was lying in faeces until carers came to her in the morning. Second, provision of services in this way would actually cause a deterioration since it would effectively compel someone who was not incontinent to become so.

> In the United Kingdom we do not oblige people who can control their bodily functions to behave as if they cannot do so, unless they themselves find this the more convenient course. We are, I still believe, a civilized society. (Lady Hale in judgment in this case para 79)

The Supreme Court majority decision in this case invoked a number of responses. Disability rights groups generally deplored the decision since it appears to allow care providers to ignore issues of dignity in the considerations as to how services should be provided. Academic lawyers have expressed concern about the way in which the court appeared generally to consent to avoiding considering wider implications, narrowing down their focus to technicalities of the law rather than considering the wider remit set out in statute to provide services that meet people's needs. The majority of the court appeared to have become preoccupied with the process of assessment and reassessment, what some would call the 'technicalisation' of law. As a result:

> The decision is not only resource sensitive; it reinforces the status quo. (Carr, 2012: 228).

So in essence the ethical debate is: should decision-making in community care be resource sensitive, or should it be based on absolute principles that relate to human dignity?

Connections to Ethics

Critical thinking exercise 7.1

1. How do these two approaches to the McDonald case relate to ethical theories? Specifically which of the two views can be most closely allied to:

    i. deontological, principle-based theories?
    ii. utilitarian ideas such as those of Mill?

2. What difference would it make if the case were approached from the standpoint of virtue ethics?
3. What difference would it make if the case were approached from the standpoint of care ethics?

Deontological or Principle-based Theories

Applying deontological or principle-based theories is relatively easy, for Lady Hale has obligingly done it for us since her argument asserts that there are clear absolutes relating to human dignity that service providers need to respect. Decisions have to be made that accord with an unassailable principle of respect for human beings, and the decision by the local authority in this case flew in the face of this since it imposed indignity on someone, and gave them a problem that they previously did not have – it obliged them effectively to become incontinent. Thus she could argue that a decision to impose indignity on someone in this way is irrational, and therefore, according to the long-standing legal Wednesbury principle (following a landmark legal case *Associated Provincial Picture Houses Ltd. v Wednesbury Corporation*, 1948), unlawful and liable to be overturned by judicial review.

There was also the argument in the case that there was some potential for considering whether it conformed to Article 8 of the European Convention on Human

Rights which appears to lay down an absolute concerning privacy and rights to family life. However the court ruled against this on the grounds that there was a margin of appreciation. In other words, international law allows that there is some discretion about the extent to which the state, here meaning local authorities as a public body, can be expected to promote privacy and family life in every single situation, and to the exclusion of all other considerations. While there is no need here to offer a detailed exposition of the 'margin of appreciation', it is worth noting that the very fact that such a margin exists concedes that privacy and family life cannot be absolutes (for more on this see Freeman, 2011: Chapter 6).

Yet what of dignity? Could dignity be the yardstick that determines how decisions are made? Implementing a categorical imperative of respect for humanity and personal respect would mean that all community care decisions must maintain or respect people's dignity. This imperative, or universal law, would certainly comply with the principle that human beings are never to be treated as a means to an end, but should always be ends in themselves. Kant argued that human beings occupy a special place, have an intrinsic 'worth' (what could easily be labelled dignity) that makes human beings valuable above all price. In this context, dignity overrides financial considerations. If there were to be a number of decisions that equally validly respected dignity, other criteria could then be adopted for deciding between them.

However, if decision-makers had to look to the consequences – such as what would be the impact on the budget and therefore the potential for meeting the needs of other service users and carers – then that would not be legitimate. In fact such decisions would be utilitarian, and might demote dignity in the quest to go for the cheapest option.

Utilitarian Theories

Utilitarians do focus on consequences, so for them it would be perfectly legitimate to address decision-making in this case by balancing the competing needs of Ms McDonald with those of all other potential service users. The desire would be to make a decision that led to good consequences for as many people as possible. Thus it could be argued that the greatest utility is achieved by adopting the cheapest option for Ms McDonald in order to release funds that would then be available to meet other people's needs. Ms McDonald's personal desire for dignity might then become secondary in the final outcome of this balancing process.

While there might be a number of people prepared to justify this mode of reasoning, it is worth noting – and this is a really important point for social work practice – that core values and principles undergirding professional practice, such as the belief in human dignity, could become compromised. For in utilitarian evaluations of competing arguments, necessarily there cannot be any overriding principles other than that which determines that the best decision is that which accords with the most beneficial consequence for the greatest number of people.

In practice, the problem that then arises is that there can be no certain way of determining that the end result will be better, since if Ms McDonald is compelled to become incontinent for the purposes of sharing the community care budget in Kensington and Chelsea more equitably, what other compromises with core values and principles might there be? For example, if the cheapest way of providing a meals-on-wheels service is to provide every service user who is entitled to the service with exactly the same meal, what would be wrong with that? The answer might be that this violates the principle of respect for people's culture. If the meal contained beef, that would simply be unacceptable to some for religious reasons and therefore the meal would be uneaten and likewise with pork and with other kinds of foods. If as a consequence a minority of service users was going without food, that presumably would not matter since the majority would be satisfied and overall this would be the cheapest way of providing the service. This example underlies the fundamental problem which is that it is always difficult to judge whether the end result will truly be better. Better for the majority might mean substantial suffering for the minority.

If this were deemed undesirable, is it possible to keep within utilitarian principles and work towards a better outcome that both meets the needs of all service users and meets the overall requirements to use resources as economically as possible? One way of doing this might be Mill-derived rule utilitarianism which, as we saw in Chapter 3 and again in our example in Chapter 5, tries to accommodate this desire by asking what rules should operate in the long-term general interests of society. Here it might be possible to introduce a rule that both respected individual desires and was fair to the majority. In the meals-on-wheels example, such a rule might be that meals had to comply with genuine dietary requirements, including cultural or religious expectations, providing that such meals cost no more than the others. In the case of Ms McDonald it might be possible to introduce a rule that said services could be provided by the most economical method consistent with keeping current levels of physical well-being. So in her case the 'solution' imposed on her through the use of incontinence pads would not be acceptable because it violated that rule by imposing a physical condition on her that she did not have.

At first glance it might seem that such a rule brings us back to the deontological approach, but it is the mode of reasoning which is different. A deontological approach would start with absolute principles that are then applied regardless of consequence. By contrast, here rule utilitarians look at desirable and undesirable consequences, and then work back to calculate what rules are necessary in order to bring about only those consequences that are desirable. So in this case a rule that paid due regard to the need not to worsen someone's condition would be devised on the basis that worsening someone's condition might be the consequences of certain provision of social care. Hence the rule would be: if worsening someone's condition is a consequence of a decision, then that decision is inadmissible.

Virtue Ethics

Virtue ethics, as explained in previous chapters, concerns itself with the nature and characteristics of people involved, rather than rules and principles per se. One of the fascinating features of the McDonald case, according to the official transcripts and as analysed by Carr (2012), is the extent to which a debate about people's virtuousness crept into the deliberations. Some people were seen as rational, logical and reasonable while others appeared to be considered to be dogmatic, irrational and difficult. Indeed Carr considers there is also a gender issue which is why her article is entitled 'Rational men and difficult women – R (on the application of McDonald) v. Royal Borough of Kensington and Chelsea'.

Carr argues that there are several examples to demonstrate this. Lady Hale was taken to task by one of her colleagues for making references to defecation in her judgment and for suggesting that a consequence of the court's majority decision would be that someone might be left lying in their faeces day and night (Carr, 2012: 262). This was considered 'deplorable'. Likewise Ms McDonald herself is perceived as a problem, someone who is 'unwilling' to try other options, who was 'unprepared' to discuss the use of incontinence pads and whose position was 'entrenched' (cited by Carr, 2012: 228).

By contrast the evidence given by the Head of Assessment from Kensington and Chelsea was held in high esteem; he was considered to be an expert in advising the court on what is standard practice in social care. There was much debate about the technical aspects of provision to address toileting needs without any apparent regard for how people might feel about methods adopted. So, in a sense, the debate then became simplified into one that concerns itself solely with the rational, logical course of action, inevitably hinging on which is the most economical. Interestingly, financial considerations are not made explicit in the judgment in the case, although they always appear to be hovering over it.

From all of this, one is left with the clear impression that the court in this case valued a decision arrived at by a logical process that balanced competing needs of people generally, and formulated a response that met the need in the most economical away. By implication, this 'solution' was a good one since it allowed the local authority to distribute its resources in a fair and equitable way, meaning that it had more money to provide services for other people. It was achieved in a valid way because the people who made that decision were rational, logical and reasonable, while those who opposed it appeared to be seen as irrational, illogical and intransigent.

It is worth noting in passing that this assumes that somehow the amount of resources potentially available is actually fixed and that the sole consideration is equitable distribution. All it is necessary to point out for our purposes here is that such an argument does not start with absolute principles of human dignity and worth and then gauge the course of action adopted to see whether it complies with that principle. The experience, competence and expertise of the assessors is lauded, and therefore their actions can be seen as more likely to be correct or even as more moral, for

> Virtue ethics sees the morality of an action as emanating from the character of the individual performing the action and not in the outcome that is envisaged as a consequence of following particular procedures. (Lloyd, 2006: 1173)

Care Ethics Approach

One of the key elements in an ethics of care or approach is responsiveness in the context of organised responses to the need for care. Responsiveness 'is not imagining how I would see things if I were in this position, but how does this person in this position see things?'

(Lloyd, 2006: 1178–9). There are strong connections between this and social work values such as empowerment, and connections can be made with personalisation, including internationally (Rummery, 2011). An ethics of care approach is more than one that focuses on the quality of the relationships between a service user and professional; it argues that care is a central feature of life and that there is a political dimension to all of this (Lloyd, 2010). Hence in the McDonald case, it was not a question of an even-handed debate between service user and service provider, for most power lay in the hands of the service provider. The Borough had the resources and they were the ones who determined the extent to which they were going to provide the financial means of meeting people's needs under the National Health Service and Community Care Act 1990.

While this may sound an obvious statement concerning the organisation of social services, the way in which the law is formulated accords the local authority considerable discretion. Section 9 Care Act 2014, for example, states:

> Where it appears to a local authority that an adult may have needs for care and support, the authority must assess whether the adult does have needs for care and support, and if the adult does, what those needs are.

There is a very similar provision in relation to carers (section 10, Care Act 2014).

Having carried out this needs assessment the local authority 'must determine whether any of the needs meet the eligibility criteria' and, where some of the needs do meet the eligibility criteria, the local authority must 'consider what could be done to meet those needs' (section 13). Although there is provision in the legislation for the service user's and carer's voice to be heard, in the last analysis it is very clear that the local authority determines how resources are allocated and therefore, however one looks at it, it is the local authority that ultimately has the power.

This position is effectively strongly reinforced by the Supreme Court's majority decision in McDonald which appears to set little store on the way in which Ms MacDonald perceived her own position, and consequently was a decision that was profoundly disappointing for the groups representing the interests of people with disabilities who rely on the care system to meet their needs in a way that respects their dignity (Carr, 2012: 219).

Critical thinking exercise 7.2

These questions are for reflection on the McDonald case study and the court's interpretation of the local authority's assessment of need in that case.

1. To what extent should a community care assessment take dignity into account?
2. What would you have done in this case, bearing in mind the consequences of different courses of action?
3. Should the characteristics of service users and carers be a factor in determining how services are provided?

CONNECTIONS TO SOCIAL JUSTICE THEORIES

The typology adopted here again follows the scheme outlined in Chapter 2, which used four headings: utilitarianism, libertarianism, egalitarianism (or maximin), and capabilities (or comparative) social justice.

> ## Critical thinking exercise 7.3
>
> How does the McDonald case study and community care law generally relate to the four headings of social justice: utilitarianism, libertarianism, egalitarianism, and comparative social justice?

Utilitarian Social Justice

The earlier discussion in this chapter set out a number of points justifying a utilitarian approach to this case, principally that by reducing the cost of provision of services to Ms McDonald, the local authority in question was enabling itself to have more resources available for other service users. A number of potential consequences for Ms McDonald were discussed, and were also highlighted in the minority judgment in the case in the Supreme Court. What would be the more general implications for adopting the social justice approach to this line of decision-making?

In analysing decision-making from a utilitarian perspective, it is obviously important to look at the desirability of consequences. Although one desirable consequence – more resources more widely available to a greater range of people – has already been indicated, there may be serious problems in developing this line of argument to its ultimate extent. One could argue that the cheapest way of providing services that meet people's needs in order to fulfil the statutory assessment requirement should always be adopted. Yet what of the consequences for that individual? In the McDonald case the major consequence was loss of dignity. In other cases, provision of the cheapest services might actually diminish the quality of life, and even in some cases shorten it.

Let us take a specific example. Let us suppose that an individual with advanced dementia is assessed as needing substantial supervision and care. There is a choice of agencies who can provide this care. One agency will simply provide a carer daily to assist with basic physical needs, meal preparation and shopping. A second, more expensive, agency will provide those services and in addition will guarantee that staff employed are skilled and experienced in offering stimulating experiences to people with dementia, including arranging outings. Which should be the choice? Looking at the options from a strictly financial point of view, the conclusion is obvious. Yet from a practice standpoint and adopting a broader perspective, the second agency would be potentially more effective in promoting the well-being of the person, and possibly prevent a deterioration in their condition. Interestingly, this might more closely meet the legislative developments enshrined in the Care Act 2014 and Social Services and Well-being (Wales) Act 2014 with their emphases on prevention or 'delaying the development by adults in its area of needs for care and support' (section 2 Care Act 2014).

A more extreme utilitarian argument could be put forward for actually withdrawing services where it is clear that the service user is nearing the end of their life, where it would be cheaper to provide residential (or nursing home) care rather than a complex package of 24-hour care in the person's own home. Ultimately this could lead us into the very dangerous argument that in these cases euthanasia might be an option if it were legally permissible, since in cases where people have very complex needs the amount of resources dedicated to a few cases would severely deplete the potential resources available to others. This point is deliberately provocative, but it does highlight some of the difficulties in adopting a strictly utilitarian approach.

One way of addressing this, yet keep to a utilitarian line of argument would be, following Mill, to adopt rule utilitarianism. This might mean saying something like: a decision in a community care case should always be one that meets the greatest need for the greatest number of people providing certain requirements in relation to people's basic rights are met. One of these might be the absolute need to preserve life, which would naturally rule out any potential for euthanasia. Here are some suggestions as to what others might be:

- people are entitled to live in their own homes for as long as possible;
- people are entitled to be treated with dignity;
- people have the absolute right to choose their own service provider.

In theory, those principles already apply, yet there are some limitations:

- In complex needs cases, residential care is the cheaper option so at what point and how is the phrase 'for as long as possible' to be interpreted?
- Whose definition of dignity is being used? This was clearly an issue in the McDonald case.
- Through direct payments people do have this right to some extent, but service users and carers only receive the amount of money which the local authority would be paying for the provision of services to meet the assessed needs.

From all of this it will be seen that a rule utilitarian approach might not solve all the problems.

Libertarianism

Perhaps predictably, libertarianism in its assertion of its particular notion of freedom, promotes a strong belief in individual responsibility, accountability, and right to make one's own decisions. In the context of community care, this translates into a free market in the provision of community care services, which people can buy as and when they need them. This of course presupposes the availability of a range of services to meet all needs, with individuals having the capacity to afford them. In a sense, these arrangements already exist in the UK, but superimposed on this is a system for providing services on the basis of need even when people cannot afford to pay for them themselves. Such services are paid for by local authorities, either by direct arrangement with the service provider, or if service users and carers choose their own services, then by providing the sum of money which the local authority considers they need to pay for appropriate services (usually referred to as direct payments).

Thus far, the community care system does not violate libertarian principles, since individuals are always free to choose to go to the market and purchase the services they think they need. In addition, by obliging local authorities to operate on a purchaser-provider model in which those who assess need have to be quite independent from those who deliver services, what operates in the private sector is effectively translated into the public.

Libertarian purists would of course object in principle to extensive state provision. Libertarians who are prepared to concede a residual approach to social welfare, whereby local authorities provide a safety net, would accept that this model broadly accords with their expectations. In such a model of delivery, where the local authority ultimately has responsibility for financing services, it is clear that local authorities would have the right to determine what services can be afforded, providing they meet the needs identified. Although theoretically this is done on the basis of individual need, in practice those individual needs have to be assessed in relation to the needs of others. After all that is why there is a system of resource allocation, formerly referred to as Fair Access to Care Services, which is now set down as the Care and Support (Eligibility Criteria) Regulations 2014 associated with the Care Act 2014 (the Welsh equivalent is the Care and Support (Eligibility) (Wales) Regulations 2015). Such regulations require needs identified by assessors to be slotted into categories that distinguish for which groups the local authority does or does not make provision.

In the McDonald case, there is clearly a dispute between the local authority and the service user about how the need is identified. It is impossible to overlook the wider context which is affordability: the local authority is bound to go for the least expensive option. The service user does not have a choice since presumably she is unable to afford the carer services that she sees as ideal. However, at least in theory, she is not obliged to accept the services the local authority offers. Instead she could opt for the payments the local authority would otherwise make for such services, although this amount would not be sufficient to pay for what she ideally wants. In this situation it is not difficult to see how service users who are dependent on the local authority to finance their community care services in practice are treated differently from those who are able to afford whatever services they need.

For a libertarian of course this is quite unproblematic. Conversely, for those who believe in certain inalienable rights for service users, particularly pertaining to dignity, this is wholly unacceptable.

Egalitarianism Rawlsian Theory

While Rawls' theories fit best to social policy and social work practice in relation to distribution of wealth and equal opportunities, it could also be suggested that his theories argue for maximising people's liberties and minimising disadvantage. In a community care context, this could be adapted and taken to mean that care services should be provided in order to encourage independence and self-reliance. Hence in this case, enabling someone to make their own way to a toilet would surely be preferable to imposing incontinence on them.

At a much broader level, what about the argument that there are finite resources to devote to community care and that by providing an expensive resource for some this reduces opportunities to maximise opportunities for all? Here someone who subscribed to Rawlsian theory might argue that the provision of social work and social care support generally is part of the redistribution of wealth. Taxes such as income tax are levied according to ability to pay with the income generated pooled, and then redistributed in the form of services provided on the basis of need: from each according to their ability to pay, to each according to their need for services. If the need is greater than had been forecast, then the answer to the resource allocation challenge is not to introduce eligibility criteria to give everyone a thin slice of cake, but instead to increase the 'size of the cake'; to this end taxes might have to be increased.

Comparative or Capabilities Approach to Social Justice

One interesting aspect of a capabilities approach to social justice is that it appears to be arguing for the adoption of the course of action that expands people's capabilities, freedom of opportunity or potential for achievement. It is plain that if one adopted this approach, an outcome that made someone less independent would clearly not be desirable. The issue therefore appears to be clear cut. It is however worth noting that such an approach does not engage with the whole issue of resource allocation, for this would be irrelevant. The argument would be that it is self-evident how one should proceed; it is, in a sense, obvious what social justice would mean in this case.

CONNECTING SOCIAL JUSTICE, ETHICS AND LAW

The fundamental challenge in this case, and indeed in nearly all community care cases, is how to balance competing needs. There is a budget within which services have to be provided. If it looks likely that the budget will be exceeded, then a strict definition of need needs to be applied in order to reduce what needs to be spent in each individual case. If the budget increases, then the criteria can be loosened. However, as virtually every article on this subject will state in its introduction, this all operates in a demographic context of increasing numbers of older people and therefore greater demands made on health and social care services.

What of fundamental, inalienable rights in this context? Do service users and carers have certain rights regardless of budgetary considerations? Strictly speaking, from a legal point of view, the answer is no. The European Convention on Human Rights is broadly silent on entitlements to services. Instead it argues for rights in terms of limitations of state powers. So in the context of child care and adoption, it is clear how the various articles might apply. In adult care services, however, much of what appears in the various articles that comprise the European Convention does not seem relevant. Those that come closest are Article 2 (right to life), Article 3 (includes prohibition of inhuman or degrading treatment), Article 5 (right to liberty and security), and Article 8 (includes right to family life).

Article 2 could be interpreted to imply a positive obligation to improve someone's chances of living longer. Under Article 3, some forms of care provision could be considered to be inhuman or degrading, although note that this is quite a high threshold (it is doubtful if it would apply in Ms McDonald's case, for example). Article 5 could be interpreted to imply positive obligations to help people leave residential care, if they wish; it might be suggested that failure to provide services to a minimum level might result in people effectively being imprisoned in their own homes. Likewise Article 8 could be interpreted to suggest a positive duty to help people remain living in their own homes with their own families. All of this involves creative use of the law (Ellis, 2004) and it is worth noting that there have been few actual instances of successful challenges to decisions in these cases. Exceptions have included cases concerning deprivation of liberty (see next chapter) and overturning decisions to close residential care or nursing homes without consultation on the basis that such homes are in effect people's own homes, so arbitrary closure decisions breached Article 8 (for example: *R v North East Devon Health Authority ex parte Coughlan*, 2000; *R (on the application of Madden and others) v Bury Metropolitan Borough Council*, 2002; *Louisa Watts v UK*, 2010).

As indicated earlier, the McDonald case was taken to the European Court where it was agreed that there had been a limited breach of Article 8 for a year due to a failure to re-assess need at the time the night-carer was withdrawn. With regard to general interpretation of Article 8, however, the European Court considered that there had to be a balance with a wide margin of 'appreciation' afforded issues of general policy, including social, economic and health care policies, especially when it came to an assessment of priorities in the context of the allocation of limited state resources (judgment in *McDonald v United Kingdom*, 2014).

As regards domestic legislation, it is notable that entitlement is all related to assessment of need. A careful examination of previous community care legislation, the Care Act 2014 and the Social Services and Well-being (Wales) Act 2014 would confirm this. Nowhere in either of these Acts does it state that people are entitled to certain kinds of services. Decisions about allocation of resources always fall to the local authorities who, in determining that allocation, are obliged to operate in accordance with regulations concerned with equitable distribution of resources according to need, rather than absolute entitlements that cannot be countermanded.

CHALLENGES FOR SOCIAL WORK PRACTICE

The key challenge for social work practice is the interpretation of personalisation. If personalisation means taking account of people's preferences and perceptions of themselves, how can it be acceptable to override those when arranging services? Yet at the same time people cannot just opt for any kind of service regardless of financial considerations since that has implications for other service users and carers.

If the policy drive towards personalisation is meant to promote empowerment, how can refusing people preferred services be compatible with this? Insisting that need is met in a particular way is surely disempowering, and if the way of meeting need is considered offensive to someone's self-perception of dignity and self-worth, then surely it cuts the ground from under their feet. In practice, legal decisions in the Gloucestershire and McDonald cases summarised in this chapter indicate that personalisation cannot be interpreted in a way that is wholly subjective. Rather, the personalisation process seems to imply that, in practice, some acknowledgement is made of people's expressed wishes but only within budget constraints, within clearly defined (financial) parameters.

How could social work practice address this and what of the future? Apart from the policy implications, such as pushing for more resources to be available, one result of this analysis might be to re-evaluate ethical considerations. Is there a case for adopting a deontological approach by asserting an absolute principle in relation to personal dignity? This might raise fundamental questions about how dignity is to be defined, and whether it is to be purely subjective or assessed by some other legal means, such as reference to the European Convention on Human Rights. This in turn presupposes that the Convention can be interpreted in this way; thus far, the European Court has confined itself to adjudicating against states only where quite extreme affronts to dignity occur.

Adopting a rule utilitarian approach might have some value but, as discussed earlier in the chapter, would not altogether resolve the issues. An ethics of care approach might have much to commend it, given that it is probably more compliant with changes introduced by the Care Act 2014 and Social Services and Well-being (Wales) Act 2014. Specifically, section 1 of the Care Act 2014 requires local authorities 'to promote that individual's well-being' (the Welsh equivalent is section 5 Social Services and Well-being (Wales) Act 2014). Well-being includes (section 1(2) Care Act 2014):

- personal dignity (including treatment of the individual with respect);
- physical and mental health and emotional well-being;
- protection from abuse and neglect;
- control by the individual over day-to-day life (including over care and support, or support, provided to the individual and the way in which it is provided);
- participation in work, education, training or recreation;
- social and economic well-being;
- domestic, family and personal relationships;
- suitability of living accommodation;
- the individual's contribution to society.

It is interesting to speculate whether, had this legislation had been in force at the time of the McDonald case, the Supreme Court would have come to the same conclusion. The additional requirements in relation to promoting well-being would surely strengthen the hand of those who want to promote service user and carer empowerment, although of course it has already been stated that the final decision on allocating resources always seems to rest with local authorities. It remains to be seen whether the introduction of the Care Act 2014 and the Social Services and Well-being (Wales) Act 2014 will result in any significant shift in adult care provision and in adjudication by the courts on community care cases.

CONCLUSION

In this chapter the focus was on community care law and the provision of services in the context of budgetary constraints. The relevant legislation lays a great deal of emphasis on local authority duties in relation to assessing need, and accords them the final decision in allocating resources to meet need, unless of course service users and carers are in the fortunate position of being able to pay for whatever care they consider they need. In interpreting the legislation, local authorities are bound to have one eye on the resources available, and in the case study examined in this chapter, this resulted in them adopting a course of action the service user considered to be an affront to her dignity. A majority of the Supreme Court did not consider this to be the major factor that should determine the decision, but instead focused on the process whereby the local authority took the service user's wishes into account. However one judge did consider that dignity should be an unassailable principle, which naturally accords with a deontological approach to ethical decision-making. The chapter then went on to consider competing approaches to ethics in the context of the case study, followed by different views of social justice. There was then an attempt to connect these together, and in doing so the discussion pointed to a changing context in light of implementation of the Care Act 2014 and Social Services and Well-being (Wales) Act 2014.

In essence, ethical considerations in this chapter have raised major questions about how policies such as personalisation and values such as empowerment should be implemented and interpreted. There is clearly a case here for thinking more deeply about the way in which ethics, social work practice and law interconnect, since there is a real risk that financial considerations determine everything.

The next chapter moves on to consider those kinds of cases where adults lose the right to self-determination, when there are major issues of concern about their ability to look after themselves or to protect themselves from harm. Needless to say, such cases raise fundamental questions about the role of social work in a legal and ethical context, and will reveal some fundamental tensions in the way in which courts try to address these.

8

Making Decisions on Behalf of Other People: Promoting the Best Interests of Vulnerable Adults

INTRODUCTION AND CHAPTER OVERVIEW

This chapter, the fifth and final chapter focusing on one specific area of social work practice, considers those kinds of cases where adults lose their rights to self-determination, where the law allows decision-making to be taken over by social workers or others, either in the interest of the person themselves, or with a view to protection of other people. This chapter will concentrate on one specific example. In this particular illustrative case, the court wrestled with how to delineate the rights of individuals where they needed a significant degree of protection.

The discussion in this chapter starts once again with a summary of legislation, here the law that applies where someone loses the ability (usually legally termed 'capacity') to make decisions for themselves. Then comes the case example itself with an exposition of the various debates that the courts had with themselves regarding how to determine when courts and social workers need to be involved in depriving people of their liberty. This inevitably raised fundamental questions about legal rights, the ethics of taking over people's entitlements to make decisions themselves, and the whole issue of how to determine what is meant by the much used phrase 'best interests'. The chapter attempts to connect these debates to considerations of social justice as well as ethical theories, concluding with some reflections on how all of this relates to social work practice, especially for those practitioners who are charged with making decisions on behalf of vulnerable adults when they are deemed to have lost the capacity to make such decisions themselves. The format of this chapter is therefore quite similar to that of the previous chapter.

Once again readers are referred back to Chapter 4 for information on how this discussion relates to the Professional Capabilities Framework (The College of Social Work, 2012), QAA Subject Benchmark Statements for Social Work (QAA, 2008) and Critical Thinking Skills.

There are two key areas where social workers are directly involved in making decisions for vulnerable adults.

The first is where there are serious mental health issues, when someone is deemed to be in need of admission to a psychiatric hospital or unit but, because of their state of mental health, they appear to be unable to recognise that need. Originally such social workers operated as 'duly authorised officers' who then became 'mental welfare officers' with the passing of the Mental Health Act 1959 (Ramon in Barker, 2011: 89). In the years following the merger of specialist mental health social workers with other kinds of social workers in 1972 with the implementation of the Seebohm Report, it became apparent that there was a need to introduce some kind of specialism where social workers learned more about mental health law. This need arose particularly with the legal developments enshrined in the Mental Health Act 1983 which still forms the backbone to current mental health legislation regarding compulsory admission and detention of people in psychiatric hospitals. The 1983 Act introduced the term Approved Social Workers which then became Approved Mental Health Professionals following the passing of the Mental Health Act 2007 (the difference primarily being that following the 2007 Act the role was not exclusively confined to social workers).

The second area of practice is more recent in its origins. This is where social workers, and in some cases other professionals, have opted to become Best Interest Assessors who have specific roles in relation to assessing cases where vulnerable adults are deprived of their liberty. These roles derive from implementation of the Mental Health Act 2007 which amended the Mental Capacity Act 2005 by introducing Schedule A1 establishing procedures for compelling someone to remain in a residential home or hospital where it is deemed to be in their best interest to do so (the next section sets out the law in more detail). This law, which has been recently criticised as 'tortuous and complex' (judgment in re *AJ (Deprivation of Liberty Safeguards)*, 2015), was devised in response to a decision by the European Court in what is generally referred to as the Bournewood case.

The Bournewood case (*HL v United Kingdom*, 2004) centred on what happened to Mr L who had autism and learning disabilities and lacked the capacity to make certain decisions regarding his own care and treatment. In 1997 following various incidents he became an inpatient at Bournewood Hospital. He was not detained under the Mental Health Act 1983; but accommodated in his own 'best interests' under the common law doctrine of 'necessity'. This was challenged in UK courts as constituting illegal detention, but his detention was deemed lawful because it was in his best interests, and this was considered permissible under common law.

The European Court did not accept this. They considered that Mr L had been detained, so that the 'right to liberty' in Article 5 of the European Convention on Human Rights (ECHR) applied, and therefore decisions had to be justified through a process that involved clear procedures, during which there were rights to advocacy. Furthermore, the court decided that detention under common law was 'too arbitrary' with insufficient safeguards, pointing out that in this respect people like Mr L were treated quite differently from people detained under mental health legislation. There was, in effect, a gap in the law – what came to be known as the 'Bournewood gap'.

The European Court's objections, drawing on comparison with mental health law, are demonstrated in Table 8.1.

The key practice issue here is that Mr L complied with those who told him he had to go hospital and stay there. However, the European Court declared that compliance is not the same as consent. It was wrong to assume consent simply because someone did not actively object. So it needed to be much clearer who was taking decisions on behalf of someone who was not able to give full, informed consent to a specific course of action (for further detailed discussion of this case see Johns, 2014a: 37–49).

The case study in this chapter focuses on the second area of practice since this raises quite specific issues concerning compulsory intervention in people's lives that are quite distinctive. In mental health, the primary consideration is whether someone has a medical condition that justifies the need for them to be admitted to hospital, confirmed by the wider considerations of the Approved Mental Health Professional concerning whether it is in the interest of the person themselves or the wider public for them to be admitted. While there have been a number of cases where decisions made by Approved Mental Health Professionals or Approved Social Workers have been scrutinised by the courts (we shall look at one in the final chapter), issues raised in deprivation of liberty safeguards cases are more wide-ranging and therefore this chapter focuses on these.

The principal case study selected, along with others that will be mentioned in passing, raise fundamental questions about the rights of the state to impose care on someone who is unable to look after themselves, and the need to have a formal system of decision-making where it is apparently patently obvious that someone needs such care. With regard to the last point, the Supreme Court had to decide what exactly was meant by deprivation of liberty, and effectively overruled previous decisions that said that deprivation of liberty was relative to the context in which the person had specific needs. For our purposes, the case offers a neat example of whether courts and care professionals should adopt an objective, absolute definition of deprivation of liberty by comparing what deprivation of liberty would mean to an 'ordinary' person, or whether it is a relative and fluid concept dependent on the perceptions of the individual concerned and what would usually happen in similar cases. If this distinction seems perplexing, and readers are puzzled about how the courts got themselves in this situation, read on!

Table 8.1 European Court's objections to law prior to Mental Capacity Act 2005

	Law that applies	What law says	Where law can be found	Who decides?	Appeal rights	Compliant with ECHR?
Mental health	Mental Health Acts 1983 and 2007	In specified circumstances people can be admitted to hospital against their will for a specified maximum period	In specific sections of statute laws	Specified professionals who have authority on basis of expertise and training	Yes, for every admission under an order with automatic appeals in some cases and there is hierarchy of appeal tribunals and courts, with procedures clearly specified	Compliant with principles laid down (see discussion below)
Learning disabilities and vulnerable adults generally	Common law	Where deemed appropriate by courts people can be deprived of their liberty for so long as is necessary	By examining case law decisions going back over time and trying to draw some general principles	Courts acting under 'inherent jurisdiction' using expert guidance as and when they see fit	Can only appeal to higher courts but this is a lengthy and expensive process, no tribunals, only courts and not clear on what grounds appeals can be put forward	No, law not specific, not obvious what is and is not allowed, decision-making cumbersome, very difficult to appeal

SOCIAL WORK LAW CONTEXT: RELEVANT LAW AND STATUTORY GUIDANCE

The previous discussion of the Bournewood case has already referred to the European Convention on Human Rights. This is because legislation and court decisions are meant to be compliant with the Convention (Human Rights Act 1998) and in this context Article 5, the right to liberty. Obviously this right is not an absolute; those who have broken the criminal law, for example, forfeit this right, but there are is also another exception in relation to people of 'unsound mind'. It is therefore lawful in principle to override rights to liberty for this group of people, but the question then arises by what process are such people identified and in what circumstances would the extension to the absolute right to liberty apply.

A number of European case-law decisions have established some general principles and safeguards, beginning with *Winterwerp v The Netherlands* (1979). The first principle deriving from Winterwerp is that there must be an expert independent assessment that confirms someone is of 'unsound mind' or in current UK legislation terminology, 'mentally disordered'. The second is that even partially overriding someone's ability to make decisions themselves counts (*Ivinovic v Croatia*, 2014). The third principle is that the plan to detain someone must be consistent with their need, so detaining someone ostensibly for psychiatric treatment but offering no medical intervention whatsoever would be unlawful (*Aerts v Belgium*, 1998). The fourth, and for our purposes the most important, principle is that it must be possible to challenge the decision to detain through due legal process within a reasonable timeframe (*Stanev v Bulgaria*, 2012; *E v Norway*, 1994). This connects to Article 6, rights to fair trial and access to independent legal decision-making bodies, in this context amplified to include the rights to representation and automatic referral (*Megyeri v Germany*, 1993). This last point was a particular issue in the Bournewood case, where procedures that then existed were considered too slow with inadequate representation rights.

For many years, the law generally relating to capacity and decision-making in England and Wales was a mixture of common law principles, case-law decisions, and odd bits of statute legislation. These have now been codified and consolidated into the Mental Capacity Act 2005 which sets out some key principles governing intervention in the lives of vulnerable adults when they appear to have lost the capacity to make certain kinds of decisions for themselves. The starting point is, for adults, a presumption of capacity: people can make whatever decision they like, including unwise decisions, if they have the capacity to do so; there should be no assumptions made concerning age or appearance concerning who has lost capacity. Someone can only be considered to have lost capacity where they are unable: to understand information relevant to a decision, or retain that information, or use or weigh that information as part of the process of making the decision, or communicate that decision by some means or another (sections 1–3 Mental Capacity Act 2005).

However if a decision has to be made on behalf of someone, the professionals should always consider the option that is least restrictive of that person's rights and freedom of action. Practitioners should consider past and present wishes and feelings, beliefs and values, and other issues that someone would probably want to consider if they had capacity (section 4 Mental Capacity Act 2005). Even so, there should be encouragement to participate in the decision–making process to the fullest possible extent.

Decisions to deprive someone of their liberty, therefore, have to be made in the context of these Mental Capacity Act 2005 principles. When that Act was amended in order to bring the law into line with European Court expectations, the new Schedule A1 simply superimposed procedures applicable in deprivation of liberty scenarios. The Schedule does not apply, say, where someone loses the ability to make financial decisions. Decisions to deprive someone of their liberty are taken by the Supervisory Body (such as a local authority) or the Court of Protection; the Supervisory Body can only take decisions in cases where someone is compelled to remain in a residential home or hospital, and the Court of Protection has a much wider remit. The key adviser to the Supervisory Body is the Best Interest Assessor, a specially trained social worker or other professional, but there must be at least one other Assessor, who usually determines whether someone is mentally 'disordered'. The Best Interest Assessor must first clarify that what is requested is a deprivation of liberty as distinct from a restriction on liberty and then confirm that the person meets certain statutory requirements relating to age and any advance decisions already registered as binding. There must be an assessment concerning capacity, mental 'disorder' and confirmation that the Mental Health Act 1983 is not more appropriate (for discussion of mental health and Deprivation of Liberty Safeguards interface see Clare et al., 2013). Finally they must advise that deprivation of liberty is in the 'best interests' of the person, is necessary to prevent harm to themselves and is appropriate and proportionate to the risk. The Supervisory Body must then decide on the length of the period of deprivation (maximum 12 months) and appoint a representative to be their advocate (Schedule A1 Mental Capacity Act 2005; re *AJ (Deprivation of Liberty Safeguards)*, 2015).

In all of this, the starting point is whether or not someone is really being deprived of their liberty. Once this threshold is crossed, the Deprivation of Liberty Safeguards procedures are engaged. Otherwise the person is considered to have their liberty restricted, in which case there are no specific legal safeguards under this legislation – although, of course, other more general legislation concerning duties of care, and responsibilities to service users, may apply. Hence the definition of deprivation of liberty is crucial, and that is the issue that came to the fore in the case study example that now follows.

CASE STUDY

Is deprivation of liberty an absolute or relative concept?

Cheshire West and Chester Council v P; P and Q (MIG and MEG) [2014]
These are two cases which the Supreme Court combined into one for the purpose of hearing the final appeal.

(Continued)

(Continued)

The Cheshire West and Chester case concerned a man (known as P), aged 39, who had cerebral palsy and Down's Syndrome. He lived in four-bed residential unit, attended day centres regularly, and was under close supervision at all times. Occasionally he had to be restrained in order to manage his behaviour. Initially the Court of Protection had to consider whether the combination of close restrictions and restraint meant that he was being deprived of his liberty. The court decided that he was, but this decision was overruled by the Court of Appeal who declared that the restrictions were nothing more than 'the inevitable corollary of his various disabilities' and were necessary regardless of the environment. He was 'inherently restricted in the kind of life he can lead' and this was a 'strong degree of normality' assessed 'as it must be by reference to the relevant comparator' (*Cheshire West and Chester County Council v P*, 2011, judgment paragraph 110). In effect the actions taken in this case were necessary restrictions of movement rather than deprivations of liberty.

In its judgment, the Court of Appeal introduced a concept labelled 'context and comparator'. This principle meant, the court suggested, that the yardstick to determine whether someone was being deprived of their liberty was not what would happen to an 'ordinary adult going about normal life' but ...'in the case of an adult with disabilities, the relevant comparator is an adult of similar age with the same capabilities and affected by the same condition or suffering the same inherent mental and physical disabilities and limitations' (*Cheshire West and Chester*, 2011, judgment paragraph 86).

The Supreme Court ruled that this was not correct. The Court of Appeal comparator test was flawed in that it risked a circular argument: are people with this kind of disability or challenging behaviour normally treated in this way? If so, it is not a deprivation of liberty. The comparator test confused the concept of deprivation of liberty with the justification for imposing such a deprivation. So the Supreme Court rejected the 'relative normality' argument and insisted that deprivation of liberty had to be objective.

The P and Q case concerned two sisters who both had severe learning disabilities. P was living with her former respite carer while Q lived in a residential home. On their behalf the Official Solicitor contended that they were being deprived of their liberty because

- they were unable to decide where they lived;
- they were not free to leave their placements and
- they were subject to continuous supervision and control, including restrictions on social contacts.

Initially, the Appeal Court did not accept this argument, declaring that it was not a deprivation of liberty just because someone lacked capacity to decide whether to remain where they were living or not. Also they did not apparently object so it was assumed they had passively consented.

The Supreme Court overruled the Appeal Court's decisions in both cases completely, declaring that it was important not to confuse benevolent justification for the care arrangements with the concept of deprivation of liberty. Human rights, the court adjudicated, were universal and objective; physical liberty was the same for everyone, regardless of their disabilities. 'What would be a deprivation of liberty for a non-disabled person is also a deprivation for a disabled person' (UKSC 19, judgment paras. 45–46).

So it was not right to take into account factors such as normality, comparisons, purpose, and lack of objection. Context is irrelevant. As one judge commented:

> The fact that my living arrangements are comfortable, and indeed make my life as enjoyable as it could possibly be, should make no difference. A gilded cage is still a cage. (UKSC 19, judgment para. 46)

The overriding question however is how does all of this fit with ethics and social work practice? Should the definition of deprivation of liberty be an absolute that has to be applied even when there is no hint of objection and for all intents and purposes someone is compliant with actions taken? If professionals know what needs to be done, is it really necessary to have those actions subject to legal processes that involve formal decision-making by Supervisory Bodies, the Court of Protection or ultimately the Supreme Court?

Connections to Ethics

Critical thinking exercise 8.1

Remembering the distinctions drawn in previous chapters between deontological, utilitarian, virtue ethics and an ethics of care approach:

1. What approach or approaches to ethics do you think were demonstrated by the arguments used by the Appeal Court and the Supreme Court in their deliberations?
2. Why is it justifiable to have exceptions to the 'right to liberty' enshrined in the European Convention on Human Rights?

Deontological or Principle-based Theories

An initial interpretation of the judgment suggests that it is the Supreme Court who went for a deontological approach, declaring firmly that deprivation of liberty is a universal concept. In order to assess whether someone is being deprived of their liberty, the comparison should be how anyone would feel under those circumstances. It is wrong in principle and practice to make the comparison relative to someone's 'condition' for that implies that if someone would 'normally' be deprived of their liberty if they had this condition then there would no need to invoke legal procedures and safeguards. The 'gilded cage is still a cage' remark indicates a principle-based approach.

Going back to Kant, it could be argued that the Supreme Court decision that deprivation of liberty means the same to everyone is the result of the reasoning process. As explained in Chapter 1, in order to determine whether something is right or wrong there are a number of questions to be asked, one of which concerns willingness for a rule to be observed at all times and in all places. Indeed is there an expectation that the rule would be universalised? There are clear indications of this Kantian approach in the Supreme Court's judgment.

However, why should there be exceptions to the right to liberty that apply to people who have lost capacity? What would a deontological explanation of such a principle be? It is obvious what the principle is: where there is a lack of capacity to understand potential dangerousness or harm to oneself then others can take over decision-making, but that vitiates the whole notion of self-determination and freedom to decide for oneself. What is the justification? Here it is useful to move beyond Kant's original theory to those of his followers, particularly intuitionists such as Ross who argues that there is a hierarchy of duties and obligations (Bowie, 2004: 69–71). At the very highest are prima facie duties that transcend all others. So in this case, the right to autonomy and duty to allow people to make whatever decisions they like must on some occasions be overridden by a higher principle, or prima facie duty, to preserve life and prevent harm. Protecting people who are unable, for clearly identifiable reasons, to protect themselves always seems the right thing to do – so, in that sense, it is intuitive. When there is a clash between such high-order principles derived from intuition and other principles that have become translated into legal rights, there needs to be an exception to the legal rights to allow for the 'correct' course of action to be followed. Hence in the European Convention on Human Rights it is allowable to break the principle of the right to liberty if someone is of 'unsound mind' so long as there is evidence to justify both the existence of the condition and the circumstances in which the exception operates.

So, in short, an exception to the right to liberty is allowable because there is a higher duty or obligation in relation to protection of the vulnerable.

Utilitarian Theories

Although the Appeal Court did not declare as much in its deliberations, they appeared to be guided by some underpinning utilitarian thinking. The case before it concerned someone who had a number of disabilities and undoubtedly presented challenging behaviour to the professionals charged with his care, and there would clearly be a number of people in this position. What would be the consequence of having to refer each and every case where there was a potential deprivation of liberty to the courts? Is it right that the court should be involved in all such cases, having to confirm a deprivation of liberty even though it is 'obvious' that there is no alternative and, as the court indicated, it would be the normal appropriate way of responding to the cluster of disabilities and behaviour issues that that person presented? What would be the implications for professional practice and for practitioners who would constantly have to have one eye on the needs of the individual and one eye on the law? Surely it is obvious, the Appeal Court seems to be saying, that the professionals should be allowed to get on with the job where it is clear what needs to happen. Even though this might entail for some a deprivation of liberty, in the context within which it operates it should be interpreted as just a necessary restriction.

The Supreme Court rejected this utilitarian approach and made no reference to the implications of their decision or its consequences, declaring instead that they would be firmly set against this. So we could interpret this decision almost as deontology versus utilitarianism!

How does this stand in relation to the exception to the right to liberty? What would be a utilitarian approach here? The starting point would have to be that it is in the interests of the majority to have a law that says that all adults are free to act as they wish, and this is best when it comes to determining such issues as accountability and responsibility for actions. To allow an exception on the grounds of someone having an 'unsound mind' would be acceptable if the aim was to serve the interests of the greatest number of people. In this case, it could justifiably be argued that the majority of people would be happier with a set of rules that allowed for some people to lose their rights to self-determination in circumstances where they were unable to perceive what was in their best interests. The end of doing good would justify the apparent overriding of their fundamental rights to autonomy.

Having conceded this justification, rule utilitarians would then go on to say that it would be in the long-term general interests of society as a whole to have the exceptions to the principle of autonomy codified into some kind of rule. This is effectively what the European Court did in the cluster of cases outlined earlier (*Winterwerp v Netherlands*, 1979, *E v Norway*, 1994, *Aerts v Belgium*, 1998, and *Megyeri v Germany*, 1993) that set out procedural stages required before someone can be deprived of their liberty on the grounds of having an 'unsound mind'. This is not the same as a deontological principle for, instead of focusing on individual circumstances as such, it looks to the overall operation of this rule generally as a means of achieving the overall long-term interests of society as a whole.

So in this case a rule utilitarian might side with the Appeal Court on the grounds that the addition of a 'comparator' rule, by which deprivation of liberty was redefined as restriction in some cases, might serve the overall interests of the majority, since it would reduce the number of cases potentially coming before the courts. Whether a comparison should be made between P and people like him or between P and a non-disabled person is a matter of utility, not of principle. The rule that needs to be devised is one that suits the interests of the majority, not one that is determined by appeal to some higher-order principle.

Virtue Ethics

Applying virtue ethics to this particular case study is rather problematic, underlining the apparent disdain of virtue ethics for rules generally since the theory 'holds life to be far too complex for rules to be of any use in guiding our actions and lives' (Stewart, 2009: 55). Rather, virtue ethics focuses on the agent rather than the action. So in this case the qualities of character and intentions of the carers and decision-makers would become important, so long as they do not underestimate the value of the whole person and show respect for the individual.

However, this does not just relate to their 'virtuousness' in relation to how they treat P, but also their integrity, honesty and probity in terms of squaring up to the everyday dilemmas that they faced. Hence one could argue that a virtuous professional involved in this case would be one who seeks to have their actions validated by a court of law, since they understand that their actions might go against the fundamental essence of human flourishing (eudaimonia). Right (ethical) actions are those that result in the well-being of the individual in a holistic sense; so in order to check that this is the case, the professional might want to have their actions confirmed as appropriate and ethical.

As regards the law more generally, virtue ethics moves beyond ethical matters being purely individual considerations towards the notion of community. Hence here we might ask what kind of rules would a virtuous community have in relation to deprivation of liberty? Would it be more virtuous to allow considerable discretion to professionals, or would it be preferable to insist on a strict definition of deprivation of liberty that would necessarily mean that professionals have to have their actions confirmed by courts, no matter how well-intentioned they were? The problem with the first approach is that this might rely too heavily on professionals to police themselves in the sense of challenging their own actions. In determining what is deprivation of liberty there is a risk of adopting purely subjective or relative considerations. If the second course of action is taken, as was the case with the Supreme Court decision, this would imply that a whole host of cases would have to be brought before the courts even when it is obvious that deprivation of liberty is essential. In such cases, the courts might end up engaging in a rubberstamping exercise in a number of cases. This seems to be a possibility indicated in Re X and others (2014) in which the President of the Court of Protection outlined procedures for 'streamlining' cases to address the anticipated upsurge in cases after the Supreme Court adjudication in Cheshire West and Chester.

Critical thinking exercise 8.2

These questions are for reflection on a virtue ethics approach to the law and professional practice generally.

1.   Is it better or more 'virtuous' to have a clearly codified system of rights which may entail courts being involved in a significant number of social work cases, or is it preferable to have wider professional discretion so that fewer cases come before the courts?
2.   Is a 'virtuous' social worker one who is prepared to take on the responsibility of deciding for other people before any court decision is made, or is it more virtuous to insist that there is legal authority, if necessary confirmed by the courts, prior to intervening in the lives of vulnerable adults who are unable to protect their own interests?

Care Ethics Approach

Again it is not transparently clear how this approach might relate to the case study given its emphasis on legal rights and obligations. However it is worth thinking through the case study in terms of a rather different perspective, which the care ethics approach does offer.

Chapter 1 referred to the work of Gilligan (1982) who would challenge the way in which justice comes to be formulated on the basis of a particular kind of reasoning. So the various 'logical' arguments adopted by the different courts may not matter quite so much as the overall intention of providing good quality care. Given that there is no hint of criticism of the actions taken by carers in the two cases that came to the Supreme Court, the question might justifiably be posed as to what purpose legal action actually achieves. This does not imply that practitioners can behave just as they wish, but rather that in terms of accountability the professional bodies responsible for overseeing quality practice may have more to offer than courts.

Hence in this case some kind of agreement about the best way forward negotiated between all those who are involved in the case might be the preferred option. While it is true that there needs to be some kind of clarity as to what kinds of cases call for such reviews, this difference of emphasis does underscore the importance of addressing professional accountability in terms of quality of practice, rather than evaluating it simply in terms of its legality or otherwise.

At the more general level, human rights would still be considered to be important, but what matters particularly in individual cases is how the service user feels, and the quality of the relationship between them and those caring for them. Empowerment is obviously important in this context but that might be better achieved through advocacy in case discussions rather than through formal representation in the court arena. So it remains an open question as to whether it was truly in service users' interests for the Official Solicitor to have initiated these proceedings which eventually resulted in a Supreme Court decision. While it might be legally interesting, it may not have any particular bearing on the outcomes in terms of quality of care.

Connections to Social Justice Theories

Critical thinking exercise 8.3

How does the Cheshire West and Chester case study relate to the four headings of social justice: utilitarianism, libertarianism, egalitarianism, and comparative social justice?

Utilitarian Social Justice

In the previous discussion of utilitarian approaches to ethics, it was suggested that utilitarianism may be what lies beneath the line of argument adopted by the Appeal Court. There appeared to be an underlying concern that too strict a definition of deprivation of liberty might have the consequence of bringing a whole multitude of cases within the ambit of the court's jurisdiction, and so tests were devised to ensure that deprivation of liberty was assessed relative to the service user's disabilities and presenting issues. At the time when the decision of the Appeal Court first became known, there was considerable disquiet on the grounds that a relative definition would in effect rule out the Deprivation of Liberty Safeguards applying to anyone. Hence some commentators referred to the judgment as the 'death' of the Deprivation of Liberty Safeguards.

It is not altogether surprising that some drew this conclusion. The reasons are fairly clear. Take, for example, someone who has advanced dementia, for whom deprivation of liberty would be considered to be an appropriate course of action to prevent them from repeatedly mistakenly leaving their accommodation at night without supervision and therefore putting their lives at risk. The fact that this behaviour might be connected directly to the dementia, in which someone loses the capacity to understand time or have any notion of risk, means that any caring person would ordinarily adopt a controlling course of action and therefore that would not constitute a deprivation of liberty. Yet the various different kinds of mental 'disorders' and associated conditions could always potentially be linked to standard practice in this way, with the consequence that deprivation of liberty only becomes a real deprivation for people for whom it is not necessary.

Presumably the justification for a utilitarian approach to the case is that on balance it is better for the majority that resources are not deployed into investigating the necessity of deprivation of liberty in a large number of cases where it is unlikely that the court would overturn the decision. Resources thus saved could be redirected into providing direct services for people in need. It is certainly an attractive argument.

However it is possible to put forward exactly the contrary argument using utilitarian principles. It could be argued that it is in the interests of the majority that the rule of law be observed and therefore exceptions should not be made. So in this context, it is in the interests of the majority that the term 'deprivation of liberty' be applied in an absolute sense; this reasserts and reaffirms the whole notion of justice. It redirects considerations to objective, rather than subjective factors, and this would command the support of the majority. Ultimately implementing a strict interpretation of the law would serve society best, and lead to the greatest happiness of the greatest number, even though there might be considerable financial costs.

Libertarianism

Libertarianism has a fundamental problem with any state intervention that imposes itself on people against their will. The libertarian American psychiatrist, Thomas Szaz, for example, argued against any form of compulsory admission or detention of people in psychiatric hospitals on the grounds that this simply gave the state the right to sanction certain kind of behaviour and that people have an absolute right to refuse treatment (Szaz, 2010). Similarly a libertarian could argue that depriving someone of their liberty without their prior agreement is an example of excessive use of state control.

At this point, most social workers would hold up their hands in horror and say: but what of the consequences? The thought of allowing people to risk death or serious injury in circumstances that clearly could be prevented is one that is unpalatable to most, but the libertarian question is what cost is attached to permitting benevolent professionals forcibly preventing people from doing something. While in extreme cases there may be the case for this, where is the line to be drawn? At what point should the state, through health care and social work professionals, cease to control people's lives absolutely?

This dilemma was brought to the fore in a mental health case that came before the House of Lords (the precursor of the Supreme Court) in 2008. This concerned a woman who was detained under the Mental Health Act 1983 who absconded from hospital and committed suicide. Here the hospital authorities were held partly responsible for the suicide and were considered to have partially failed to comply with their obligations under Article 2 of the European Convention on Human Rights (*Savage v South Essex Partnership NHS Foundation Trust*, 2008). A libertarian would have to argue against this interpretation, and assert instead the rights of a person to commit suicide even though they were an inpatient in a psychiatric hospital. However the consequence of affirming that there is some kind of responsibility on health staff to prevent suicide may well result in their practice becoming more risk averse. The libertarian fear would be that this would increase the role of the state in controlling people's lives generally.

Egalitarianism Rawlsian Theory

Whereas libertarianism starts from a position of being naturally antagonistic towards state intervention, Rawls would allow some measure of state involvement in maximising people's opportunities and minimising disadvantage. In this sense, deprivation of liberty could be permissible if its intention was to prolong people's lives and allow them to participate in other areas of their lives they found pleasurable or satisfying.

Another interpretation might be that in controlling one aspect of people's lives someone is enabled to participate in society, so that in an ironic way a deprivation of liberty is empowering. Although this argument might seem somewhat perverse, it is consistent with the principles laid down in the Mental Capacity Act 2005 which insist that even where people lose rights to self-determination in some respects – this may not be liberty, it could be finance, for example – nevertheless they must be encouraged to be involved in decision-making in as many other areas as possible. In that sense the principles enshrined in sections 1–5 Mental Capacity Act 2005 are compliant with notions of encouraging vulnerable adults to be regarded as citizens on the same basis as everyone else, except that in certain clearly defined areas of their lives they do not have absolute rights to make their own decisions. Participation is the key to this interpretation, alongside the absolute insistence that professionals act in people's 'best interests' (section 1(5) Mental Capacity Act 2005). The most telling aspect of the Mental Capacity Act 2005 in this regard is the contrast between the best interest requirement and the right to make unwise decisions in section 1(2).

Rawls also addresses issues of egalitarianism. Here one could easily argue that the Supreme Court's decision is egalitarian because it affirms quite emphatically the need to have one standard for everyone. Deprivation of liberty for a non-disabled person is also a deprivation for a disabled person, as the Supreme Court averred. There must be no distinction – no set of standards that applies to people with certain kinds of disabilities and another set of standards that applies to everyone else.

Comparative or Capabilities Approach to Social Justice

If we take this approach to social justice, meaning that law and practice should be directed towards expanding people's capabilities (including freedom of opportunity or potential for achievement), then once again the Mental Capacity Act 2005 is to be applauded for its various provisions in this regard. The whole tenor of the Act is to promote the encouragement of participation in decision-making to the very fullest possible extent.

The existence of the European Convention on Human Rights allows comparisons to be made with different jurisdictions, and some sort of consistency achieved in relation to interpretation of people's basic rights. A review of cases where the court has had to adjudicate on cases where vulnerable adults have lost rights to make their own decisions makes interesting reading for this reveals some quite extraordinary inconsistencies. For example, in *Stanev v Bulgaria* (2012) a man was placed in a remote care home without being consulted or informed. He was not allowed to leave at all, being brought back by the police when he did so. Physical conditions were so horrendous that they were considered to constitute 'inhuman or degrading treatment'. Food was inadequate and the home did not return clothes to the same people after they were washed. Hearing this case in the European Court had a dramatic effect on improving conditions in such homes in Bulgaria as well as promoting radical legislative reforms in that country.

CONNECTING SOCIAL JUSTICE AND THE LAW

What is just? What is fair? What is reasonable? What is proportionate? What is right? All of these are questions addressed by ethical theories and by the law, and clearly all impinge on social work practice in challenging cases. In this chapter's key case study, there were additional complex issues to address. How are competing rights to be balanced? When can someone's rights to self-determination and autonomy be overridden? How should the decision to do this be arrived at?

The Supreme Court decision provides a definitive answer to nearly all of these questions in relation to the operation of Schedule A1 Deprivation of Liberty Safeguards. This decision rests on interpretation of the European Convention on Human Rights and in many ways reasserts the principle declared by the European Court in the Bournewood case: the exception to the right to liberty can only be implemented on grounds of 'unsound mind' through a precise legally oriented process and different standards must not apply to vulnerable people. Just as in the Bournewood case it was not acceptable to treat HL as a person with fewer rights than people detained under the Mental Health Act 1983 because he had a learning disability, so in this case different standards cannot operate that enable a lower threshold to apply to people with certain disabilities compared to others. This is interpreted as an absolute, so in this way the Supreme Court appears to be a good example of a deontological principle being applied.

So much for the process. What of the wider issues that relate to fundamental human rights in this context? In the last chapter the point was made that the European Convention on Human Rights is largely silent on entitlements to services, yet it does have something to say about compelling people to accept treatment or care. Compulsory care cases mainly fall under Article 5, the right to liberty, with its 'unsound mind' exemption. Why this exception? Presumably because preceding this Article is Article 2, the right to life which appears to place some kind of positive obligations on the state to protect the most vulnerable from potential loss of life. This duty is particularly pertinent in the cases of people admitted to psychiatric units, as was demonstrated and confirmed in another suicide case that reached the Supreme Court, *Rabone and another v Pennine Care NHS Foundation Trust* (2012). Here, the Supreme Court declared that hospital authorities had a responsibility towards an inpatient when they allowed her home leave knowing that there was a real and immediate risk of suicide. She was under its control, even though she was not a detained patient. In her case the authorities could and should have exercised their powers under the 1983 Act to prevent her from leaving hospital and, by not doing so, had failed in their duty to protect life under Article 2 of the European Convention on Human Rights. So the right to life appears to supersede all other rights.

CHALLENGES FOR SOCIAL WORK PRACTICE

One merit of this case study is that at least we now have, legally, a definitive answer to questions about the interpretation of the term 'deprivation of liberty'; in this sense it truly is a 'watershed' (Care Quality Commission, 2015: 6). Justice to the individual is not interpreted as meaning that individuals have absolute autonomy; this has to be tempered with the need to safeguard in the interests of attaining the higher-order principle, the preservation of life and safeguarding from harm (SCIE, 2015). In determining what is deprivation of liberty, the same yardstick has to apply. The definition of deprivation of liberty has to be an absolute. With a strong commitment to empowerment and rights, many social work practitioners welcomed the decision, and the message it conveys about the position of the most vulnerable in society. The Supreme Court is considered to have shown itself concerned with principles derived from absolutes, uninfluenced by consequences.

One consequence, however, has been a dramatic rise in Deprivation of Liberty Safeguards cases. When the Supreme Court judgment was first declared, there was consternation as some considered there would be a massive upsurge in requests for assessment under the Safeguards. Indeed figures from the government Health and Social

Care Information Centre (2015) confirm this: between April and December 2014 (9 months) there were 83,100 Deprivation of Liberty Safeguards applications, whereas for all 12 months of 2013–14 the number was 11,300. Some feared that resources would have to be deployed from adult social care budgets in order to pay for large numbers of assessments (Association of Directors of Adult Social Services, 2014). Others were concerned that

> the aftermath of this judgement will effectively capsize existing Deprivation of Liberty Safeguards and Court of Protection infrastructures. (Whitaker, 2014: 1491)

Whichever is the case, it would certainly be a 'wake-up call' (Whitaker, 2014: 1494).

CONCLUSION

In this chapter, the discussion focused on the ethics of depriving vulnerable adults of their liberty when they lose capacity to determine what is their own best interests. The legal example centred on the operation of the Deprivation of Liberty Safeguards under the Mental Capacity Act 2005. The origin of these Safeguards lies in the decision of the European Court in the 'Bournewood' case in which objections were raised to reliance on common law provision. The everyday operation of the Safeguards hinges on the definition of deprivation of liberty, an issue that has preoccupied the courts on several occasions, principally in the Cheshire West and Chester case used as the chapter case study. Here the Appeal Court's attempt to introduce a relative definition has been superseded by the Supreme Court's insistence that deprivation of liberty is an absolute, objective concept applied equally to disabled and non-disabled people.

The court's deliberations and associated social work practice issues were then considered related to various ethical theories. Under virtue ethics, readers were asked to consider what constitutes a 'virtuous' social worker when it comes to seeking legal authority for protecting vulnerable adults. The case study was then connected, briefly, to different approaches to social justice. Finally, exploring the interconnections between social justice, ethics, law and social work suggests that human rights legislation is of more direct relevance to this area of practice and that there is an expectation that practitioners will be prepared to use the law to override people's rights to liberty when there is a risk to life. So Article 2 of the European Convention on Human Rights trumps Article 5. As a result of all of this there may well be a significant increase in the amount of work in this area in future.

9

Acting Legally, Acting Ethically

INTRODUCTION AND CHAPTER OVERVIEW

This concluding chapter highlights selected cases that crystallise the ethical issues that arise when someone is accusing of acting illegally. It therefore directly connects practice to the discussion in Chapters 1–3, for in all cases the social worker concerned considered that they were acting in someone's 'best interests' – although as we shall see, in whose best interests is a pertinent question. These case examples provide a platform for a broader discussion of how ethics, law and social work practice relate to each other in the context of the theories and approaches to ethics and social justice covered in this book.

As with all other chapters in this book, this chapter is directly relevant to the values and ethics aspect of the Professional Capabilities Framework (The College of Social Work, 2012) concerning the application of social work ethical principles and values to guide professional practice. This chapter focuses particularly on critical reflection and analysis, another Professional Capabilities Framework expectation (Context and Organisations heading in the Framework).

Exercises integrated into this chapter are designed to promote the attainment and development of the Critical Thinking Skills 2, 3, 4, 7 and 8 (as listed in Chapter 4). In addition, the chapter relates to Subject Benchmarks for Social Work (QAA, 2008) 5.1.1 (6), 5.1.2 (5) and 5.1.3 (2)–(3) (for list see Introduction).

The structure of this chapter is rather different from the previous chapters. Previous chapters included a case study that was related to relevant law and then explored in respect of ethical theories and approaches to social justice. By this time, it is anticipated that readers will be familiar with these, so each of the case studies in this chapter is not analysed in respect of all of these theories and approaches. Instead, after presenting expositions of the cases, there will be an invitation to decide how best to analyse the ethical and social justice dimensions of them.

The chapter begins with an overview of three cases in which the lawfulness of someone's actions were considered by the courts. The first of these concerns allegations that a social worker took advantage of someone's medical condition in order to 'persuade' them to agree to their child being accommodated, knowing that in other circumstances they would probably refuse. A parental request for a child to be accommodated may be made under section 20 Children Act 1989. Accepting such an application would be one way of avoiding forcing the issue by bringing care proceedings under section 31. Acting to avoid children being involved in court proceedings is a duty under Schedule 2 of that Act.

CASE STUDY 1

Was this really a voluntary request for a child to be accommodated?

Coventry City Council v C and others [2013]

The case concerned baby C, who was the fourth child of the mother, all three previous children having been placed for adoption following placement orders made by the court. The judge made it clear that the mother had never harmed any of her children, had always co-operated with those trying to help her, including the court itself. Nevertheless, it was generally agreed that she had significant learning difficulties and, while she could manage well under supervised contact, appeared to have no 'instinctive or intuitive feel for parenting'. Because of this, the local authority plan was to remove the new-born baby as soon as the mother was discharged from hospital, and the mother appeared to consent to this, or rather did not object.

At the time of the birth, there were medical complications and mother needed life-sustaining surgery. She was offered accommodation for her baby under section 20 Children Act 1989, which initially she refused. However, once she had been treated with morphine, she agreed. Questions were raised in court about the ethics and legality of a 'request' made under the influence of morphine. Specifically, was this a valid consent since there were clearly questions about whether the mother had capacity?

The court made it clear that it was not acceptable for the social worker to say that the mother had given consent to her child being accommodated under section 20. From a legal perspective, the social worker was obliged to consider section 3 Mental Capacity Act 2005 Act, especially with regard to the ability to evaluate information. They had to reassure themselves that their way of obtaining consent was fully compliant with that Act and that it was truly informed consent. Above all the method of obtaining parental consent had to be fair.

In this particular case, the social worker effectively misled the parent by reassuring her that removal was a temporary arrangement when in reality the social worker knew that it was extremely unlikely that the child would be returned. The actions taken, the local authority had conceded, were unfair and not proportionate.

In the next case there are implications that the social worker took advantage of particular circumstances in order to get round the anticipated refusal of a nearest relative to agree to the admission of his son to a psychiatric hospital under section 3 Mental Health Act 1983. Compulsory admission in these circumstances requires the social worker to attempt to consult with the nearest relative and, if it is known that the nearest relative objects, admission cannot take place unless that relative is displaced by order of a court (sections 13, 11(4), 29 Mental Health Act 1983).

CASE STUDY 2

Was this an attempt to deny the nearest relative their rights?

GD v Edgware Community Hospital and London Borough of Barnet [2008]

This case concerned an application by a social worker (at that time designated an Approved Social Worker) who was authorised to apply for the compulsory admission and detention of someone in a psychiatric hospital. GD's nearest relative, as defined in the Mental Health Act 1983 (section 26) was his father who had rights to block the application (section 11). The patient himself had a diagnosis of schizophrenia, and was well-known to mental health services. His father was antagonistic to conventional hospital treatment, believing that natural remedies were preferable and so, on previous occasions, had taken his son into hiding to avoid an assessment under the Mental Health Act 1983.

In the light of this history, the social worker decided to delay contacting the nearest relative before carrying out the assessment, but waited until the assessment was in progress at which time he telephoned him and left a message, knowing that he was probably somewhere which did not have a reliable phone signal. By the time the call was returned 20 minutes later, the papers had been completed, with the relevant section of the form filled in to say that it had been 'impracticable' to consult with the nearest relative. The nearest relative strenuously objected and supported his son's complaint to the court that GD had been detained without authorisation.

The judge confirmed that this was the case. As a consequence of the actions taken by the social worker GD had been illegally detained since the social worker had deliberately failed to make adequate attempts to consult with the nearest relative as he (correctly) anticipated that the nearest relative would object. This amounted to 'a misuse of power, albeit for the best of motives'.

In our final example, a local authority were so concerned about the challenging behaviour of a young man with learning disabilities that they extended the respite care that they had originally agreed with his principal carer, his father. While not disputing that actions were well-intentioned, the accusation here is of operating with scant regard to the law and, questionably, ethics. The relevant law here is the Deprivation of Liberty Safeguards under the Mental Capacity Act 2005 which was covered in Chapter 8.

CASE STUDY 3

Was this well-motivated heavy handedness?

Hillingdon v Neary [2011]

Stephen Neary, who was then aged 21, had autism and a severe learning disability, needing substantial support and supervision. The local authority were providing community services to support his carer father, who lived on his own. When he became ill in December 2009, Stephen's father requested respite care which the local authority provided for an agreed period of two weeks.

After the agreed period, the local authority, London Borough of Hillingdon, decided not to return Stephen to the care of his father, citing as their reasons for doing so the challenging behaviour which Stephen had exhibited while in respite care. His father insisted on Stephen being returned to him but this did not happen. Instead, after a further incident in which Stephen snatched glasses from a complete stranger, the local authority as a Supervisory Body invoked the Deprivation of Liberty Safeguards procedures under the Mental Capacity Act 2005 by appointing a Best Interest Assessor to assess the need for deprivation of liberty. The social worker allocated to this Best Interest Assessor task recommended that Stephen should be compelled to remain where he was and so in April 2010 Hillingdon authorised itself to deprive Stephen of his liberty.

Mr Neary (senior) challenged this procedure in court claiming that

during the period until the local authority invoked the Deprivation of Liberty Safeguards Stephen was being unlawfully deprived of his liberty and

the way in which they had conducted themselves demonstrated a failure to respect family life in accordance with European Convention on Human Rights Article 8.

The court agreed that it was deprivation of liberty because neither Stephen nor his father had agreed to respite care beyond the first two weeks and Stephen was under total and effective control 'every waking moment' in an environment that was not his home. There was no authorisation for this period of three months and even when such authorisation was issued, the court was not happy about the fact that the Best Interest Assessor was employed by the same body as was responsible for the case management. The court also agreed that by disregarding the father's views without authority Hillingdon had violated Article 8. The court also declared that where the local authority and family disagree, the Deprivation of Liberty Safeguards ought not to be used as a way of the local authority getting its own way in deciding what was in someone's best interests.

There are, of course, other examples that could have been selected in order to demonstrate conflicts between ethics, law and social work practice (a summary of a selection will be found in Preston-Shoot, 2010: 468–70). In some of these, it is clear that the organisational demands and constraints have impinged on the ethics of social work practice. For example Preston-Shoot (2011: 182) refers to the case of *F (a child) (2008)* in which a local authority acted in accordance with the Adoption and Children Act 2002 by making an application for a child to be placed for adoption but during this process denied the birth father any opportunity to be considered as the potential carer for his child. Judges complained that they could not see how the local authority had made the decision to act in this way, so accountability was virtually impossible.

Clearly there are occasions when law, ethics and social work practice are not congruent, so the remainder of this chapter is devoted to exploring this a little further using the three selected case studies above.

Critical thinking exercise 9.1

Try to read the case studies above from different perspectives. Is it possible to see why the social worker acted as they did? How would the social worker or local authority's actions come across to the service user or carer?

Specifically, in relating these to the earlier theoretical discussions in this book what would you say in answer to the following questions?

1. What to do all these case examples have in common in relation to the behaviour of the social workers concerned?
2. How does the behaviour of the professionals relate to different ethical theories?
3. How does the interpretation and adjudication by the court relate to the different ethical theories?

From this point onwards, these questions are going to be answered. They will be addressed under three headings that relate to the questions: professional behaviour; social work practice ethics; legal interpretation and ethics.

PROFESSIONAL BEHAVIOUR

The key common feature here is that all the professionals acted with the best of intentions and were genuinely trying to do the best for people.

In the first example, the social worker could see that it was in the best interests of the child to be safe and to have as good a start in life as possible. At the same time, she was under an obligation to attempt to work in partnership and co-operation with parents, and to avoid legal action wherever possible. So when the mother became ill during pregnancy, it seemed an obvious opportunity to approach her once again and ask for her co-operation in making plans for the child, and to this end to agree to section 20 Children Act 1989 accommodation. Yet it is clear in retrospect how the mother could interpret this as taking advantage of her medical state, thereby completely undermining her parental rights. So again the question is: in whose best interests was the professional acting?

The second case has many similarities with the first insomuch as the social worker was trying to attain a certain goal with the minimum of legal hassle. In this case, the social worker genuinely believed the best plan for GD was readmission to a psychiatric hospital, and knew that there would be objections from the nearest relative which would stop this going ahead. So effectively he short-circuited the system. The judge conceded that he was acting 'for the best of motives'. Yet as a consequence there was a judicial review, compensation awarded, and increased hostility between professionals and the nearest relative. In whose long-term best interests was the professional acting?

The third case also represents an attempt to avoid proper use of the law. The social workers responsible for case management perceived it to be in the best interests of Stephen to be kept where he was, so their motivation in terms of seeking the best for him was unchallengeable, yet as a consequence of their actions they acted without proper lawful authority. Once more the risk was of alienating Stephen's family so again the question should still be posed: in whose long-term best interests were they acting?

SOCIAL WORK PRACTICE ETHICS

In case study 1 there are number of reasons why the social worker's actions could not be regarded as entirely ethical using a deontological line of reasoning. Going back to Kant, the argument is that for a principle to be adopted, it needs to be tested by considering the extent to which it could be universalisable. Here, while the social worker has not actually lied, they have taken advantage of the parent's vulnerability, albeit with the best of intentions. Presumably they were trying to achieve the very best for the child in terms of their future. They may also have been subscribing to the principle of trying to work in partnership and co-operation with parents. Yet it is difficult to avoid the conclusion that the end, the best future of the child, somehow justified the means. The question then is what would happen if everyone operated by this principle, in other words it was acceptable to exploit the potential of any particular situation that arose.

Exactly the same considerations apply in case studies 2 and 3. In the mental health case, the social worker took advantage of the temporary absence of the nearest relative in order to secure the objective of carrying out a compulsory admission under the Mental Health Act 1983, which he considered to be in the best interests of GD. In the deprivation of liberty case, the local authority took advantage of the period of respite care by extending it on the grounds that it was concerned about Steven's behaviour, again presumably with his best interests at heart.

From a utilitarian perspective, it is possible to draw quite the opposite conclusion. Here the consequences of the social worker's actions will be what matters. In all three cases, the social workers concerned were focused on the needs of one person (in case study 1, the child) and overrode the strict legal rights of someone else. So in each case it could be argued that the end justified the means. While strictly speaking their actions might not have been entirely legal, they would have had the result of attaining the desired objective, and therefore would have been ethical (but note only from a utilitarian perspective).

When it comes to virtue ethics, the situation is more complex. What would a good, conscientious, magnanimous, gentle, truthful, witty, friendly, modest, just, wise, careful, respectful, courageous, reflective, empathetic and sensitive social worker have done? (This list of attributes is derived and adapted from McBeath and Webb, 2002, and Pullen-Sansfacon, 2010: 403.) Readers will have to decide for themselves on that one but one point that may be worth considering, however, is that a virtuous social worker should surely show respect for people's legal rights, in which case it would be difficult to see how the actions could be defended as entirely ethical. In case study 1, the issue of capacity was not properly addressed, as the judgment of the court indicates. In case study 2, it looks as though the social worker anticipated the nearest relative exercising their rights to object and therefore circumvented this by taking certain pragmatic steps. In case study 3, the local authority tried to assume, once a period of respite care came to an end, that it was acceptable for them to keep Stephen in their care so long as he did not actively try to go home, even though they knew that his father wanted to resume care. This, however, has echoes of the situation that arose in the original Bournewood case (*HL v the United Kingdom*, 2004) where a hospital kept a compliant HL in their care despite the entreaties of carers to discharge him to their care. So again there was a demonstration of a somewhat cavalier approach to people's rights.

Examining these three cases from the vantage point of care ethics, there is clearly going to be a conflict as to how the social worker should have proceeded. For in all three cases there was a breach of trust. In case study 1, the social worker paid insufficient regard to the mother's capacity to consent thereby imperilling that relationship. Yet it could also be argued that there was greater attention and priority given to the child's needs. This dilemma is ever present in child safeguarding work, as we saw in Chapter 4. This means that, while it is always sensible, if at all possible, to try to negotiate an agreement with parents, in some circumstances the needs of the child will be placed above those of the parents. However, it never seems right from the care ethics perspective to be perceived to be taking advantage of someone's medical state in order to secure their 'agreement' to accommodation. This seems not only legally wrong but ethically dubious. Likewise in case studies 2 and 3, action was taken which inevitably had the consequence of jeopardising relationships between professionals and carers. Although it could be argued that in focusing on the needs of GD and Stephen, social workers were showing a commitment to doing what was best for them in the long term, this fails to take adequate account of the impact on personal relationships.

LEGAL INTERPRETATION AND ETHICS

Judgments in some cases can follow a line of reasoning that is almost classic utilitarianism. For example, in *W v Edgell*, 1990, a consultant psychiatrist breached the confidentiality rule by sharing information on a patient whom he considered posed a public danger. The court decided that if the consequence of the breach was enhanced public safety then that would clearly be acceptable (Gallagher and Hodge, 2012: 96–7). The end in this case really did justify the means, even if the means meant violating a principle that is actually written into medical practice in the form of the Hippocratic oath. Following on from this case, textbooks written for health-care professionals now make it quite clear that there is an exception to the principle of confidentiality if issues of public safety are involved (see for example Mason and Laurie, 2013: Chapter 6).

As regards the social work cases, it is interesting to note that in all of them the court made explicit reference to the virtues of the professionals involved. In each case they were considered to have acted with the highest of motives and best of intentions, demonstrating a clear commitment to the needs of the child in case study 1, and the person detained in case studies 2 and 3. However, courts do not decide cases on such grounds. Rather, in all three they stuck with the absolute principle that the law as it is written down must be observed (note in passing the contrast with Edgell where there is no statute specifically setting down a medical confidentiality rule). In case study 1, this law constituted the Mental Capacity Act 2005, in case study 2 the nearest relative's rights under the Mental Health Act 1983, and in case study 3 the failure to implement the Deprivation of Liberty Safeguards and then, when belatedly such procedures were initiated, a failure to implement them correctly.

SOCIAL JUSTICE

Rather than explore different approaches to social justice individually, the discussion that follows focuses on competing rights, and differing interpretations of those rights.

Critical thinking exercise 9.2

How do the three case examples in this chapter fit with the different approaches to social justice? Whose rights appear to count most?

Analysing the three case studies from a social justice perspective is quite challenging. For a utilitarian, the question will always be: do the actions of the social workers concerned accord with the principle of utility? However, it can be quite difficult to calculate what was truly in the interest of the majority. Hence rule utilitarians would probably say that it is in the interests of the majority to have certain rules concerning the way in which the law was implemented. So in each of these cases, the social workers' actions would be deemed unjust since they failed to respect the explicit legal rights of specific individuals. In the Coventry case, the right of the parent to be fully informed of the implications of a section 20 application for accommodation for a child was breached. In the Edgware case, the social worker was fully aware of the father's rights as 'nearest relative' under the Mental Health Act 1983, but adopted a course of action to avoid those rights being exercised. In the Hillingdon case, the local authority simply refused to discharge Stephen from respite care despite the fact it had no legal authority to do so, thereby violating both his rights and those of his parent.

A libertarian would no doubt agree with this conclusion but come at this from a different angle. The actions of the social workers in each case will be seen as simply an example of the state exercising too much power over an individual, acting in a paternalistic fashion, and riding roughshod as a consequence over people's rights to make their own decisions.

From a more egalitarian (Rawlsian) perspective, the fundamental question remains as to whose needs counts most. Does a child have more rights than a parent? Does someone in need of urgent psychiatric care have more rights than their relative? Does someone who cannot understand their own long-term needs have fewer rights than a parent who claims to have this understanding, especially when that interpretation is challenged by a professional? All of these are challenging questions and, while it is not possible to give definitive answers from a social justice perspective, these questions recur constantly in social work and need to be addressed in a careful and reflective manner.

However, if, following Sen, the question posed concerns which course of action is most likely to expand people's capabilities or potential for achievement, it may be possible to come to different conclusions. In the Coventry case, the social worker was clearly focused on the needs of the child, and was attempting to engage in a course of action that was least disruptive to that child and best met the child's future needs – hence the push for adoption. In the Edgware case, the social worker was focused totally on the needs of GD, believing that these had to be met by immediate psychiatric intervention. What was standing in the way was an awkward relative who had their own beliefs about what was best, and so a pragmatic course of action was adopted that avoided his interference. In the Hillingdon case, there is no doubt that the local authority's motives were well-intentioned and also geared at promoting Stephen's well-being, hence once again a pragmatic course of action was adopted to attain this end.

This is an opportune point at which to bring all of this together and summarise what has been covered in this book about the interconnections between the law, ethics and social work practice.

BRINGING IT ALL TOGETHER: CONNECTING LAW, ETHICS AND SOCIAL WORK PRACTICE

One way of exploring this interconnection is by adopting the distinction first put forward by Braye and Preston-Shoot (2006) between 'doing things right', that is acting in accordance with the law and procedures, 'doing right things', that is acting in accordance with ethical principles or values, and 'right-thinking', which is adopting a social justice approach that incorporates both law and ethics.

Adopting 'doing things right' is fundamentally de-skilling for social workers since it takes away the essence of social work which is to act in a reflective and person-centred manner. Following the rules exactly as they are written down might appear to be a sensible course of action, but it is also one which is inevitably legalistic, bureaucratic and can lead to profound injustices – for example, refusing to allow a parent to see their child for supervised contact because the parent turns up late. Slavish observance of legal requirements does not require much thought or compassion; it simply requires a knowledge of what the laws, rules and regulations are. If a practitioner does not know how to act in a given situation, the answer appears to be to look it up in a manual of procedures based on interpretation of the law.

On the other hand, 'doing right things' may mean acting in accord with one's own values or conscience, interpreting ethical codes or theories in one's own particular way. If this is done without due regard to the law, the consequence can be sensitive and passionate social work that may inadvertently cause injustices. So for example, a youth justice worker who condones deviations from supervision requirements may ultimately be doing a young person a disservice, since the consequence may be a return to court and a harsher sentence. One of the reasons why law became a mandatory part of social work qualifying courses in the 1990s is because social workers had sometimes been practising in the past without due regard to what the law actually said. An extreme example was the failure to protect a child which was in large part due to the social worker's ignorance of basic childcare law, including understanding what a care order actually meant (Blom-Cooper, 1985).

'Right-thinking' is not so much a different approach to social work, but an approach to social work that holds in balance an unquestioned commitment to people with a thorough understanding of the legal context within which social work operates. Both aspects are absolutely essential for quality social work. Yet for this to be attained, it is not just a question of maintaining this balance, but in exploring how the two elements interact, and sometimes conflict, with each other. Compassionate social work practice has to pay due regard to what the law says; at the same time it is perfectly legitimate to adopt a critical approach to law, sometimes challenging what the law actually says, and at other times questioning how it is implemented. There is considerable evidence that there is sometimes a disjunction between law, ethics and practice especially in a 'resource-constrained' environment where social workers could be hard pushed to justify professional decision-making while remaining committed to social justice (Preston-Shoot, 2011). Consequently, it could be argued that too little attention has been paid to exploring the complex interface between law, ethics and practice 'especially when one orientation may be critical of another, or when each or all may find employer expectations, as expressed in a procedural orientation, indefensible' (Preston-Shoot, 2012: 32).

The question is: how is this to be achieved?

Critical thinking exercise 9.3

This is an opportunity to reflect on how, as a social work practitioner, you intend to bring together law, ethics and justice into your social work practice.

While the answer to this question has to be essentially personal, there are some steps that need to be taken as a move in the right direction. In order to achieve 'right-thinking', it is clearly going to be essential for practitioners to combine knowledge with a plan of action.

A first essential step is clearly going to be to gain a thorough knowledge of what the law says about social work practice. This will include a commitment to updating knowledge since the law is constantly evolving, and the courts daily have to decide on how the statutes are to be interpreted and how the law is to be applied to particular circumstances.

The second step is to gain and develop knowledge of ethical theories and approaches. It is hoped that this book has facilitated that, and has done so in a way that furthers the ambition of connecting ethics to law and practice.

The third step is more personal. Social workers need to be self-aware in the sense that they are able to relate their own values to their work. Everyone brings into social work their own culture and values, and some come with a very clear understanding of what they stand for, with a mission to help people who are disadvantaged and disempowered. That is, of course, to be applauded, yet social workers do need to guard against imposing their own values on others and particularly, in this context, need to be alert to the dangers of pushing too far against the boundaries of what is legal. The three case studies in this chapter have provided examples of well-intentioned practitioners stepping over the boundary of what is actually lawful.

The fourth step is to learn how to approach the law critically by reflecting on how the law interacts with ethics. In some cases the law embodies and enshrines in statute what are excellent principles: the Mental Capacity Act 2005 (sections 1–5) clarification of capacity, decision-making and best interests being a case in point. In other cases, the law does not sit quite so well with ethical principles, and indeed may be experienced as oppressive. It is important to be able to distinguish good and bad law, and particularly law that is empowering and disempowering.

So much for knowledge. This book has attempted to clarify different approaches to ethics and to social justice. The expectation is that practitioners start with a clear commitment to social justice which, generally, focuses on empowerment, is committed to equitable and fair treatment for all (this obviously includes anti-discriminatory practice), and more generally involves working alongside disadvantaged people, enhancing their capabilities and potential. Inevitably there are echoes of a Rawlsian and a Sen approach to social justice in this, but as the book was demonstrated, these are not the only approaches.

Likewise practitioners need to be clear about ethical approaches and, having read this book, should be able to analyse and reflect on these. In drawing on these ethical approaches, it is hoped that practitioners will be able to use the law imaginatively and constructively, yet being wary of any well-intentioned breaches of people's rights – breaches committed by other people or themselves.

CONCLUSION

This book began by issuing a challenge: how to marry ethics, social work law and social justice. It is hoped that this book has itself equipped beginning and more experienced practitioners with some tools that enable them to do this.

There are many other examples that the book could have offered as to how these three interrelate and interact, so inevitably the choice of case examples has been highly selective. Yet it is hoped that the book has offered a range of case studies that has proved instructive, and by learning lessons from some of these, readers will have acquired a much greater understanding of the fascinating interrelationships between social work law, ethical theories and social justice.

List of Cases

Aerts v Belgium [1998] 29 EHRR 50

AJ (Deprivation of Liberty Safeguards) [2015] EWCOP 5

Associated Provincial Picture Houses Ltd. v Wednesbury Corporation [1948] 1 KB 223

B (A Child) [2013] UKSC 33

B-S (Children) (Adoption: Application of Threshold Criteria) [2013] EWCA Civ 1146

Cheshire West and Chester Council v P; P and Q (MIG and MEG) [2014] UKSC 19

Cheshire West and Chester County Council v P [2011] EWCA Civ 1257

Coventry City Council v C and others [2013] 1 FCR 54

E v Norway [1994]17 EHRR 112

EH v London Borough of Greenwich [2010] 2 FLR 661

F (A Child) [2008] EWCA Civ 439

G v E and A Local Authority [2010] EWCA Civ 822

GD v Edgware Community Hospital and London Borough of Barnet [2008] EWHC 3572 (Admin)

Hillingdon v Neary [2011] EWHC 1377 (COP)

HL v the United Kingdom [2004] 40 EHRR 761

Ivinovic v Croatia [2014] ECHR 964

J (Children) [2012] EWCA Civ 1330

Louisa Watts v UK [2010] ECHR 793

McDonald v United Kingdom [2014] ECHR 4241/12

Megyeri v Germany [1993] 15 EHRR 584

N (A Child) (placement order: alternative option to adoption) [2013] All ER (D) 246 (Mar)

P (Children) (adoption: parental consent) [2008] EWCA Civ 535

R (on the application of Madden and others) v Bury Metropolitan Borough Council [2002] EWHC (Admin) 1882

R (on the application of McDonald) v. Royal Borough of Kensington and Chelsea [2011] UKSC 33

R (Shoesmith) v OFSTED and others [2011] EWCA Civ 642

References

Association of Directors of Adult Social Services (2014) *ADASS Advice Note: Guidance for Local Authorities in the Light of the Supreme Court Decisions on Deprivation of Liberty*. London: ADASS.

BAAF (British Association for Adoption and Fostering) (2013) *Adoption Statistics England*. Available at: www.baaf.org.uk/res/statengland (accessed 19 March 2015).

Banerjee, M.M. (2011) 'Social work scholars' representation of Rawls: a critique', *Journal of Social Work Education*, 47(2): 189–211.

Banerjee, M.M. and Canda, E.R. (2012) 'Comparing Rawlsian justice and the capabilities approach to justice from a spiritually sensitive social work perspective', *Journal of Religion and Spirituality in Social Work*, (31): 9–31.

Banks, S. (2004) *Ethics, Accountability and the Social Professions*. Basingstoke: Palgrave.

Banks, S. (2008) 'Critical commentary: social work ethics', *British Journal of Social Work*, (38): 1238–49.

Banks, S. (2012) *Ethics and Values in Social Work* (4th edition). Basingstoke: Palgrave.

Barker, P. (ed.) (2011) *Mental Health Ethics: The Human Context*. London: Routledge.

Beckett, C. and Maynard, A. (2013) *Values and Ethics in Social Work* (2nd edition). London: Sage.

Beckett, C., Pinchen, I. and McKeigue, B. (2014) 'Permanence and "permanence": outcomes of family placements', *British Journal of Social Work*, 44(5): 1162–79.

Biehal, N., Ellison, S., Baker, C. and Sinclair, I. (2010) *Belonging and Permanence: Outcomes in Long-Term Foster Care and Adoption*. London: BAAF (British Association for Adoption and Fostering).

Blom-Cooper, L. (1985) *A Child in Trust: The Report of the Panel of Inquiry into the Circumstances Surrounding the Death of Jasmine Beckford*. London: London Borough of Brent.

Boot, M. (2011) 'The aim of a theory of justice', *Ethical Theory and Moral Practice*, 15: 7–21.

Bowie, R. (2004) *Ethical Studies* (2nd edition). Cheltenham: Nelson Thornes.

Box, S. (1980) 'Where have all the naughty children gone?' in National Deviancy Conference (eds), *Permissiveness and Control: The Fate of the Sixties Legislation*. Basingstoke: Macmillan.

Brammer, A. (2015) *Social Work Law* (4th edition). London: Pearson.

Braye, S. and Preston-Shoot, M. (2006) 'The role of law in welfare reform: critical perspectives on the relationship between law and social work practice', *International Journal of Social Welfare*, 15: 19–26.

Braye, S. and Preston-Shoot, M. (2010) *Practising Social Work Law* (3rd edition). Basingstoke: Palgrave.

Brayne, H. and Carr, H. (2013) *Law for Social Workers* (12th edition). Oxford: Oxford University Press.

Brayne, H., Carr, H. and Goosey, D. (2015) *Law for Social Workers* (13th edition). Oxford: Oxford University Press.

Burton, F. (2012) *Family Law*. London: Routledge.

Care Council for Wales (2011) *Code of Practice for Social Care Workers*. Available at: www.ccwales.org.uk/code-of-practice-for-workers (accessed 19 March 2015).

Care Council for Wales (online) Hearing outcomes. Available at: www.ccwales.org.uk/hearings/outcomes (accessed 6 March 2015).

Care Quality Commission (2015) *The Operation of the Deprivation of Liberty Safeguards 2013–14*. Newcastle: Care Quality Commission.

Carr, H. (2012) 'Rational men and difficult women – R (on the application of McDonald) v. Royal Borough of Kensington and Chelsea [2011] UKSC 33', *Journal of Social Welfare and Family Law*, 34(2): 219–30.

Carr, S. (2010) *SCIE Report 36: Enabling Risk, Ensuring Safety: Self-directed Support and Personal Budgets*. London: SCIE.

Clare, I.C.H., Redley, M., Keeling, A., Wagner, A.P., Wheeler, J.R., Gunn, M.J. and Holland, A.J. (2013) *Understanding the Interface between the Mental Capacity Act's Deprivation of Liberty Safeguards (MCA-DoLS) and the Mental Health Act (MHA)*. Cambridge: Cambridge Intellectual and Developmental Disabilities Research Group, University of Cambridge.

Cohen, S. (1972) *Folk Devils and Moral Panics*. London: Paladin.

Corby, B. (2006) 'The secret of Bryn Estyn: the making of a modern witch hunt by Richard Webster', *Child Abuse Review*, 15: 285–7.

Corby, B., Doig, A. and Roberts, V. (2001) *Public Inquiries into Abuse of Children in Residential Care*. London: Jessica Kingsley.

Coventry Safeguarding Children Board (2013) *Final Overview Report of Serious Case Review re Daniel Pelka*. Coventry: Coventry Safeguarding Board.

Department for Children, Schools and Families (2008) *The Children Act 1989 Guidance and Regulations, Volume 1: Court Orders*. London: Department for Children, Schools and Families.

Department for Education (2012) *An Action Plan for Adoption: Tackling Delay*. London: Department for Education.

Department for Education (2013) *Further Action on Adoption: Finding More Loving Homes*. London: Department for Education.

Department for Education (2014a) *Children Looked After in England (Including Adoption and Care Leavers) Year Ending 31 March 2014*. London: Department for Education.

Department for Education (2014b) *Court Orders and Pre-proceedings for Local Authorities*. London: Department for Education.

Department of Health (1989) *Introduction to the Children Act 1989*. London: Department of Health.

Department of Health (2000a) *Adoption: A New Approach*. London: Department of Health.

Department of Health (2000b) *Lost in Care, Report of the Tribunal of Inquiry into the Abuse of Children in Care in the Former County Council Areas of Gwynedd and Clwyd since 1974 [Waterhouse Inquiry]*. Norwich: The Stationery Office.

Department of Health (2002) *Requirements for Social Work Training*. London: Department of Health.

Department of Health (2003) *Fair Access to Care Services LAC 2002(13)*. London: Department of Health.

Department of Health (2005) *Independence, Well-being and Choice*. Norwich: The Stationery Office.

Department of Health (2006) *Our Health, Our Care, Our Say: A New Direction for Community Services*. Norwich: The Stationery Office.

Department of Health (2010) *Practical Approaches to Safeguarding and Personalisation*. London: Department of Health.

DHSS (Department of Health and Social Security) (1988) *The Report of the Inquiry into Child Abuse in Cleveland 1987 [Butler-Sloss Inquiry]*. London: HMSO.

Doel, M. and Shardlow, S. (2005) *Modern Social Work Practice*. London: Ashgate.

Ellis, K. (2004) 'Promoting rights or avoiding litigation? The introduction of the Human Rights Act 1998 into adult social care in England', *European Journal of Social Work*, 7(3): 321–40.

Fisher, C. and Lovell, A. (2009) *Business Ethics and Values* (3rd edition). Harlow: Prentice Hall.

Fitzpatrick, T. (2011) *Welfare Theory: An Introduction to Theoretical Debates in Social Policy*. Basingstoke: Palgrave.

Freeman, M. (2011) *Human Rights*. Cambridge: Polity Press.

Gallagher, A. and Hodge, S. (2012) *Ethics, Law and Professional Issues*. Basingstoke: Palgrave.

General Social Care Council (2002) *National Occupational Standards for Social Work*. Leeds: Training Organisation for the Personal Social Services.

General Social Care Council (2012) *Regulating Social Workers 2001–2012*. Available at http://social welfare.bl.uk/subject-areas/services-activity/social-work-care-services/generalsocialcarecouncil/regulating121.aspx (accessed 27 April 2015).

Gilligan, C. (1982) *In a Different Voice: Psychological Theory and Women's Development*. Cambridge, MA: Harvard University Press.

Glasby, J. (2011) *Whose Risk is it Anyway? Risk and Regulation in an Era of Personalisation*. York: Joseph Rowntree Foundation.

Goldson, B. (1999) *Youth Justice: Contemporary Policy and Practice*. Aldershot: Ashgate.

Gray, M. (2010) 'Moral sources and emergent ethical theories in social work', *British Journal of Social Work*, 40: 1794–811.

Gray, M. and Lovat, T. (2007) 'Horse and carriage: why Habermas's discourse ethics gives virtue a praxis in social work', *Ethics and Social Welfare*, 1(3): 310–28.

Gray, M. and Webb, S.A. (2010) *Ethics and Value Perspectives in Social Work*. Basingstoke: Palgrave.

Griffiths, R. (1988) *Community Care: Agenda for Action*. London: HMSO.

Haines, K. and Drakeford, M. (1998) *Young People and Youth Justice*. Basingstoke: Macmillan.

Health and Care Professions Council (2012) *Standards of Practice for Social Workers in England*. Available at www.hpc-uk.org/publications/standards/ (accessed 27 April 2015).

Health and Social Care Information Centre (2015) *Mental Capacity Act 2005, Deprivation of Liberty Safeguards (England) Quarter 3 Return, 2014*. Available at www.hscic.gov.uk/catalogue/PUB16793/dols-q3-1415-keyfindings-DQ.pdf (accessed 16 February 2015).

HM Government (2007) *Putting People First: A Shared Vision and Commitment to the Transformation of Adult Social Care*. Norwich: The Stationery Office.

HM Government (2010) *Building the National Care Service*. Norwich: The Stationery Office.

HM Government (2012) *Caring for Our Future: Reforming Care and Support*. Norwich: The Stationery Office.

HM Government (2013) *Working Together to Safeguard Children*. Norwich: The Stationery Office.

Holland, S. (2010) 'Looked after children and the ethic of care', *British Journal of Social Work*, 40: 1664–80.

Home Office (1960) *Report of the Committee on Children and Young Persons* [the Ingleby Report]. London: HMSO.

Home Office (1965) *The Child, the Family and the Young Offender*. London: HMSO.

Home Office (1968) *Children in Trouble*. London: HMSO.

House of Lords Select Committee on the Mental Capacity Act 2005 (2014) *Report of Session 2013–14 – Mental Capacity Act 2005: Post-Legislative Scrutiny*. Norwich: The Stationery Office.

Hugman, R. (2013) *Culture, Values and Ethics in Social Work*. London: Routledge.

IFSW (International Federation of Social Workers) and IASSW (the International Association of Schools of Social Work) (2004) *Code of Ethics, Statement of Principles*. Berne: IFSW.

Jenkins, J. (1999) *Ethics and Religion*. Oxford: Heinemann.

Johns, R. (2011a) *Social Work, Social Policy and Older People*. Exeter: Learning Matters.

Johns, R. (2011b) *Using the Law in Social Work* (5th edition). Exeter: Learning Matters.

Johns, R. (2014a) *Capacity and Autonomy*. Basingstoke: Palgrave.

Johns, R. (2014b) *Using the Law in Social Work* (6th edition). London: Sage.

Kirton, D. (2013) '"Kinship by design" in England: reconfiguring adoption from Blair to the coalition', *Child and Family Social Work*, 18: 97–106.

Kline, R. and Preston-Shoot, M. (2011) *Professional Accountability in Social Care and Health*. London: Sage.

LAG (Legal Action Group) (2012) What price dignity? Conference report. Legal Action, January, 2012: 6.

Lloyd, L. (2006) 'A caring profession? The ethics of care and social work with older people', *British Journal of Social Work*, 36: 1171–85.

Lloyd, L. (2010) 'The individual in social care: the ethics of care and the "personalisation agenda" in services for older people in England', *Ethics and Social Welfare*, 4(2): 188–200.

Mason, K. and Laurie, G. (2013) *Mason and McCall Smith's Law and Medical Ethics* (2nd edition). Oxford: Oxford University Press.

McBeath, G. and Webb, S.A. (2002) 'Virtue ethics and social work: being lucky, realistic and not doing one's duty', *British Journal of Social Work*, 32: 1015–36.

McGhee, J., Alice, L. and Waterhouse, M. (2012) 'Massachusetts and Scotland: from juvenile justice to child welfare?', *Child Welfare*, 91(5): 169–91.

McLaughlin, K. (2010) 'The social worker versus the General Social Care Council: an analysis of care standards tribunal hearings and decisions', *British Journal of Social Work*, 40: 311–27.

Ministry of Justice (2008) *Deprivation of Liberty Safeguards Code of Practice*. Norwich: The Stationery Office.

Ministry of Justice (2009) *Preparation for Care and Supervision Proceedings*. London: Ministry of Justice.

Ministry of Justice (2010) *The Public Law Outline: Guide to Case Management in Public Law Proceedings*. London: Ministry of Justice.

Morris, A. and Giller, H. (1983) *Providing Criminal Justice for Children*. London: Edward Arnold.

Muncie, J. (1999) *Youth and Crime: A Critical Introduction*. London: Sage.

Muncie, J. (2011) 'Illusions of difference: comparative youth justice in the devolved United Kingdom', *British Journal of Criminology*, 51(1): 40.

Munro, E. (2011) *The Munro Review of Child Protection Final Report*. London: Department for Education.

Northern Ireland Social Care Council (2002) *Northern Ireland: Codes of Practice for Social Care Workers and Employers of Social Care Workers*. Available at: www.niscc.info/files/Codes/2010Jun_Codes OfPracticeLargePrint_report_Approved_AFMCK.pdf (accessed 27 April 2015).

Northern Ireland Social Care Council (online) *Northern Ireland Social Care Council Registrants Conduct Hearings and Decisions*. Available at: www.niscc.info/index.php/registrants/conduct-work force-regulation/conduct-hearings-decisions (accessed 6 March 2015).

Palmer, M. (2005) *Moral Problems* (2nd edition). Cambridge: Lutterworth Press.

Parrott, L. (2015) *Values and Ethics in Social Work Practice* (3rd edition). Exeter: Learning Matters.

Parton, N. (2010) 'Risk, social work and social care: the example of children's social care', in L.-A. Long, J. Roche and D. Stringer (eds), *The Law and Social Work: Contemporary Issues for Practice*. Basingstoke: Palgrave.

Pearson, G. (1983) *Hooligan: A History of Respectable Fears*. Basingstoke: Macmillan.

Pickford, J. and Dugmore, P. (2012) *Youth Justice and Social Work* (2nd edition). London: Sage.

Pojman, L.P. (2002) *Ethics: Discovering Right and Wrong*. Belmont, CA: Wadsworth.

Preston-Shoot, M. (2010) 'On the evidence for viruses in social work systems: law, ethics and practice', *European Journal of Social Work*, 13(4): 465–82.

Preston-Shoot, M. (2011) 'On administrative evil-doing within social work policy and services: law, ethics and practice', *European Journal of Social Work*, 14 (2): 177–93.

Preston-Shoot, M. (2012) 'The secret curriculum', *Ethics and Social Welfare*, 6(1): 18–36.

Pullen-Sansfacon, A. (2010) 'Virtue ethics for social work: a new pedagogy for practical reasoning', *Social Work Education*, 29(4): 402–15.

QAA (Quality Assurance Agency for Higher Education) (2008) *Social Work Subject Benchmark Statements*. York: QAA.

Rai, L. and Stringer, D. (2010) 'Partnership or participation?', in L.-A. Long, J. Roche and D. Stringer (eds), *The Law and Social Work: Contemporary Issues for Practice*. Basingstoke: Palgrave.

Ramon, S. (2011) 'The social worker', in P. Barker (ed.), *Mental Health Ethics*. London: Routledge.

Raphael, D. (2001) *Concepts of Justice*. Oxford: Oxford University Press.

Rawls, J. (1972) *A Theory of Justice*. Oxford: Oxford University Press.

Rawls, J. (1993) *Political Liberalism*. New York: Columbia University Press.

Rawls, J. (1999) *A Theory of Justice* (2nd revised edition). Oxford: Oxford University Press.

Robinson, M. (2010) 'Assessing criminal justice practice using social justice theory', *Social Justice Research*, 23: 77–97.

Rossiter, A. (2011) 'Unsettled social work: the challenge of Levinas's ethics', *British Journal of Social Work*, 41(5): 980–95.

Rummery, K. (2011) 'A comparative analysis of personalisation: balancing an ethic of care with user empowerment', *Ethics and Social Welfare*, 5(2): 138–52.

SCIE (Social Care Institute for Excellence) (2010) *Personalisation: A Rough Guide* (revised edition). London: Social Care Institute for Excellence.

SCIE (Social Care Institute for Excellence) (2015) *Deprivation of Liberty Safeguards: Putting Them into Practice*. London: Social Care Institute for Excellence.

Scottish Social Services Council (2009) *Code of Practice for Social Service Workers and Employers*. Available at: www.sssc.uk.com/about-the-sssc/multimedia-library/publications/60-protecting-the-public/61-codes-of-practice/1020-sssc-codes-of-practice-for-social-service-workers-and-employers (accessed 27 April 2015).

Seebohm, F. (1968) *Report of the Committee on Local Authority and Allied Personal Social Services*. London: HMSO.

Sen, A. (2010) *The Idea of Justice*. London: Penguin Books.

Seymour, C. and Seymour, R. (2013) *Practical Child Law for Social Workers: A Guide to English Law and Policy*. London: Sage.

Simmonds, J. (2012) 'Adoption: from the preservation of the moral order to the needs of the child', in M. Davies (ed.), *Social Work with Children and Families*. Basingstoke: Palgrave.

Sinclair, I., Baker, C., Lee, J. and Gibbs, I. (2007) *The Pursuit of Permanence: A Study of the English Child Care System*. London: Jessica Kingsley.

Smith, R. (2014) *Youth Justice: Ideas, Policy, Practice* (3rd edition). London: Routledge.

Standley, K. and Davies, P. (2013) *Family Law* (8th edition). Basingstoke: Palgrave.

Stewart, N. (2009) *Ethics: An Introduction to Moral Philosophy*. Cambridge: Polity Press.

Szasz, T. (2010) *The Myth of Mental Illness: Foundations of a Theory of Personal Conduct*. New York: Harper Perennial.

Taket, A. (2012) *Health Equity, Social Justice and Human Rights*. London: Routledge.

The College of Social Work (2012) *Professional Capabilities Framework*. London: The College of Social Work.

Thorpe, D. (1983) 'De-institutionalisation and justice', in A. Morris and H. Giller (eds), *Providing Criminal Justice for Children*. London: Edward Arnold.

Triseliotis, J. (2002) 'Long-term foster-care or adoption? The evidence examined', *Child and Family Social Work*, 7(1): 23–33.

Vardy, P. and Grosch, P. (1999) *The Puzzle of Ethics*. London: Harper Collins.

Webster, R. (2009) *The Secret of Bryn Estyn: The Making of a Modern Witch Hunt*. Suffolk: Orwell Press.

Welbourne, P. (2002) 'Adoption and the rights of children in the UK', *The International Journal of Children's Rights*, (10): 269–89.

Welbourne, P. (2010) 'Accountability in the law and social work: contemporary issues for practice', in L.-A. Long, J. Roche and D. Stringer (eds), *The Law and Social Work: Contemporary Issues for Practice*. Basingstoke: Palgrave.

Welsh Assembly Government (2008) *The Children Act 1989 Guidance and Regulations, Volume 1: Court Orders*. Cardiff: Welsh Assembly Government and NHS Wales.

Whitaker, D. (2014) 'Social justice for safeguarded adults deprived of their liberty in the United Kingdom?', *Disability & Society*, 29(9): 1491–5.

Zink, J.R. (2011) 'Reconsidering the role of self-respect in Rawls' *A Theory of Justice*', *Journal of Politics*, 73(2): 331–44.

Index